A TEXT BOOK OF
SURVEYING

FOR
Semester – I
Second Year Degree Course in Civil Engineering

As Per New Revised Syllabus of
North Maharashtra University, Jalgaon, June 2013

A. S. SHELAR
B.E. Civil, M.Tech. (Town & Country Planning),
Senior Lecturer, Civil Engg. Deptt.,
Cusrow Wadia Institute of Technology,
PUNE - 1

Dr. S. T. MALI
B.E. Civil, M.E. (Construction Management), Ph.D.
Assistant Professor, Civil Engg. Deptt.,
STE's Sinhgad College of Engineering,
Vadgaon (Bk.) PUNE

U. S. PATIL
B.E. Civil, M. Tech (Construction Management),
Associate Professor, Civil Engg. Deptt.,
Bharati Vidyapeeth's Group of Institutes Technical Campus,
College of Engineering,
Lavale, PUNE - 43

Surveying (S.E. Civil - Semester I - NMU)　　　　ISBN 978-93-83525-14-0

Third Edition　　:　　August 2015
©　　　　　　　:　　Authors

　　The text of this publication, or any part thereof, should not be reproduced or transmitted in any form or stored in any computer storage system or device for distribution including photocopy, recording, taping or information retrieval system or reproduced on any disc, tape, perforated media or other information storage device etc., without the written permission of Authors with whom the rights are reserved. Breach of this condition is liable for legal action.

　　Every effort has been made to avoid errors or omissions in this publication. In spite of this, errors may have crept in. Any mistake, error or discrepancy so noted and shall be brought to our notice shall be taken care of in the next edition. It is notified that neither the publisher nor the authors or seller shall be responsible for any damage or loss of action to any one, of any kind, in any manner, therefrom.

Published By :	Printed By :
NIRALI PRAKASHAN	**REPRO INDIA LTD.**
Abhyudaya Pragati, 1312, Shivaji Nagar,	50/2 T.T.C. MIDC,
Off J.M. Road, PUNE – 411005	Industrial Area, Mahape, Navi Mumbai
Tel - (020) 25512336/37/39, Fax - (020) 25511379	Tel - (022) 2778 2011
Email : niralipune@pragationline.com	

☞ **DISTRIBUTION CENTRES**

PUNE
Nirali Prakashan　　:　119, Budhwar Peth, Jogeshwari Mandir Lane, Pune 411002, Maharashtra
　　　　　　　　　　　　Tel : (020) 2445 2044, 66022708, Fax : (020) 2445 1538
　　　　　　　　　　　　Email : bookorder@pragationline.com, niralilocal@pragationline.com
Nirali Prakashan　　:　S. No. 28/27, Dhyari, Near Pari Company, Pune 411041
　　　　　　　　　　　　Tel : (020) 24690204 Fax : (020) 24690316
　　　　　　　　　　　　Email : dhyari@pragationline.com, bookorder@pragationline.com

MUMBAI
Nirali Prakashan　　:　385, S.V.P. Road, Rasdhara Co-op. Hsg. Society Ltd.,
　　　　　　　　　　　　Girgaum, Mumbai 400004, Maharashtra
　　　　　　　　　　　　Tel : (022) 2385 6339 / 2386 9976, Fax : (022) 2386 9976
　　　　　　　　　　　　Email : niralimumbai@pragationline.com

☞ **DISTRIBUTION BRANCHES**

JALGAON
Nirali Prakashan　　:　34, V. V. Golani Market, Navi Peth, Jalgaon 425001,
　　　　　　　　　　　　Maharashtra, Tel : (0257) 222 0395, Mob : 94234 91860

KOLHAPUR
Nirali Prakashan　　:　New Mahadvar Road, Kedar Plaza, 1st Floor Opp. IDBI Bank
　　　　　　　　　　　　Kolhapur 416 012, Maharashtra. Mob : 9850046155

NAGPUR
Pratibha Book Distributors　:　Above Maratha Mandir, Shop No. 3, First Floor,
　　　　　　　　　　　　Rani Jhanshi Square, Sitabuldi, Nagpur 440012, Maharashtra
　　　　　　　　　　　　　Tel : (0712) 254 7129

DELHI
Nirali Prakashan　　:　4593/21, Basement, Aggarwal Lane 15, Ansari Road, Daryaganj
　　　　　　　　　　　　Near Times of India Building, New Delhi 110002
　　　　　　　　　　　　Mob : 08505972553

BENGALURU
Pragati Book House　:　House No. 1, Sanjeevappa Lane, Avenue Road Cross,
　　　　　　　　　　　　Opp. Rice Church, Bengaluru – 560002.
　　　　　　　　　　　　Tel : (080) 64513344, 64513355,Mob : 9880582331, 9845021552
　　　　　　　　　　　　Email:bharatsavla@yahoo.com

CHENNAI
Pragati Books　　　:　9/1, Montieth Road, Behind Taas Mahal, Egmore,
　　　　　　　　　　　　Chennai 600008 Tamil Nadu, Tel : (044) 6518 3535,
　　　　　　　　　　　　Mob : 94440 01782 / 98450 21552 / 98805 82331,
　　　　　　　　　　　　Email : bharatsavla@yahoo.com

niralipune@pragationline.com | www.pragationline.com

Also find us on www.facebook.com/niralibooks

PREFACE

It gives us an immense pleasure to present this book on **'Surveying'** to the Students of Second Year of Degree in Civil Engineering of North Maharashtra University, Jalgaon.

One of the main concerns of Civil Engineer is survey work either in stage of planning or execution of different types of Civil Engineering Projects. He/she shall be well acquainted with the principles, concepts, facts and procedures in surveying. With this knowledge and skills, he/she will be able to develop or select and use appropriate techniques and instruments to establish controls, locate details, measure distances and directions, reduce positions, areas, volumes etc. during the survey for construction or maintenance or repair or extension of various civil engineering works in different roles.

The text book has been thoroughly prepared according to five units as per revised curriculum of 2013. An attempt is made to give due justice to the use of modern equipments in routine survey activities. The authors with their professional and academic experience have taken all efforts to present the text in lucid manner. The theoretical matter has been explained with number of diagrams and illustrations supported by solved examples.

In the preparation of this book we owe greatly to the authors and publishers of various books and the literature on all kind of survey equipments and techniques by various manufacturers.

We are thankful to our colleagues, friends and family members for their valuable assistance by variety of ways during the preparation of this book.

We sincerely thank to Shri. Dineshbhai K. Furia, Shri. Jigneshbhai C. Furia, Shri. M.P. Munde and the entire team of Nirali Prakashan namely Mr. Ilyas Shaikh and Mrs. Roshan Shaikh for their keen interest in publishing this book in attractive form in very short time.

We hope that the book will be well received by the students as well as the teaching faculty. We will like to welcome any kind of suggestions for the improvement of contents of this book.

September 2013 — *Authors*

SYLLABUS

SECTION I

UNIT I : Surveying and Levelling (16 Marks)

Part - A : Introduction to Surveying

(a) Surveying - Definition, principle of surveying, various types of surveying.

(b) Bench mark and its types, reduced level, rise and fall method, height of instrument method.

Part - B : Leveling

(a) Instrument used in leveling, dumpy level, automatic level, types of leveling staffs.

(b) Principal axes of dumpy level, reciprocal leveling curvature and refraction correction, distance to the visible horizon.

(c) Profile leveling : L-section and cross-sections.

UNIT II : Theodolite (16 Marks)

(a) Principal axes and temporary adjustments of transit theodolite.

(b) Uses of theodolite : Measurement of horizontal angles, vertical angles, magnetic bearings, measuring deflection angles.

(c) Theodolite Traversing : Computation of consecutive and independent co-ordinates, adjustments of closed traverse, Gales traverse by co-ordinate method.

UNIT III : Tachometry (16 Marks)

(a) Principle of stadia method, fixed hair method with vertical staff to determine horizontal distances and elevations of the points.

(b) Use of tachometry in surveying, contour, characteristics and uses, methods of interpolation, tachometric contour survey.

UNIT IV : Curves (16 Marks)

(a) Horizontal and vertical curves and their purposes.

(b) Simple circular curves - Elements and setting out by linear and angular methods.

(c) Compound curves - Elements and setting out of compound curves.

(d) Transition curves - Types and uses, length of transition curves, (No numerical problem to be asked).

UNIT V : Plane Table Surveying (16 Marks)

(a) Objective and equipment required for plane table survey.

(b) Methods of plane tabling - radiation, intersection, traversing and resection.

(c) Advantages, disadvantages, limitations and errors of plane table surveying.

(d) Minor instruments : Study and use of abney level, box sextant, digital planimeter.

CONTENTS

1. **Surveying and Levelling** — 1.1 – 1.48

2. **Theodolite** — 2.1 – 2.46

3. **Tachometry** — 3.1 – 3.42

4. **Curves** — 4.1 – 4.52

5. **Plane Table Surveying** — 5.1 – 5.20

   University Question Paper — P.1 – P.2

Unit - I

SURVEYING AND LEVELLING

PART - [A] INTRODUCTION TO SURVEYING

1.1 INTRODUCTION

Surveying is an important branch of Civil Engineering, which includes linear and angular measurements, vertical measurements are made in the vertical plane and are grouped under the term 'Levelling'.

Surveying is carried out to obtain information about the piece of land or a plot or features in a particular locality. Surveying is preliminary and very important work in all of the civil engineering projects like buildings, roads, railways, tunnels, dams, canal etc.

These measurements enable the surveyor to locate the boundaries of the plot or features of an area and to show them on paper by drawing a plan of these features.

1.1.1 Definition

Surveying is the art of determining the relative positions of points on, above or beneath the surface of earth by means of direct or indirect measurements of distance, direction and elevation. It also includes the art of establishing points by predetermined angular and linear measurements.

Objectives of Surveying :
1. To collect field data.
2. To prepare plan or map of the areas surveyed.
3. To analyse and to calculate the field parameters for setting out the operation of actual engineering works.
4. To set out field parameters at the site for further engineering works.

1.1.2 Principle of Surveying

The two main principles of surveying are :
(1) To work from the whole to the part.
(2) To locate a point by at least two independent processes :
    (a) Linear measurement,
    (b) Angular measurement, or
    (c) Both linear and angular measurement.

(1) To Work from the Whole to the Part
[According to work form whole to part]:
- It is essential to fix first, system of control points with high precision of the whole area to be surveyed.
- This area is divided into large traverse or triangles or both, and further subdivided into smaller ones by locating other control points in-between the main control points with less precision.
- The details are then located.
- By this method, minor errors are controlled and localized. Accumulation of errors is thus, avoided.
- On the other hand, if we work from part to the whole, small errors will increase in process of expansion and thus, become uncontrollable at the end. The whole survey then will go wrong.

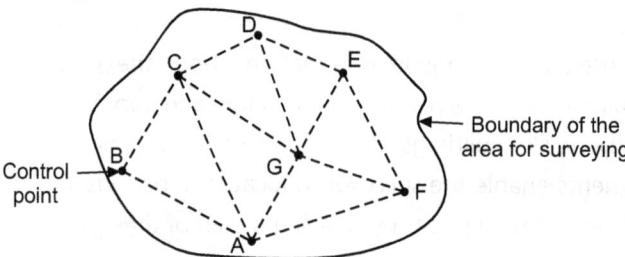

Fig. 1.1 : Work from whole to the part

- Suppose a very large area like town is to be surveyed. Firstly, fixed the control points A, B, C, D, E, F with grate core.
- This area is divided into number of triangles. The details within these triangles are surveyed with less accurate method.

(2) To Locate a Point by At Least Two Points of References
- In this method, two points are selected in the field and distance between them is measured. The relative positions of the points can be located from these reference points.
- To locate a point M with respect to two more given points of references say A and B, the following methods are used.

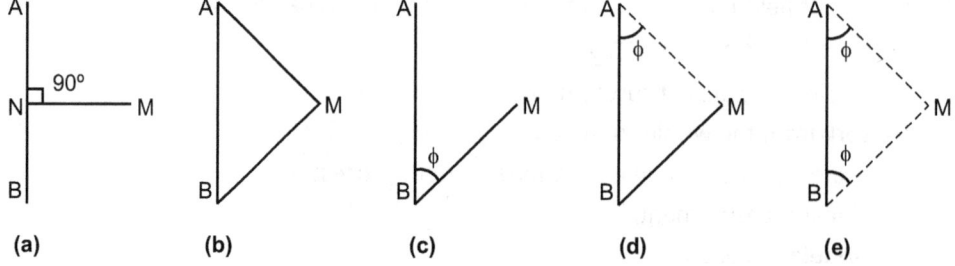

Fig. 1.2 : Locating a point M with reference to A and B

The position of point M can be located by any one of the methods described below :

(a) A perpendicular MN can be dropped on the reference line AB and lengths AN and NM are measured. The point M can then be plotted and measured. This principle is used in chain surveying for defining details.

(b) Distance AM and BM can be measured and point M can be plotted by swinging the two arcs to the same scale to which AB has been plotted. The principle is very much used in chain surveying.

(c) The distance BM and angle ABM can be measured and point M is plotted either by means of a protractor or trigonometrically. This principle is used in traversing.

(d) An angle MAB and distance BM is measured and point M is plotted either by protracting an angle and swinging an arc from B or plotted trigonometrically. This is used in traversing.

(e) In this method, the distances AM and BM are not measured, but angle MAB and angle MBA are measured with angle measuring instrument. Knowing the distance AB, the point M is plotted either by means of a protractor or by solution of triangle AMB. The principle is very much used in triangulation and for extensive work.

1.1.3 Types of Surveying

Based upon the consideration of the shape of the earth, surveying is broadly classified as :
1. Plane surveying
2. Geodetic surveying.

1. Plane Surveying :

In plane surveying, the mean surface of the earth is considered as a plane and the spheroidal shape is neglected. The earth's surface is considered as a plane, the line connecting any two points as a straight line and the angles of polygons as plane angles. The degree of accuracy required in this type of surveying is comparatively low. As a rough estimate, American surveyors put the limit 250 km^2 for treating the survey as plane. Most of the civil engineering works are concerned only with a small portion of the earth which seems to be plane surface.

Classification :

Surveys may be classified as :

(A) Classification based upon the nature of the field survey :
1. Land surveys :
    (a) Topographical survey
    (b) Cadastral survey
    (c) City survey
2. Marine or hydrographic survey
3. Astronomical survey

(B) Classification based upon the object of survey :
1. Engineering survey
2. Military survey
3. Geological survey
4. Mine survey

(C) Classification based upon the methods employed in survey :
1. Triangulation for survey
2. Traverse survey

(D) Classification based upon the instrument employed :
1. Chain survey
2. Theodolite survey
3. Tacheometric survey
4. Compass survey
5. Plane table survey
6. Photographic survey
7. Aerial survey

2. Geodetic Surveying :

In geodetic surveying, the shape of earth is taken into account. All lines lying in the surface are curved lines and the triangles are spherical triangles. All geodetic surveys include work of larger magnitude and high degree of precision.

1.2 TYPES OF BENCH MARK

There are four types of bench marks in a levelling work.

1. Great Trigonometric Survey Bench Mark (G.T.S.B.M.) : These bench marks are established throughout the country with high precision by the Survey of India Department. Their elevations are shown in a G.T.S. map. These are established at an interval of about 100 km all over the country with respect to the mean sea level at Karachi datum.

2. Permanent Bench Mark (P.B.M.) : These are established between the G.T.S. bench marks by the state government agencies like Public Work Department (P.W.D.) on clearly defined and permanent points such as the top of a parapet wall of a bridge or culvert, kilometre stone, railway platform etc. Its exact location and reduced level is marked on the top of permanent object.

3. Arbitrary Bench Mark (A.B.M.) : These are reference points whose elevations are arbitrarily assumed for small levelling operations. Their elevations do not refer to any fixed datum. It is used when elevation difference is important rather than elevation.

4. Temporary Bench Mark (T.B.M.) : These are the reference points on which a day's work is closed and from where levelling is continued the next day. Such a B.M. is carefully established on permanent objects like kilometre stones, parapets etc.

1.2.1 Reduced Level

There are two methods of calculation of reduced level or elevation of points from the staff readings observed in the field.
   (a) Collimation plan or height of instrument method (H.I.)
   (b) Rise and Fall.

(a) Collimation Plane Method or Height of Instrument Method (H.I. Method)

In this method, the reduced level of the collimation plane is found out for each setup of dumpy level and then the reduced levels of other points are found out with respect to the respective plane of collimation.

The procedure of finding R.L. is as given below :

1. First take a reading on bench mark and then find the R.L. of collimation plane by adding back sight reading and R.L. of bench mark.
   Height of Instrument = R.L. of collimation plane
                        = R.L. of bench mark + B.S.
2. Calculate the reduced levels of intermediate points or change point by subtracting the I.S. or F.S. readings from the R.L. of collimation plane.
3. After the instrument is shifted and setup and levelled at new position, take a back sight reading on change point. Determine the R.L. of new collimation plane.
   R.L. of new collimation plane = R.L. of change point + B.S. reading
4. Obtain the reduced levels of the remaining points from the R.L. of new collimation plane.
5. Repeat the procedure till all the levelling work is finished.

On completing the observations, the arithmetical check is applied as given below :

$$\boxed{\Sigma \text{ B.S.} - \Sigma \text{ F.S.} = \text{Last R.L.} - \text{First R.L.}}$$

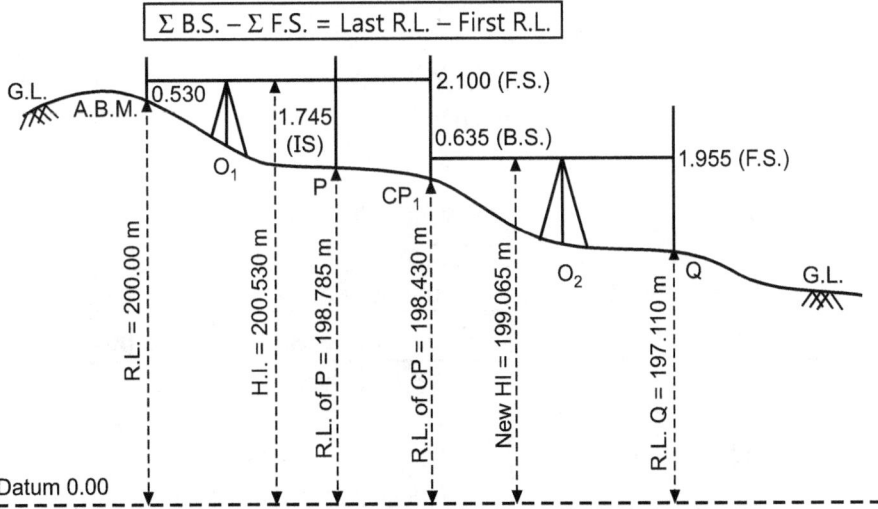

Fig. 1.3 : Sketch Illustrating Collimation Plane or H.I. Method

Sketch illustrates collimation plane or H.I. method.
- Let the dumpy level height setup at O_1 and all the temporary adjustments are done.
- The telescope will revolve in a horizontal plane and reading is taken on Arbitrary Bench Mark (A.B.M.) which is 0.530 m.
- It is required to find the reduced levels of P and Q.
- R.L. of A.B.M. is 200.000 m.
- Then readings are taken at station P and change point (CP_1) respectively i.e. 1.745 and 2.100 m.
- Dumpy level is shifted to new position O_2 and all the temporary adjustments are done.
- Back sight reading is taken on CP_1 i.e. 0.635 m and fore sight reading taken on station Q i.e. 1.955 m.

$\therefore$ Height of Instrument or R.L. of collimation plane at O_1
$$= \text{R.L. of ABM} + \text{B.S.}$$
$$= 200.000 + 0.530$$
$$= 200.530 \text{ m}$$

R.L. of St. P $= \text{H.I.} - \text{I.S.}$
$$= 200.530 - 1.745$$
$$= 198.785 \text{ m}$$

R.L. of CP_1 $= \text{H.I.} - \text{F.S.}$
$$= 200.530 - 2.100$$
$$= 198.430 \text{ m}$$

New H.I. at O_2 $= \text{R.L. of } CP_1 + \text{B.S.}$
$$= 198.430 + 0.635$$
$$= 199.065 \text{ m}$$

R.L. of Q $= \text{New H.I.} - \text{F.S.}$
$$= 199.065 - 1.955$$
$$= 197.110 \text{ m}$$

The readings will be tabulated as under in the page of a level book.

Station	B.S.	I.S.	F.S.	H.I.	R.L. (m)	Remark
–	0.530	–		200.530	200.000	ABM
P	–	1.745	–	–	198.785	–
	0.635		2.100	199.065	198.430	CP_1
Q	–		1.955	–	197.110	
Σ	1.165	–	4.055	–	–	–

Arithmetical Check :

$$\Sigma \text{ B.S.} - \Sigma \text{ F.S.} = \text{Last R.L.} - \text{First R.L.}$$
$$1.165 - 4.055 = 197.110 - 200.000$$
$$-2.890 = -2.890$$

(b) Rise and Fall Method :

In this method, the difference of elevation between two consecutive points is determined by comparing each point after the first with that immediately preceding it, i.e. two consecutive staff readings.

Rise or Fall = Previous Reading − Current Reading

If difference is + ve → Rise

If difference is − ve → Fall

Reduced level of any point = Reduced level of preceding point ± Rise or fall

+ → when Rise

− → when Fall

The R.L. of collimation plane is not required to find out. The difference of readings will indicate a rise or a fall depending on whether the staff reading at that point is smaller or greater than that at the preceding point.

The arithmetical check in the reduction of level is applied as follows :

$$\boxed{\Sigma \text{ B.S.} - \Sigma \text{ R.S.} = \Sigma \text{ Rise} - \Sigma \text{ Fall} = \text{Last R.L.} - \text{First R.L.}}$$

Thus, there is a check on the intermediate reduction of levels.

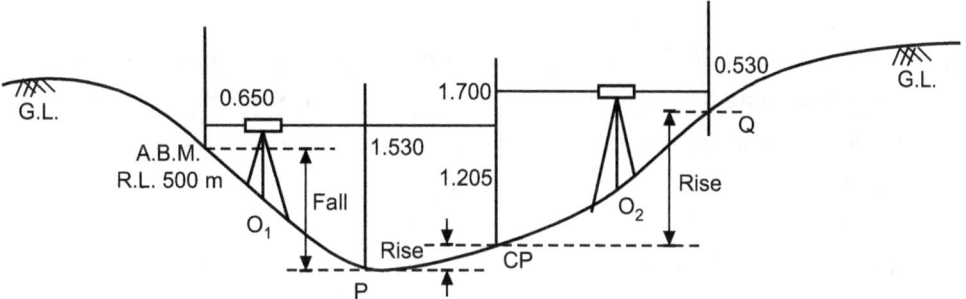

Fig. 1.4 : Illustrative Sketch of Rise and Fall Method

Rise or Fall between ABM and P = Previous reading − Current reading
$$= 0.650 - 1.530$$
$$= -0.880 \text{ m}$$

R.L. of P = R.L. of AMB ± Rise or Fall
$$= 500 - 0.880$$
$$= 499.120 \text{ m}$$

Rise or Fall between P and CP = 1.530 − 1.205
= 0.325 m
R.L. of CP = R.L. of P ± Rise or Fall
= 499.120 + 0.325
= 499.445 m
Rise or Fall between CP and Q = 1.700 − 0.530
= 1.170 m
R.L of Q = R.L. of CP ± Rise or Fall
= 499.445 + 1.170
= 500.615 m

Station	B.S.	I.S.	F.S.	Rise	Fall	R.L. (m)	Remark
−	0.650	−			−	500.000	ABM
P	−	1.530	−	−	0.880	499.120	−
−	1.700	−	1.205	0.325	−	499.445	CP
Q	−	−	0.530	1.170	−	500.615	−
Σ	2.350	−	1.735	1.495	0.880	−	−

Arithmetic Check :

Σ B.S. − Σ F.S. = Σ Rise − Σ Fall = Last R.L. − First R.L.
2.350 − 1.735 = 1.495 − 0.880 = 500.615 − 500.000
∴   0.615 = 0.615   = 0.615

Comparison between Collimation Plane (H.I) Method and Rise and Fall Method

Collimation Plane (H.I.) Method	Rise and Fall Method
1. It is more rapid and involve less number of calculations.	1. This method is more tedious as it involves more calculations.
2. Since there is no check on R.L. of I.S., errors if any, in the I.S. are not detected.	2. Since there is complete check on the R.L. of I.S., errors if any, in the I.S. are also detected.
3. Most suited for longitudinal or cross-sectional levelling and controlling.	3. It is well suited for determining the difference of levels of two points where precision is required. e.g. establishing new bench marks.
4. There are two arithmetical checks. Σ B.S. − Σ F.S. = Last R.L. − First R.L.	4. There are three arithmetical checks. Σ B.S. − Σ F.S. = Σ Rise − Σ Fall = Last R.L. − First R.L.

SOLVED EXAMPLES

Example 1.1 : Determine the Reduced Levels of all the stations by H.I. method from the following. The readings during a road profiling working from a point P to another point Q, 2 km apart using a dumpy level and a 4 m levelling staff were :

0.500, 1.525, 2.150, 0.985, 0.450, 0.870, 1.850, 2.585, 1.710, 2.850, 3.415, 3.855

While obtaining the above readings, the instrument was shifted after fourth, sixth and tenth readings. Enter all the readings in a level field book page. The R.L. of 1st point P was happened to be a P.B.M. with R.L. = 150.000 m. Also apply usual Arithmetic check.

Solution :

- The readings are entered in a level book page by noting that the instrument was shifted after 4th, 6th and 10th readings. Therefore, 4th, 6th and 10th readings (0.985, 0.870 and 2.850) will be entered in fore sight column.
- Consequently 5th, 7th and 11th readings (i.e. 0.450, 1.850 and 3.415) will be entered in back sight column.
- The first reading is entered in the B.S. column, whereas, the last reading is entered in the fore sight column. The remaining readings are entered in intermediate sight column.
- It is noted that number of B.S. readings is equal to the number of F.S. readings on a level book page.
- Here No. of B.S. = No. of F.S. = 4.

Station	B.S.	I.S.	F.S.	H.I. (Collimation plane)	R.L. in m	Remark
P	0.500	-	-	150.500	150.000	P.B.M.
1	-	1.525	-	-	148.975	-
2	-	2.150	-	-	148.350	-
3	0.450	-	0.985	149.965	149.515	CP$_1$
4	1.850	-	0.870	150.945	149.095	CP$_2$
5	-	2.585	-	-	148.360	-
6	-	1.710	-	-	149.235	-
7	3.415	-	2.850	151.510	148.095	CP$_3$
Q	-	-	3.855	-	147.655	Last Pt.
SUM (Σ)	6.215		8.560	-	-	-

The R.L.s of staff stations are calculated as follows by using Collimation Plane Method (H.I.)

1. First H.I. = R.L. of P.B.M + B.S. on station P
   = 150.00 + 0.500
   = 150.500 m

2. R.L. of St. 1 = H.I. − I.S. on St. 1
   = 150.500 − 1.525
   = 148.975 m

3. R.L. of St. 2 = H.I. − I.S. on St. 2
   = 150.500 − 2.150
   = 148.350 m

4. R.L. of St. 3 [CP_1] = H.I. − F.S. on St. 3
   = 150.500 − 0.985
   = 149.515 m

Now the instrument is shifted, hence new H.I. will be calculated.

5. Second H.I. = R.L. of CP_1 (St. 3) + B.S. on St. 3
   = 149.515 + 0.450
   = 149.965 m

6. R.L. of St. 4 [CP_2] = Second H.I. − F.S. on St. 4
   = 149.965 − 0.870
   = 149.095 m

As the instrument is shifted; third H.I. is to be found out.

7. Third H.I. = R.L. of St. 4 [CP_2] + B.S. on St. 4
   = 149.095 + 1.850
   = 150.945 m

8. R.L. of St. 5 = Third H.I. − I.S. on St. 5
   = 150.945 − 2.585
   = 148.360 m

9. R.L. of St. 6 = Third H.I. − I.S. on St. 6
   = 150.945 − 1.710
   = 149.235 m

10. R.L. of St. 7 = Third H.I. − F.S. on St. 7
    = 150.945 − 2.850
    = 148.095 m

As the instrument is shifted, fourth H.I. is to be found out.

11. Fourth H.I. = R.L. of St 7 [CP₃] + B.S. on St. 7
                = 148.095 + 3.415
                = 151.510 m
12. R.L. of St. Q = Fourth H.I. − F.S. on St. Q
                  = 151.510 − 3.855
                  = 147.655 m

Note : It can be noted from above calculations that B.S. is always 'plus' sight and is always added; whereas R.S. and I.S. are 'minus' sights and are always subtracted.

Check : The arithmetical check on calculation is

Σ B.S. − Σ F.S. = Last R.L. − First R.L.
6.215 − 8.560 = 147.655 − 150.000
− 2.345 = − 2.345

Example 1.2 : Readings taken successfully on staff positions in a levelling work are : 2.065, 1.470, 1.226, 3.198, 2.458.

Level was shifted after second reading. If R.L. of first staff position is 260 M, find the R.Ls of other staff positions. Use rise and fall method. Show arithmetical check and simple calculations.

Solution : From the data, first reading (i.e. 2.065) will be entered in back sight column. The level was shifted after second reading (i.e. 1470), so it will come in fore sight column and next consecutive reading 1.226 will come in back sight column in the same row as it is change point.

Last reading (i.e. 2.458) will be in fore sight column and remaining will be in intermediate sight column.

Explanation of Calculation :

In the rise and fall method, each staff reading is compared with respect to previous one, to find out whether it is a rise or fall of next point. The rise or fall is added to or subtracted from the R.L. of previous point to get R.L. of next point.

Station	B.S.	I.S.	F.S.	Rise	Fall	R.L. (m)	Remark
1	2.065	-	-	-	-	260.000	First Pt.
2	1.226	-	1.470	0.595	-	260.595	C.P.1
3	-	3.198	-	-	1.972	258.623	-
4	-	-	2.458	0.740	-	259.363	Last Pt.
Sum (Σ)	3.291	-	3.928	1.335	1.972	-	-

1. For station 2 rise will be = B.S. on St. 1 – F.S. on St. 2
   = 2.065 – 1.470
   = 0.595

The second reading being smaller than previous one indicates that it is rise.

2. ∴ R.L. of St. 2 = R.L. of St. 1 + Rise of St. 2
   = 260.00 + 0.595
   = 260.595 m

3. As I.S. of station 3 is greater than B.S. of station 2, so it indicates that it is fall.
   For St. 3 fall = B.S. on St. 2 – I.S. on St. 3
   = 1.226 – 3.198
   = 1.972

4. R.L. of St. 3 = R.L. of St. 2 – Fall
   = 260.595 – 1.972
   = 258.623 m

5. As F.S. of station 4 is smaller than I.S. of station 3, so it is rise
   For St. 4, Rise = I.S. on St. 3 – F.S. on St. 4
   = 3.198 – 2.458
   = 0.740

6. R.L. of St. 4 = R.L. of St. 3 + Rise of St. 4
   = 258.623 + 0.740
   = 259.363 m

Arithmetical Check :

Σ B.S. – Σ F.S. = Σ Rise – Σ Fall = Last R.L. – First RL
3.291 – 3.928 = 1.335 – 1.972 = 259.363 – 260.000
– 0.637 = – 0.637 = – 0.637

Example 1.3 : During a fly levelling work the staff readings were obtained at a regular interval of 25 m. The readings were as under –

B.S. → 0.565, 0.990, 2.775 and 2.350
F.S. → 1.685, 1.350, 2.055 and 3.450

The work was beginned with a point whose R.L. known to be 255.555. Enter the readings for Rise and Fall method to determine the R.L.s of all stations. Also, find the nature and magnitude of gradient. Apply usual check.

Solution: From the data of B.S. and F.S. readings, it is observes that there are continuous change points. Readings are tabulated accordingly.

Station	B.S.	I.S.	F.S.	Rise	Fall	R.L. (m)	Remark
0	0.565	-	-	-	-	255.555	ABM
25	0.990	-	1.685	-	1.120	254.435	CP_1
50	2.775	-	1.350	-	0.360	254.075	CP_2
75	2.350	-	2.055	0.720	-	254.795	CP_3
100	-	-	3.450	-	1.110	253.695	-
Σ	6.680	-	8.540	0.720	2.580	-	-

$$\text{Gradient} = \frac{\text{Last R.L.} - \text{First R.L.}}{\text{Horizontal distance}}$$

$$= \frac{-1.860}{100}$$

$$= 0.0186 \text{ or 1 in 53.76} \quad \text{(Falling gradient)}$$

Arithmetical Check:

Σ B.S. $- \Sigma$ F.S. $= \Sigma$ Rise $- \Sigma$ Fall $=$ Last R.L. $-$ First R.L.

∴ 6.680 − 8.540 = 0.720 − 2.580 = 253.695 − 255.555

∴ − 1.860 = − 1.860 = − 1.860

Example 1.4: A fly levelling work was carried out, starting from a P.B.M. of R.L. 239.685 (Refer Fig. 1.5) and finishing the work on C. Tabulate the readings shown in Fig. 1.5 and find R.L. of A, B and C. Use any method of your choice. Apply usual check.

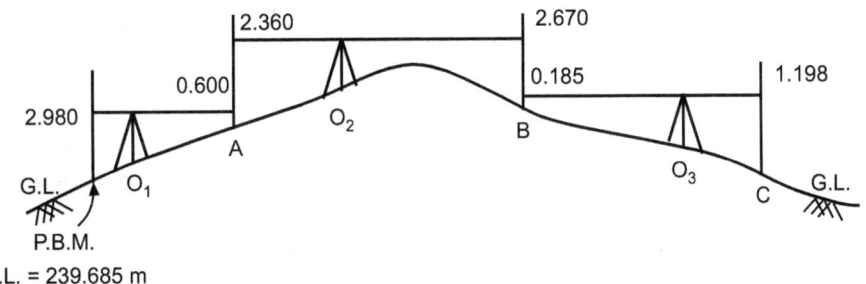

Fig. 1.5 : Fly Levelling (Not to Scale)

Solution: As Fly levelling work was carried out, so they will be only back sight and fore sight and no intermediate sight. The problem is solved by collimation plane (H.I.) method.

Station	B.S.	I.S.	F.S.	H.I. (Collimation plane)	R.L. in m	Remark
-	2.980	-	-	242.665	239.685	P.B.M.
A	2.360	-	0.600	242.425	242.065	CP_1
B	0.185	-	2.670	241.940	241.755	CP_2
C	-	-	1.198	-	240.742	-
Sum (Σ)	5.525	-	4.468		-	-

Arithmetical Check :

$$\Sigma \text{ B.S.} - \Sigma \text{ F.S.} = \text{Last R.L.} - \text{First R.L.}$$
$$5.525 - 4.468 = 240.742 - 239.685$$
$$1.057 = 1.057$$

The problem can also be solved by rise and fall method.

Station	B.S.	I.S.	F.S.	Rise	Fall	R.L. (M)	Remark
-	2.980	-	-	-		239.685	P.B.M.
A	2.360	-	0.600	0.2380	-	242.065	CP_1
B	0.185	-	2.670	-	0.310	241.755	CP_2
C	-	-	1.198	-	1.013	240.742	-
Sum (Σ)	5.525	-	4.468	2.380	1.323	-	-

Arithmetical Check :

∴ Σ B.S. − Σ F.S. = Σ Rise − Σ Fall = Last R.L. − First R.L.

$$5.525 - 4.468 = 2.380 - 1.323 = 240.742 - 239.685$$

∴ $1.057 = 1.057 = 1.057$

Example 1.5 : Starting from an A.B.M. of R.L. = 200 m, levelling was done on a continuous sloping ground and following readings were successfully recorded.

3.090, 3.840, 1.370, 2.660, 3.410, 0.955 and 1.820

Rule out the page of a level book for Collimation Plane Method' outer the readings and calculate R.L. value of each staff station. Apply usual check show two simple calculations.

Solution : In the continuously sloping ground, change point occurs where the reading abruptly changes from bigger value to smaller value abruptly as in the case of a falling ground.

Station	B.S.	I.S.	F.S.	H.I. (Collimation plane)	R.L. in m	Remark
1	3.090	-	-	203.090	200.000	A.B.M.
2	1.370	-	3.840	200.620	199.250	CP_1
3	-	2.660	-	-	197.960	-
4	0.955	-	3.410	198.165	197.210	CP_2
5	-	-	1.820	-	196.345	-
Σ	5.415	-	9.070	-	-	-

Arithmetical Check :

$$\Sigma \text{ B.S.} - \Sigma \text{ F.S.} = \text{Last R.L.} - \text{First R.L.}$$
$$5.415 - 9.070 = 196.345 - 200$$
$$-3.655 = -3.655$$

1. First H.I. = R.L. of A.B.M. + B.S.
   = 200 + 3.090
   = 203.090 m

2. R.L. of St. 2 = H.I. − F.S. on St. 2
   = 203.090 − 3.840
   = 199.250 m

3. Second H.I. = R.L. of CP_1 + B.S. on St. 2. (CP_1)
   = 199.250 + 1.370
   = 200.620 m

4. R.L. of St. 3 = Second H.I. − I.S. on St. 3
   = 200.620 − 2.660
   = 197.960 m

Example 1.6 : The following staff readings were observed on the continuously sloping ground along the centre line of a road, with the help of a dumpy level and 4 m staff of 20 m interval. The first staff reading was taken on B.M. and the second reading was taken on the starting point of the road. Reduced level of B.M. was 350.00 m, 0.540, 0.935, 1.245, 3.885, 0.450, 1.635, 2.220, 3.665, 0.775, 1.555, 2.785, 3.450.

(a) Enter the readings in a level field book page.
(b) Calculate the reduced level by rise and fall method.
(c) Determine the gradient of road.

Solution :

Distance	B.S.	I.S.	F.S.	Rise	Fall	R.L. (m)	Remark
0	0.540	–	–	–	–	350.000	BM
20	–	0.935	–	–	0.395	349.605	First point on road
40	–	1.245	–	–	0.310	349.295	–
60	0.450	–	3.885	–	2.640	346.655	CP_1
80	–	1.635	–	–	1.185	345.470	–
100	–	2.220	–	–	0.585	344.885	–
120	0.775	–	3.665	–	1.445	343.440	CP_2
140	–	1.555	–	–	0.780	342.660	–
160	–	2.785	–	–	1.230	341.430	–
180	–	–	3.450	–	0.665	340.765	–
Σ	1.765	10.375	11.000	–	9.900	3454.205	–

Arithmetical Check :

$$\Sigma \text{ B.S.} - \Sigma \text{ F.S.} = \Sigma \text{ Rise} - \Sigma \text{ Fall} = \text{Last R.L.} - \text{First R.L.}$$
$$1.765 - 11 = 0 - 9.235 = 340.765 - 350.00$$
$$-9.235 = -9.235 = -9.235$$

$$\text{Gradient of Road} = \frac{\text{Last R.L.} - \text{First R.L.}}{\text{Distance between first and last point}}$$

$$= \frac{340.765 - 350.000}{180} = \frac{-9.235}{180}$$

$$= 0.0513 \quad \text{(Falling gradient)}$$
$$= 1 \text{ in } 19.491$$

Example 1.7 : Find the missing values marked as X in the below levelling page of book. Also carryout the arithmetical check.

Station	B.S.	I.S.	F.S.	Rise	Fall	R.L. (m)	Remark
1	0.930	-	-	-	-	200.00	BM
2	-	2.820	-	-	1.890	X	-
3	X	-	X	X	-	198.580	CP_1
4	0.935	-	1.850	0.230	-	X	CP_2
5	-	X	-	-	X	197.495	-
6	-	-	2.785	-	0.535	X	Last Pt.

Solution : Starting from the known data of reduced levels, the missing readings are Calculated as under :

1.   R.L. of Stn. 2 = R.L. B.M. − Fall Stn. 2
                                          = 200 − 1.890
                                          = 198.110 m

2. As we know R.L. of Stn. 2 and Stn. 3, the difference between these two R.L.s will give amount of Rise of Stn. 3

          Rise of Stn. 3 = R.L. of Stn. 3 − R.L. of Stn. 2
                              = 198.580 − 198.110
                              = 0.470 m

3.   Rise of Stn. 3 = I.S. of Stn. 2 − F.S. on Stn. 3
                    0.470 = 2.820 − F.S. on Stn. 3

∴   F.S. on Stn. 3 = 2.350 m

4.   Rise of Stn. 4 = B.S. of Stn. 3 − F.S. on Stn. 4
                    0.230 = B.S. of Stn. 3 − 1.850

∴   B.S. of Stn. 3 = 2.080 m

5.   R.L. of Stn. 4 = R.L. of Stn. 3 + Rise of Stn. 4
                              = 198.580 + 0.230
                              = 198.810 m

6.   Fall of Stn. 5 = R.L. of Stn. 4 − R.L. of Stn. 5
                              = 198.810 − 197.495
                              = 1.315 m

7.   I.S. of Stn. 5 = B.S. of Stn. 4 + Fall of Stn. 5
                              = 0.935 + 1.315
                              = 2.250 m

8.   R.L. of Stn. 6 = R.L. of Stn. 5 − Fall of Stn. 6
                              = 197.495 − 0.535
                              = 196.960 m

Arithmetical Check :

∴   Σ B.S. − Σ F.S. = Σ Rise − Σ Fall = Last R.L. − First R.L.
            3.945 − 6.985 = − 0.700 − 3.740 = 196.960 − 200.000

∴   − 3.040 = − 3.040   = − 3.040

The result in tabulated form :

Station	B.S.	I.S.	F.S.	Rise	Fall	R.L. (m)	Remark
1	0.930	-	-	-	-	200.00	BM
2	-	2.820	-	-	1.890	198.110	-
3	2.080	-	2.350	0.470	-	198.580	CP_1
4	0.935	-	1.850	0.230	-	198.810	CP_2
5	-	2.250	-	-	1.315	197.495	-
6	-	-	2.785	-	0.535	196.960	Last Pt.
Sum Σ	3.945	-	6.985	0.700	3.740	-	-

Example 1.8 : Find the values shown as X in the following level field book page. Also show usual arithmetic check.

Station	B.S.	I.S.	F.S.	H.I.	R.L. in M	Remark
P	X	-	-	X	105.000	P.B.M.
Q	-	1.525	-	-	X	-
R	-	1.600	-	-	104.250	-
S	X	-	2.450	X	103.400	X
T	-	1.250	-	-	103.050	-
U	-	1.855	-	-	X	-
V	-	-	-	-	101.315	Last Point

1.   H.I. at Stn. P = R.L. of Stn. R + Fall on Stn. R
   = 104.250 + 1.600
   = 105.850 m
2.   B.S. on Stn. P = H.I. – R.L. of Stn. P
   = 105.850 – 105.000
   = 0.850 m
3.   R.L. of Stn Q = H.I. – I.S. on Stn. Q
   = 105.850 – 1.525
   = 104.325 m
4.   H.I. at Stn. S = R.L. of Stn T + I.S. on Stn. T
   = 103.050 + 1.250
   = 104.300 m

5.   B.S. on Stn S = H.I. at Stn. S – R.L. of Stn. S
          = 104.300 – 103.400
          = 0.900 m

6.   R.L. of Stn U = H.I. at Stn S – I.S. on Stn. U
          = 104.300 – 1.855
          = 102.445 m

7.   F.S. on Stn Y = H.I. at Stn. S – R.L. of Stn V
          = 104.300 – 101.315
          = 2.985 m

Station	B.S.	I.S.	F.S.	H.I.	R.L. (m)	Remark
P	0.850	-	-	105.850	105.000	P.B.M.
Q	-	1.525	-	-	104.325	-
R	-	1.600	-	-	104.250	-
S	0.900	-	2.450	104.300	103.400	CP_1
T	-	1.250		-	103.050	-
U	-	1.855	-	-	102.445	-
V	-	-	2.985	-	101.315	Last Point
(Σ) Sum	1.750	-	5.435	-	-	-

Arithmetical Check :

     Σ B.S. – Σ F.S. = Last R.L. – First R.L.
     1.750 – 5.435 = 101.315 – 105.000
       – 3.685 = – 3.685

Example 1.9 : The following readings were taken with a 4 m levelling staff. The staff was held inverted at 3rd reading. Readings were 1.585, 2.630, 2.465, 3.285. Calculate the R.L's. of the staff stations. The first reading was taken on a B.M. of R.L. 200.000 m.

Solution : The problem is solved by collimation plane method. Since, the instrument was not shifted during the exercise, only one H.I. will be obtained.

1.   H.I. = R.L. of B.M. + B.S. on B.M.
          = 200.000 + 1.585
          = 201.585 m

2.   R.L. of Stn. 2 = H.I. – I.S. on Stn. 2
          = 201.585 + 2.630
          = 198.955 m

3.   R.L. of Stn. 3 = H.I. – (–I.S. on Stn. 3)
          = 201.585 + 2.465
          = 204.050 m

Here, the I.S. is added to H.I. as the staff is held inverted at the point. Therefore, the point is above the line of sight i.e. H.I. and hence the staff reading will have to be added to get R.L. of the point above H.I. as shown in Fig. 1.6.

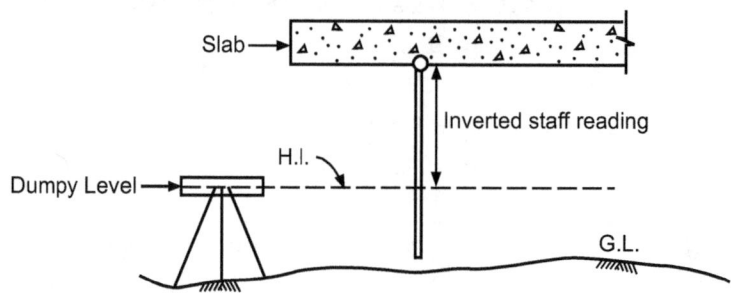

Fig. 1.6

4.   R.L. of Stn. 4 = H.I. − F.S. on Stn. 4
                  = 201.585 − 3.285
                  = 198.300 m

The readings are entered as follows. The reading of staff held inverted is entered as negative since, it is above H.I.

Station	B.S.	I.S.	F.S.	H.I.	R.L. in M	Remark
1	1.585	-	-	201.585	200.000	B.M.
2	-	2.630	-	-	198.955	-
3	-	−2.465	-	-	204.050	Inverted staff
4	-	-	3.285	-	198.300	Last Point
Σ	1.585	-	3.285	-	-	-

Arithmetical Check :

Σ B.S. − Σ F.S. = Last R.L. − First R.L.
1.585 − 3.285 = 198.300 − 200.000
− 1.700 = − 1.700

Example 1.10 : Find the height of a Tee-beam above the floor level. The R.L. of the floor is 100.855 m and the staff reading on the floor is 2.055 m. The reading on the staff held upside down against the under side of the beam is 3.565 m.

Solution : R.L. of plane of collimation,

H.I. = 100.855 + 2.055
    = 102.910 m

R.L. of the under side of Tee-beam,
$$= 102.910 + 3.565$$
$$= 106.475 \text{ m}$$
Hence, the height of the Tee-beam above the floor level,
$$= 106.475 - 100.855$$
$$= 5.620 \text{ m}$$

Example 1.11 : During a levelling work started from A.B.M. of known R.L. = 100.000 m, the following staff readings were obtained :

1. 0.850　　2. 1.555　　3. 1.725
4. 0.455　　5. 1.800　　6. 1.750
7. 0.950　　8. 1.555

The instrument was shifted after 3rd and 6th readings. Enter correctly all the readings in a field book page and determine the reduced levels of all stations showing calculations by Rise and Fall method. Apply usual arithmetic check.

Solution : The readings are entered in a field book page by noting that the instrument was shifted after 3rd and 6th reading will be entered in fore sight column and consequently 4th and 7th reading will be entered in back sight column.

The first reading is entered in back sight column, whereas last reading will be entered in fore sight column and remaining readings in intermediate sight column.

Station	B.S.	I.S.	F.S.	Rise	Fall	R.L. in m	Remark
1	0.850	-	-	-	-	100.000	A.B.M.
2	-	1.555	-	-	0.705	99.295	-
3	0.455	-	1.725	-	0.170	99.125	CP_1
4	-	1.800	-	-	1.345	97.780	-
5	0.950	-	1.750	0.05	-	97.830	CP_2
6	-	-	1.555	-	0.605	97.225	Last point
(Σ) Sum	2.255	-	5.030	0.050	2.825	-	-

Arithmetical Check :

$$\Sigma \text{ B.S.} - \Sigma \text{ F.S.} = \Sigma \text{ Rise} - \Sigma \text{ Fall} = \text{Last R.L.} - \text{First R.L.}$$
$$2.255 - 5.030 = 0.050 - 2.825 = 97.225 - 100$$
∴
∴ $$-2.775 = -2.775 = -2.775$$

PART - [B] LEVELLING

1.3 INTRODUCTION

Vertical measurements are measurements which are made in the vertical plane and grouped under the term levelling.

- The operation of determining the difference of elevation of points with respect to each other on the surface of the earth is called *levelling*.
- Determination of elevations of points is necessary in selecting alignments of highways, railways, water supply and drainage pipelines and in the construction of engineering structures such as dams, bridges, industrial sheds etc.
- Levelling helps in locating industries or different shops of an automobile on a large piece of land.
- The profile of ground can be plotted in the form of longitudinal and cross-sections from spot level. This data can be used to calculate the magnitude of the cutting, filling of earth work involved in the project.

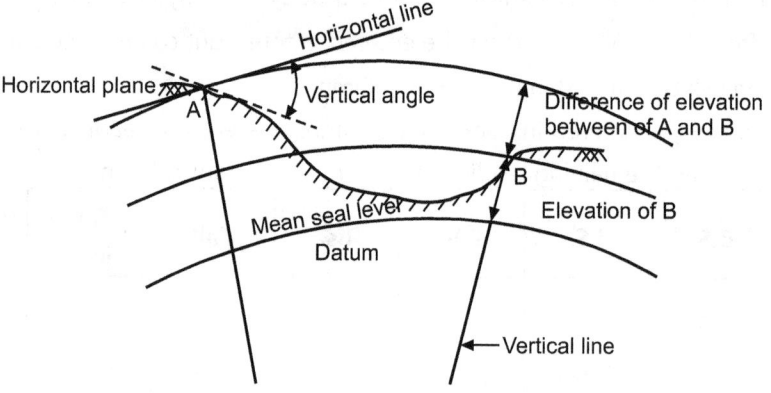

Fig. 1.7 : Levelling Terms

Level Surface : A surface parallel to the mean spheroidal surface of the earth is called level surface, e.g. a still lake. It is normal to the plumb line at all points.

Level Line : It is a line lying on a level surface. It is normal to the plumb line at all the points.

Horizontal Plane : It is a plane tangential to the level surface at the point under consideration. It is perpendicular to the plumb line.

Horizontal Line : It is line lying in the horizontal plane. It is a straight line tangential to the level line.

Vertical Line : It is a line from any point on the earth's surface to the centre of the earth. It is commonly considered to be the line defined by a plumb line.

Datum Surface : It is an arbitrarily assumed level surface from which vertical distances are measured. The mean sea level at Karachi is taken as the datum surface for India or datum level from which G.T.S. bench marks are established.

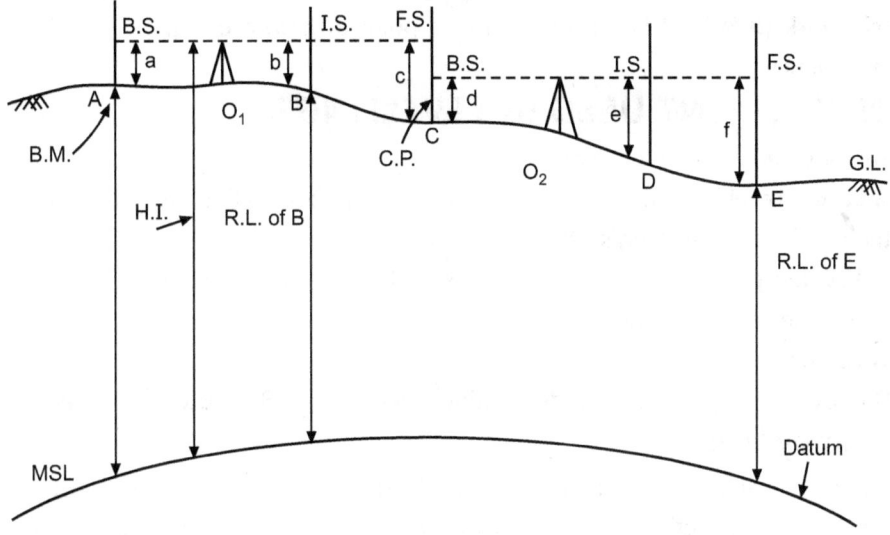

Fig. 1.8

Reduced Level (R.L.) : It is the vertical distance of a point measured above or below the datum. It is also called as elevation of a point. It is abbreviated as R.L.

Back Sight (B.S.) : It is a staff reading taken on a point of known elevation e.g. sight on a benchmark (station A) or on a change point, i.e. station C. In Fig. 1.8, 'a' and 'd' are back sights. It is also called a **plus** sight since the reading is added to the reduced level of the bench mark.

Fore Sight (F.S.) : It is a staff reading taken on a point whose elevation is to be determined e.g. a sight on a change point i.e. station C and E. In Fig. 1.8, 'c' and 'f' are fore sights. It is also called as **minus** sight since this reading is subtracted from the reduced level of collimation plane to get the R.L. of point.

Intermediate Sight (I.S.) : It is a staff reading taken on a point of unknown elevation between back sight and fore sight e.g. a sight on station B and D. In Fig. 1.8, 'b' and 'e' are the intermediate sights. It is also called as minus sight since this reading is subtracted from the reduced level of collimation plane to get the R.L. of the point.

Change Point (C.P.) or Turning Point (T.P.) : It is a point on which fore sight and back sight readings are taken. Change point indicates the shifting of the level. Any well defined object whose top surface is level such as boundary stone, man hole cover, kilometre stone can be selected as change point. It is also called as Turning point. In Fig. 1.8, station C is the change point.

Height of Instrument (H.I.) : It is the elevation of the plane of collimation when the instrument is levelled. It should be noted that the height of an instrument does not mean the height of the centre of the telescope above the ground, where the level is set up.

Bench Mark (B.M.) : It is a fixed reference point of known elevation. Levelling work is started with bench mark.

1.4 INSTRUMENT USED IN LEVELLING

Instruments required for levelling are :
1. **A Level :** Level is an instrument used to obtain horizontal line of sight while observing the readings on levelling staff.
2. **A Levelling Staff :** It is used to measure the vertical distances of points below or above the horizontal line of sight.

Types of Levels :
  1. Dumpy level
  2. Modern tilting level
  3. Automatic level.

1.4.1 Dumpy Level

The dumpy level is commonly used for levelling work because it is compact and stable type of instrument. It consists of a telescope mounted upon a level bar which is rigidly fastened to the spindle. Inside the tube of the telescope there are objective and eye piece lens at the either end of the tube. A diaphragm fitted with cross-hairs is present near the eye piece end. A focusing screw is attached with the telescope. A level tube housing a sensitive plate bubble is attached to the telescope and parallel to it. The levelling head consists of tribrach and trivet with three foot screws known as levelling screws in between. The trivet is attached to a tripod stand.

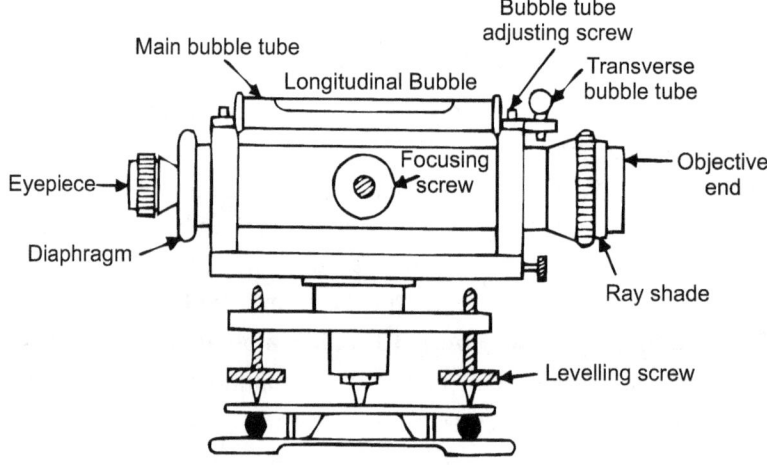

(a) Dumpy Level and its Parts

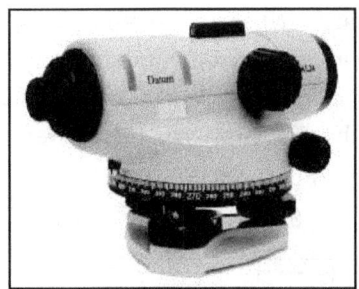

(b) Dumpy Level
Fig. 1.9

Functions of Salient Parts :
1. **A Levelling Head :** To bring the bubble in the centre of its run.
2. **Telescope :** Used to sight a staff placed at desired station and to read staff distinctly.
3. **Diaphragm :** Holds the cross hairs (fitted with it).
4. **Eye Piece :** Magnifies the image formed in the plane of the diaphragm and thus to read staff during levelling.
5. **Level Tube :** Used to make the axis of the telescope horizontal and thus the line of sight.
6. **Levelling Screws :** To adjust instrument (level) so that the line of sight is horizontal for any orientation of the telescope.
7. **Tripod Stand :** To fix the instrument (level) at a convenient height of an observer.

Advantages of Dumpy Level :
1. It is stable and compact type of instrument.
2. It is simple in construction with very few movable parts.
3. The adjustments are not easily disturbed.

1.4.2 Automatic or Adjusting Level

It is similar to the dumpy level with its telescope fixed to the tribrach. For approximate levelling a circular spirit bubble is attached to the side of the telescope. For accurate levelling, a stabilizer or compensate [Fig. 1.10 (a)] is fitted inside the telescope, which automatically levels the instrument. Whatever may be the type of automatic level used, it must be levelled within approximately 15-30' of the vertical, to allow the compensator to work. This is usually achieved by using a three footscrew arrangement in conjunction with a small circular level (sometimes called a pond bubble) which is mounted somewhere on the level.

The automatic levelling uitlizes the action of gravity in its operation. A prismatic device called compensator is suspended on fine non-magnetic wires. A compensator is an optical system consisting of two fixed prisms [Fig. 1.10 (b)] placed in the optical path between the eyepiece and the objective. An inverted pendulum supported by four non-magnetic wires, operates the compensating prism that keeps the image of the sighted point at the intersection of the cross-hairs at D. When the instrument becomes approximately level, the action of gravity on the compensator causes the optical system to swing into the position that provides a horizontal line of sight. the pendulum moves until its centre of gravity is over the intersection of the lines of the wire supports. This moves the compensating prism so that the horizontal line of sight is brought to the horizontal cross-hairs at D [Fig. 1.10 (c)].

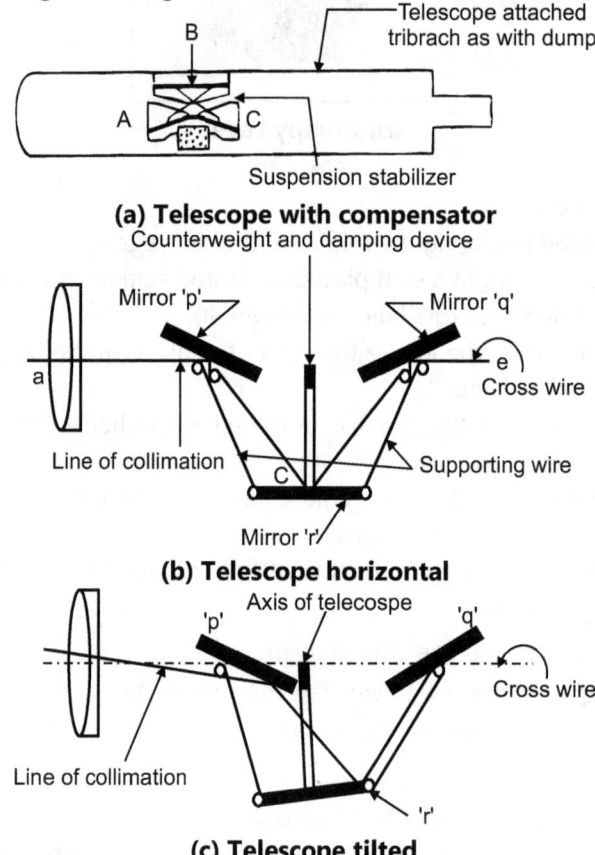

(a) Telescope with compensator

(b) Telescope horizontal

(c) Telescope tilted

Fig. 1.10 : Automatic Level

In addition to the levelling procedure, a test should be made to see if the compensator is functioning before readings commence. One of the levelling foot-screws should be moved slightly off level and, if the reading to a levelling staff remains constant, the compensator is working. If the reading changes, it may be necessary to gently tap the telescope to free the compensator. On some automatic levels, this procedure is not necessary since a button is attached to the level which is pressed when staff has been sighted. If the compensator is working, the horizontal hair is seen to move and then return immediately to the horizontal line of sight.

It is much simpler to use as it gives an erect image. It is very rapid in operation. There is no chance of errors due to bubble setting. The main disadvantages is that it cannot be used in strong winds and at places susceptible to vibrations. An automatic level AP-7 manufactured by Nikon Corporations shown in Fig. 1.11.

Fig. 1.11

1.4.3 Types of Levelling Staff

The levelling staff is a device which enables the surveyor to measure the vertical distance by which the staff station i.e. the foot of the staff is above or below the horizontal line of sight. A levelling staff is a straight rectangular piece of wood or aluminium about 75 mm wide and 25 mm thick. The foot of the staff represents zero reading since graduations are marked from the foot of the staff upwards. A self reading staff is one the reading on which can be directly read by the instrument man sighting through the telescope. In modern levels, the erect image of the staff is seen through the telescope. Hence reading the staff is very easy and convenient.

1. Telescopic Staff (Sopwith pattern) : The telescopic staffs may be made of seasoned timber or aluminium. However, the aluminium staffs are in common use now. It is usually 4 metres long and made in three telescopic lengths. The top solid piece about 1.2 m long slides into the central box of about 1.3 m length. The lower base of 1.5 m length receives the central box. Fig. 1.12 shows a sopwith pattern staff arranged in three lengths.

The inner pieces can be pulled out one after the another and kept in position by metal spring clamps at the back of each piece. On the front face decimetre, markings are neatly painted in black against a white background. The red dot indicates completed metre marking. The least count of the staff is 5 mm. One tenth of a metre is subdivided into twenty equal parts.

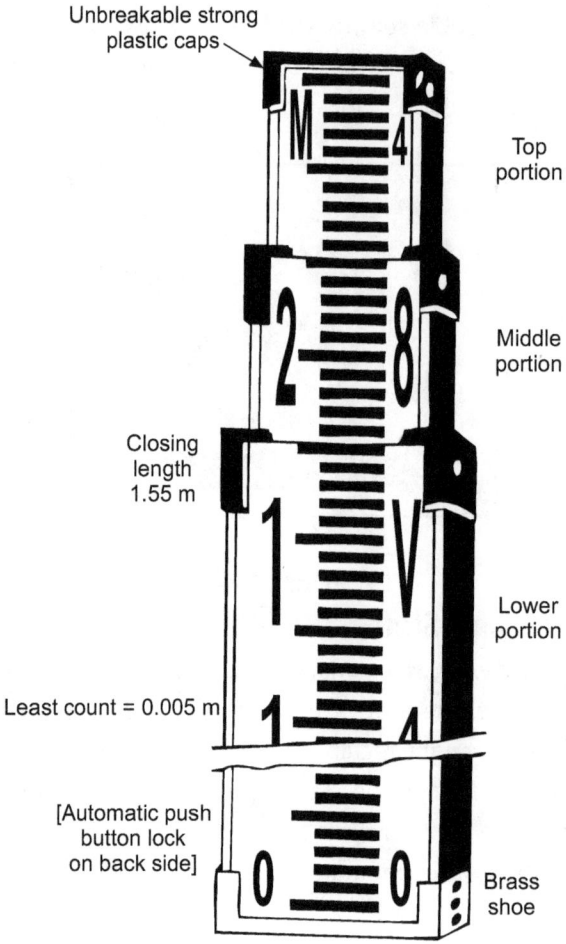

Fig. 1.12 : Telescopic Staff

2. Folding Staff : The staff is 4 metre long and consists of two 2 metre wooden pieces with hinged joint in the centre. The width is 75 mm and thickness is about 18 mm. The folding joint has a locking device at the back. When the two pieces are locked together, the two pieces become rigid and straight. The foot of the staff is protected by a brass cap at the bottom. To keep the staff vertical, a circular bubble is fitted at the back. Each metre is subdivided into 200 divisions, the thickness of the graduation being 5 mm. The metre numeral is painted in red and the decimetre numeral is painted in black colour. The decimetre numerals are marked continuously throughout the staff for folding staff.

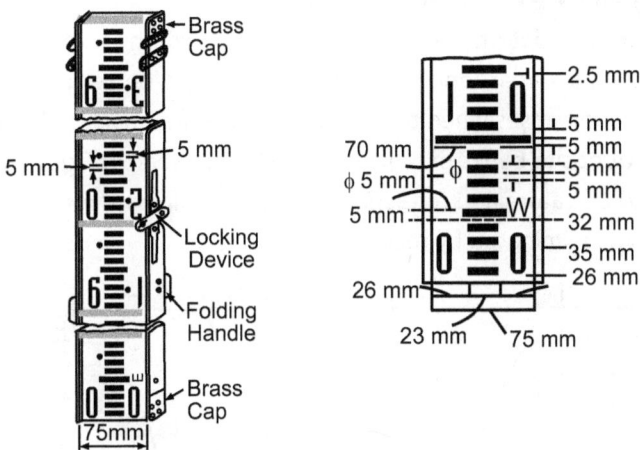

Fig. 1.13 : Folding staff

1.5 PRINCIPAL AXES OF DUMPY LEVEL

The following are the principal axis of dumpy level :

(1) Line of collimation. (2) Axis of telescope.
(2) Vertical axis. (4) Axis of the level tube

(1) **Line of collimation :** The imaginary line joining the centre of the cross-wires of the diaphragm to the centre of the object glass and its continuation.

(2) **Axis of the telescope :** It is the line joining the centre of the eye piece and centre of object glass.

(3) **Vertical axis :** It is the axis which is obtained by the rotation of the telescope in a horizontal plane.

(4) **Axis of the level tube :** It is the straight line which is tangential to the longitudinal curvature of the bubble tube as its mid-point.

For 'Fundamental Lines in a Level' refer Fig. 1.14.

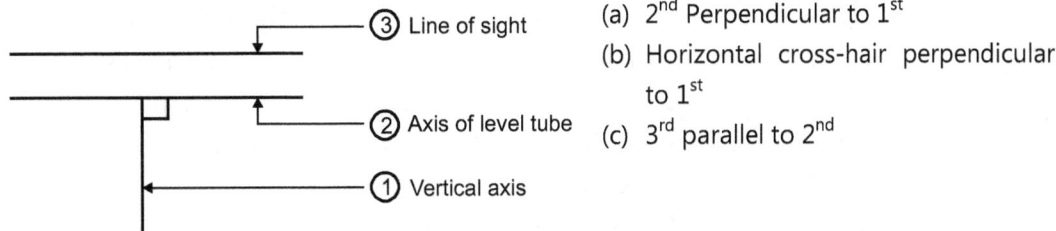

(a) 2nd Perpendicular to 1st
(b) Horizontal cross-hair perpendicular to 1st
(c) 3rd parallel to 2nd

Fig. 1.14 : Desired Relationship between Fundamental Lines

1.6 RECIPROCAL LEVELLING

It is a method used to determine the difference of elevation correctly between two points spaced at a long distance apart and when the level cannot be set up midway between the two points. This situation arises when two-points whose difference of elevation is to be found out are located on opposite banks of a river or a valley. (as seen in Fig. 1.15).

The error due to curvature and refraction and line of collimation not remaining parallel to the bubble line can be eliminated by reciprocal levelling.

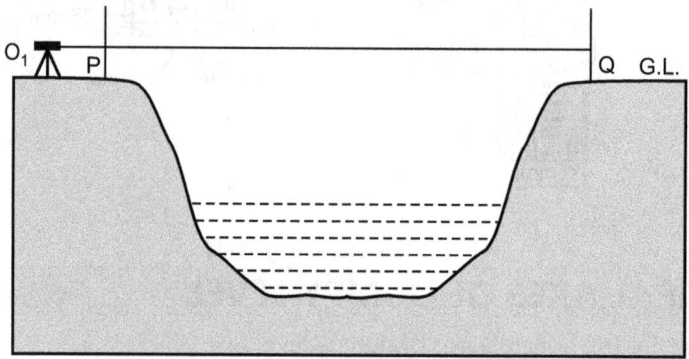

Fig. 1.15 : Reciprocal Levelling (Along Gorge)

Procedure :

(1) P and Q are the two points located on opposite banks of a river. It is derived to find the difference of elevation between P and Q accurately.

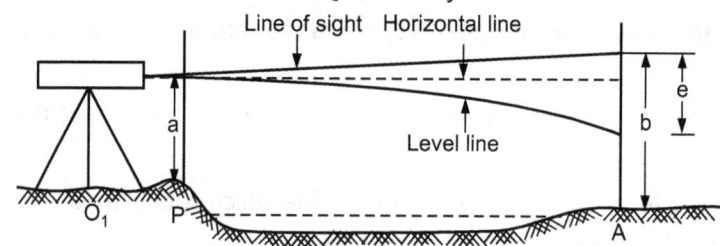

Fig. 1.16

(2) (i) Set up the instrument at O_1 very near to the point P and take reading on the staff held at P and Q with the bubble in the centre. The reading on the staff at 'P' may not be clearly seen, hence this reading will have to be taken through objective. Let the staff readings at P and Q be denoted as 'a' and 'b'.

(ii) Shift the instrument i.e. level to a point O_2 nearer to the station Q.

(iii) With the bubble in the centre, take the readings on the staff held at P and Q again. Let the staff readings be denoted as 'a_1' and 'b_1'.

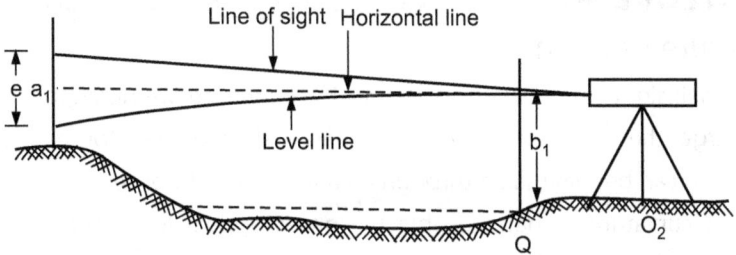

Fig. 1.17

Let 'e' be the total error due to curvature, refraction and error in the line of collimation and 'h' be the true difference of level between P and Q.

Let the point 'Q' be lower than the point 'P' as shown in Fig. 1.17. When the instrument is at O_1, the staff at P being very near to O_1, the error is negligible, hence reading on staff at P can be taken as correct. Correct reading on staff at Q = (b − e).

∴ True difference of levels in the first case

$$h = (b - e) - a$$
$$h = (b - a) - e \quad \ldots (1.1)$$

When the instrument is shifted to O_2, the reading on the staff held at 'A' can be taken as correct.

∴ Correct reading on staff held at P = a_1 − e.

Hence, the true difference of levels in the second case

$$h = b_1 - (a_1 - e)$$
$$h = (b_1 - a_1) + e \quad \ldots (1.2)$$

Add equations (1.1) and (1.2).

∴ $$h = \frac{(b - a) + (b_1 - a_1)}{2}$$

Thus, the mean of the two apparent differences of level between the two points gives the true difference of level between P and Q. In order to find the total error, equating the value of h from (1.1) and (1.2).

∴ $(b_1 - a_1) + e = (b - a) - e$

∴ $$\boxed{e = \frac{(b - a) - (b_1 - a_1)}{2}}$$

It is to be noted that refraction error is not fully eliminated. Hence, two levels are set up very near to P and Q and the staff readings are taken on P and Q simultaneously to eliminate refraction error.

1.7 CURVATURE AND REFRACTION CORRECTION

1.7.1 Curvature of Earth

In case of small sight distance, errors due to the curvature are negligible, but if the sight distances are large, the errors should be estimated and accounted for, as discussed below. However, the error can be minimized through balancing of sight or reciprocal observation.

The effect of curvature is that the objects sighted appear lower than they actually are. The effect of refraction is to make the objects sighted appear higher than they really are.

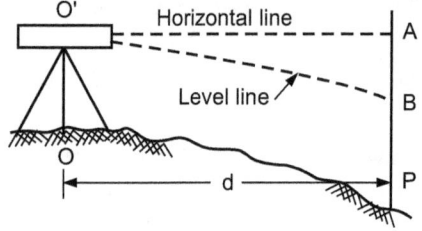

Let the level be set up at O and the staff held at point P. Although the line 'OA' is horizontal. It is not a level line. The actual level line is O'B (see Fig. 1.18).

Fig. 1.18

If the staff reading is taken on the staff held at P, the reading will be obtained as PA. The true reading will be PB. Thus, the apparent reading obtained (PA) is more than the true reading (PB). Hence, the difference between the observed reading PA and the true reading PB represents the error introduced on account of the curvature of earth.

The expression for correction for curvature of earth can be derived as follows.

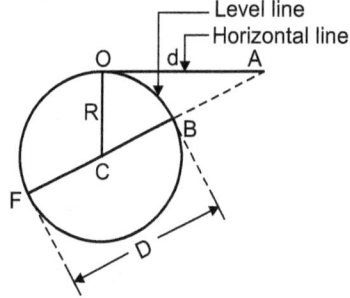

In Fig. 1.19, Let OA be the line of collimation i.e. horizontal line and 'c' be the centre of earth. Let OB be the level line. Let 'd' be the distance from the instrument station O to the staff station A in km and 'R' be the radius of earth (CO) in km and 'D' be the diameter of earth in km. From the Fig. 2.25, AB is the correction for curvature.

Fig. 1.19

Now, $AB \times AF = AO^2$
But $AF = AB + BF$
∴ $AB^2 + AB \times AF = AO^2$
(Neglecting AB^2 which is very small)
∴ $AB \times AF = AO^2$
$$AB = \frac{AO^2}{BF} = \frac{AO^2}{2R}$$

$$AB = \frac{d^2}{2R} = \frac{d^2}{12734} \quad \text{(Taking R = 6367 m)}$$
$$AB = 7.85 \times 10^{-5} d^2 \text{ (km)}$$

And $AB \text{ in (metre)} = 0.0785 d^2$

Thus, correction for curvature = $0.0785 d^2$

Where, 'd' is the distance of staff in km from the level. This correction is subtractive.

True staff reading = Observed staff reading − $0.0785 d^2$

1.7.2 Refraction

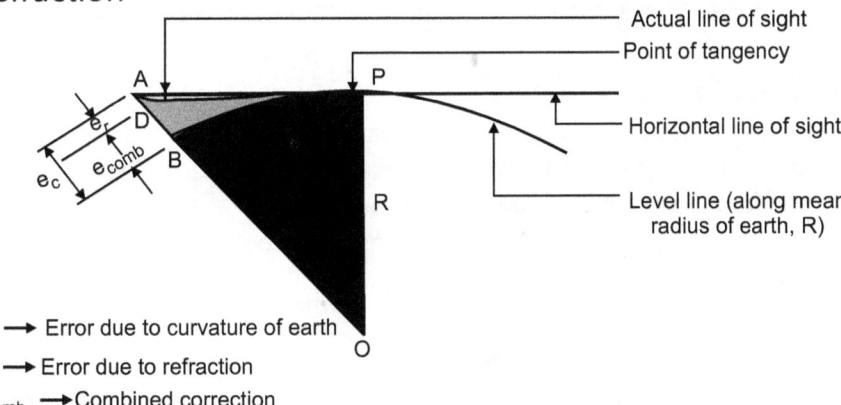

$e_c \rightarrow$ Error due to curvature of earth
$e_r \rightarrow$ Error due to refraction
$e_{comb} \rightarrow$ Combined correction

Fig. 1.20 : Calculation for Curvature and Refraction Error

The ray of light from the staff to the instrument does not follow a straight path (PA) but is refracted or bent down while passing through air of different densities. The ray of light follows a curved path PD as shown in Fig. 1.20. The length AD represents the error in the staff reading due to refraction. Thus, the effect of refraction is to reduce the staff reading. The curved path followed by the refracted ray can be assumed to be an arc of a circle of radius equal to seven times of the earth average conditions of the atmosphere.

∴ Correction for refraction in metres = $AD = \frac{1}{7} \times AB$

$$= \frac{1}{7} \times (0.0785 d^2)$$

Correction for refraction = 0.0112

The correction for refraction is additive to the staff reading.

1.7.3 Combined Correction for Curvature and Refraction

The correction for curvature of earth being substractive and having greater numerical value than the correction. For refraction, the combined correction is substractive and obviously its effect is to increase the staff reading.

∴ Combined correction = BD = $-0.0785 d^2 + 0.0112 d^2 = -0.673 d2$

The distance 'd' is measured in km.

The correction is applied in the following ways :
(i) After computing the value of combined correction, each staff reading is decreased by the value of combined correction.
(ii) After obtaining the R.L. of the point by the usual methods of reduction, the R.L. of the points is increased by the value of combined correction.

The correction for curvature and refraction is not applied in ordinary levelling, as the length of the sights is usually less than 200 m and the combined correction for 200 m length is only about 3 mm. The error can be eliminated by equalizing foresight and back sight distances.

1.8 DISTANCE TO VISIBLE HORIZON

Let 'E' be the point of observation at on elevation of 'h' metres as shown in Fig. 1.21. Let 'C' be the point on the horizon where the tangent from E meets. The distance CE of the visible horizon from the point E can be obtained as follows.

$$h = 0.0673\, d^2 \text{ (considering both curvature and refraction)}$$

$$d = \sqrt{\frac{h}{0.0673}} \text{ km} \quad \text{where h is in metres}$$

$$d = 3.853\sqrt{h} \text{ km}$$

where 'd' is distance to the visible horizon in km from the point of observation and 'h' be the height of the point of observation above mean sea level in km.

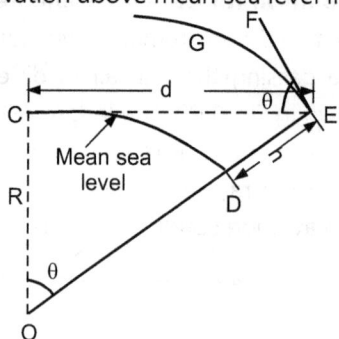

Fig. 1.21

SOLVED EXAMPLES

Example 1.12 : A dumpy level was set up very near to the station 'A' on one bank of a river. The distance from the station peg 'A' upto the centre of the eyepiece was measured as 1.560 m and reading on the staff held at B was 0.975 m. The level was shifted to other bank very near to station B. The distance upto the centre of eyepiece was measured likewise from station peg B and was found to be 1.120 M and the reading on the staff held at A was 1.725 m. Find the true R.L. of station 'B' if R.L. of station peg A was 555.555 m.

Solution :

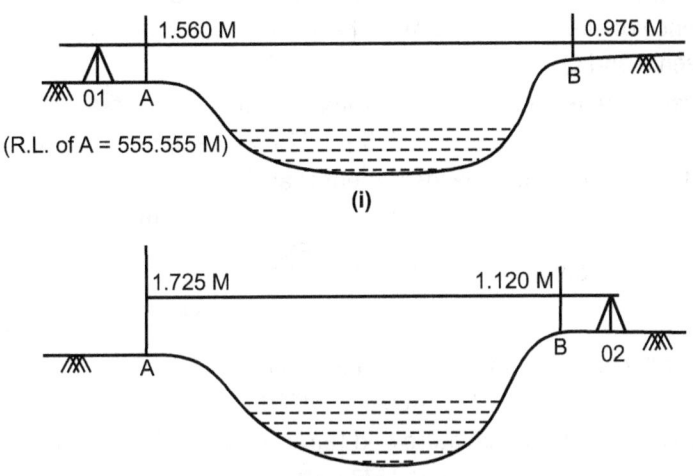

Fig. 1.22

The data in the problem pertains to reciprocal levelling

(i) When the level is set up near to station 'A', the reading on the staff at, A = 1.560 m and the reading on the staff at B = 0.975 m.

Apparent difference in elevation between A and B = 0.585 m

(ii) Similarly, when the level is shifted at B,

$$\begin{aligned}
\text{Reading on the staff at A} &= 1.725 \text{ m} \\
-\text{ Reading on the staff at B} &= 1.120 \text{ m} \\
\hline
\text{Apparent difference in elevation} &= 0.605 \text{ m}
\end{aligned}$$

∴ True difference in elevation $= \dfrac{0.585 + 0.605}{2} = 0.595$ m

To find the reduced level of 'B'

R.L. of peg A = 555.555 m
+ Difference in elevation between A and B (rise) = 0.595 m

∴ R.L. of station B = 556.150 m

Example 1.13 : Following notes refer to reciprocal levels taken with one level.

Instrument at	Staff reading on		Remarks
	P	Q	
P	1.625	2.545	Distance PQ = 782 m
Q	0.725	1.405	R.L. of P = 460.530 m

Determine :
(i) True of R.L. of Q.
(ii) Combined correction for curvature and refraction.
(iii) Angular error in collimation adjustment.

Solution : From the observations, it is clear that there is a fall from P to Q.

$$\begin{bmatrix} \text{True difference of elevation} \\ \text{between P and Q} \end{bmatrix} = \frac{\text{Sum of the apparent differences}}{2}$$

(i) (a) Apparent difference when the instrument is at P

$$= 2.545 - 1.625 = 0.920 \text{ m}$$

(b) Apparent difference when the instrument is at Q

$$= 1.405 - 0.725 = 0.680 \text{ m}$$

$$\text{True difference} = \frac{0.920 + 0.680}{2}$$

$$= 0.800 \text{ m}$$

(c) Reduced level of Q = R.L. of P − Fall from P to Q

$$= 460.530 - 0.800 = 459.730 \text{ m}$$

(ii) Combined correction for curvature and refraction for a distance of 782 m

$$C = 0.0673 \times d^2 \quad \text{(d is in km)}$$

$$= 0.0673 \times (0.782)^2$$

$$= 0.041 \text{ m}$$

(iii) Let, the line of collimation be inclined upwards and e_c be the error in collimation in a distance of 782 m.

$$\begin{bmatrix} \text{When the instrument is at P} \\ \text{the corrected staff reading on Q} \end{bmatrix} = [\text{Observed staff reading}]$$

$$- [\text{Correction for curvature and refraction}]$$
$$- [\text{Collimation error}]$$

∴ Corrected staff reading on Q $= 2.545 - 0.041 - e_c$

And staff reading on P $= 1.625 \text{ m}$

∴ $\begin{bmatrix} \text{True difference of level} \\ \text{between P and Q} \end{bmatrix} = (2.545 - 0.041 - e_c) - (1.625) = 0.800$

∴ $0.879 - e_c = 0.800$

The same answer could be found out by finding the true difference of level between P and Q from the observation at station Q − The corrected staff reading on P and will be equal to $(0.725 - 0.041 - e_c)$.

∴ True difference of level between P and Q

$$= 1.405 - (0.725 - 0.041 - e_c) = 0.721 + e_c = 0.800$$

$$e_c = \text{Error in collimation} = 0.800 - 0.721 = 0.079 \text{ m}$$

Angular error in collimation adjustment will be

$$= \frac{0.079}{782} \times \frac{180}{\pi} \times 60 \times 60$$

$$= 20.83 \text{ seconds}$$

Example 1.14 : Reciprocal levels were taken with dumpy level as under :

Instrument at	Staff reading on		Remarks
	A	B	
P	1.500	2.250	Distance between
Q	0.600	1.320	P and Q = 880 m

Assuming collimation error to be – 0.005 m in 100 m, calculate the difference between P and Q and the corrections of curvature, refraction and collimation.

Solution : The true difference of level between P and Q will be calculated from the following formula,

$$h = \frac{(b-a) - (b_1 - a_1)}{2}$$

$$= \frac{(2.250 - 0.600) - (1.500 - 1.320)}{2}$$

$$= 0.735 \text{ m}$$

Thus, the true difference of level between P and Q = 0.735 m.

The total error due to curvature, refraction and collimation $e = e_{c_1} + e_c - e_r$

Correction for curvature for 880 m will be

$$= 0.0785 \, d^2$$
$$= (0.0785) \times (0.88)^2$$
$$= 0.06079 \text{ m}$$

Similarly,

$$\text{Collimation error in 100 m} = -0.005$$
$$\text{Collimation error in 880 m} = \frac{-0.005 \times 880}{100}$$
$$= -0.044 \text{ m}$$

Let e_r be the error due to refraction, when the level is at 'P'.

[Corrected reading on 'Q'] = [Observed reading on Q] – [Curvature – Refraction] + [Collimation error].

Now, [True difference of level between P and Q] = [Corrected reading on Q] – [Reading on P].

$$2.250 - (0.06079 - e_r) + 0.044 - 1.500 = 0.735$$
$$0.733 + e_r = 0.735$$
$$e_r = 0.002 \text{ m in the correction for refraction}$$

Example 1.15 : In precise levelling between two points M and N, situated on the opposite sides of a deep valley, the level was set up near M and the staff readings on M and N were 1.625 m and 3.785 m respectively. The level was then shifted and set up near staff station, N and the respective staff readings on M and N were 0.305 m and 2.485 m. Find
1. The true R.L. of a staff station N, if the R.L. of M is 575 m and
2. The total error, due to curvature, refraction and imperfect collimation adjustment.

Solution :

1. When the level was set up near M, the apparent difference in elevation between M and N will be,

$$3.785 - 1.625 = 2.160 \text{ m (N is higher than M)}.$$

When the level was set up near N, apparent difference in elevation between M and N will be,

$$= 2.485 - 0.305 = 2.180 \text{ m}$$

True difference in elevation $= \dfrac{2.160 + 2.180}{2}$

$$= 2.170 \text{ m}$$

True R.L. of staff station N $= 575 - 2.170$

$$= 572.830 \text{ m}$$

2. To find the total error, due to curvature, refraction and imperfect collimation adjustment. When the level was at M, the apparent difference in elevation = 2.160 m.

Since the true difference in elevation is 2.170 m

Total error in observation = 2.170 − 2.160 = 0.01 m

(due to curvature, refraction and imperfect collimation adjustment)

1.9 PROFILE LEVELING

It is the operation to determine elevations of points spaced apart at known distances (say 20 m, 30 m etc.) along a given line in order to obtain the accurate outline of the surface of the ground profile. The purpose of profile levelling is to provide data from which a vertical section of the ground surface along a survey line can be plotted. This line is called *profile*.

From the plotting of longitudinal section, it is possible for the engineer to decide the longitudinal slope to be given to the road surface or to decide the location of culuerts, bridges, railways, canals etc. and to determine volume of cutting and filling of earth work. It is essential to run a longitudinal section along various proposed centre lines and to compare their costs to select a suitable one.

It uses the principle of differential levelling. A number of change points along with intermediate sights may be required. The intermediate sights are taken on stations, at breaks in the ground surface, at points of change of slope and other critical points. The readings are entered in the field in tabular form. The information regarding the various features like bed level of stream, road, railway, culvert etc. lying on the section line must also be noted.

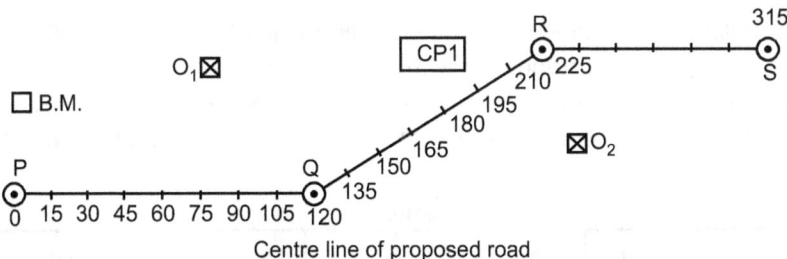

Fig. 1.23 : Plan of a Road Alignment

1.9.1 Field Work in Profile Levelling

- As shown in Fig. 1.23, let PQRS represent the centre line of a proposed road. The ranging rods are fixed at the points P, Q, R and S. If it is decided to take levels at a common interval of 15 m, chain is stretched in the direction of PQ and ranging is done.
- Chain is laid straight and level is set up on a firm ground in such a way that it is possible to take reading on bench mark and maximum points are covered along the line PQ.
- Let the instrument station chosen be O_1 and back sight reading on bench mark is taken and entered in the column of back sight. Reduced level of collimation plane is found out.
- Then staff is held at chainage 0, 15 m, 30 m, 45 m etc. and readings are taken at these chainages and entered as intermediate sight readings and the reduced levels of the respective points are found out.
- The chain is stretched further and chainages are marked at proper intervals.
- After taking certain readings, if it is found that it is not possible to read the staff, then a suitable change point say CP_1 is chosen and the level is shifted to a new position 'O_2'. Before shifting the level, the fore sight reading is taken on the change point and after shifting the level to a position 'O_2', the back sight reading is taken on CP_1.
- New R.L. of collimation plane (H.I.) is found out. Then staff readings are continued along the centre line in the usual manner. After reaching the final station 'S' and noting its chainage, the staff reading is taken and then fly levelling is carried out returning to the bench mark.
- If the closing error on the bench mark is more than the permissible limit, the entire work has to be repeated. It is to be noted that although staff readings are taken at some uniform interval of chainage, if in a particular length, the slope of the ground suddenly changes, the interval at which the staff readings are taken should be closer than before in order to accurately determine the profile of the ground in that stretch.
- The fore and back bearings of the lines PQ, QR and RS should be taken and recorded in the field book. Location sketches of the stations, sketches of bench marks and features such as road, streams and nalla crossed by the alignment should be drawn and described in the field book.

- The tabulation of readings in profile levelling is illustrated in the following example. In the example the readings along the line PQ and along line QR are tabulated as shown in Fig. 1.23. Although the stations Q and R are shown to end, at chainages 120 m and 226 m, in actual practice, the chainages of those stations will be some odd figures.

Table 1.1

Station	Distance	Fore Bearing	Back Bearing	B.S.	I.S.	F.S.	H.I.	Reduced Levels	Remarks
							321.640	320.400	ABM
P	0	72° 30'	-	1.240				320.780	
1	15				0.860			320.025	
2	30				1.615			319.770	
3	45				1.870			320.190	
4	60				1.450			319.980	
5	75				1.660			319.665	
6	90				1.975			318.810	
7	105				2.830			318.660	
Q	120	48° 15'	252° 30'		2.980			319.300	
				1.770	2.340	2.810	320.600	318.830	CP$_1$
8	135				1.690			318.910	
9	150				1.815			318.785	
10	165				1.960			318.640	
11	180				2.370			318.230	
12	195				2.650			317.950	
13	210				2.890			317.710	
R	225	113° 30'	228° 15'			2.940		317.660	
Total				+3.010	-	5.750			

Arithmetical Check :

$$\Sigma \text{ B.S.} - \Sigma \text{ F.S.} = 3.010 - 5.750 = -2.740$$

Last R.L. − First R.L. = 317.660 − 320.400 = − 2.740

Fig. 1.20 (a) and (b) show the readings as tabulated in Table 1.1 in elevation and plan.

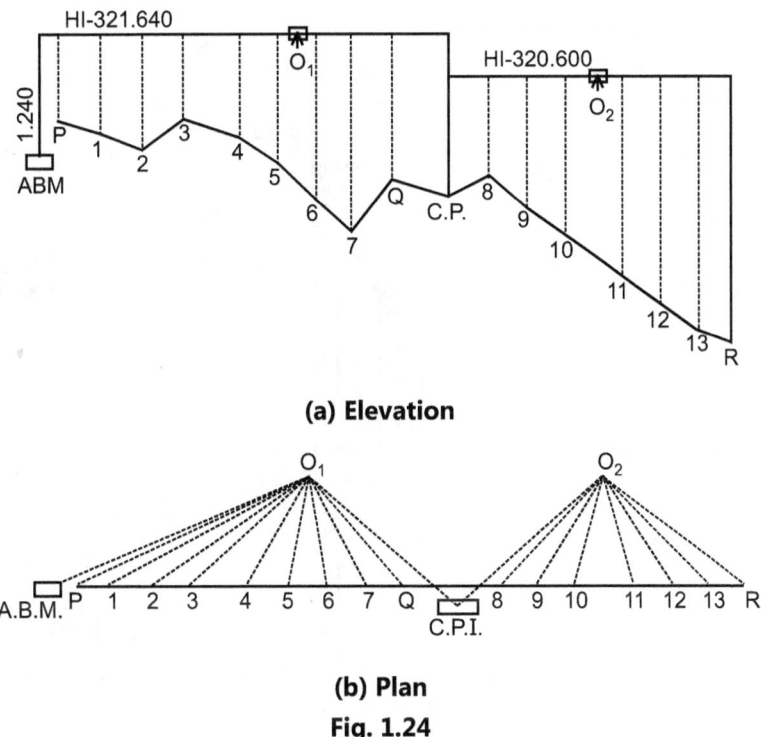

(a) Elevation

(b) Plan

Fig. 1.24

1.9.2 Points to be Kept in Mind While Carrying Out Longitudinal Sectioning

1. The chainages of the centre line of alignment should be continuous though there may be change in the alignment.
2. While shifting the instrument, the readings of back sight and fore sight on change point should be taken accurately, with bubble in the centre of its run.
3. While taking the readings, the back sight distance should be equal to fore sight distance as far as possible.
4. Important features such as streams, canal, road, river crossed by the line should be located by measuring bearings of their centre lines, width etc.

1.9.3 Plotting the Profile (Longitudinal Section)

- First a horizontal line is drawn and the chainages of staff points along the alignment are marked on this line to a suitable horizontal scale.
- Then ordinates are drawn at each of the chainages.
- The reduced level at each chainage is written over these ordinates. A horizontal line is drawn over this, which serves as a datum line.
- The minimum and maximum R.L's are found out from the field book and a suitable R.L. is selected to serve as Datum R.L. considering minimum R.L., such that the minimum height of ordinate when plotted to suitable vertical scale will be about 5 cm.

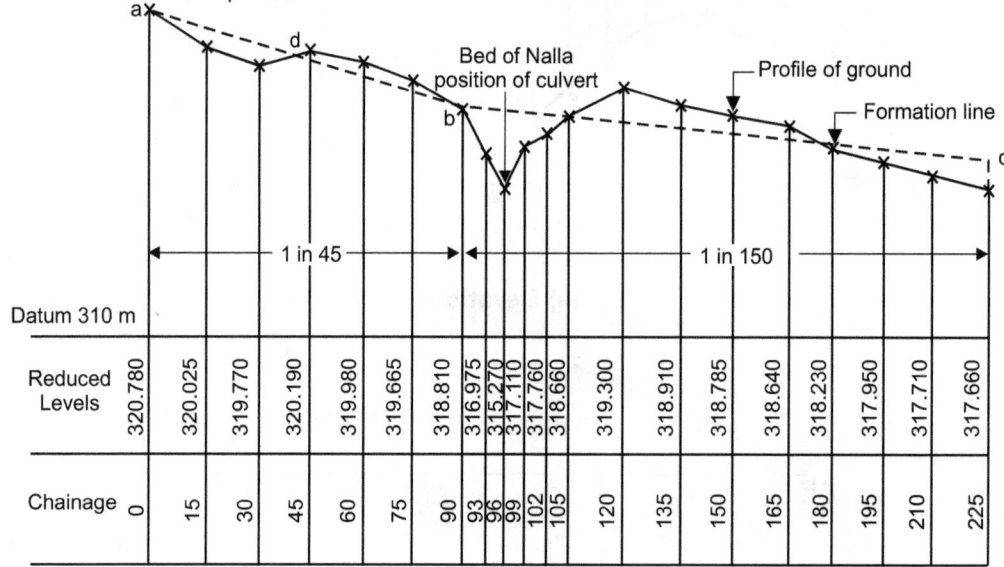

Scale – Horizontal 1 : 100
Vertical 1 : 100

Fig. 1.25

- After selecting the datum, the heights of ordinates at each chainage are calculated and plotted to the vertical scale.
- Then the plotted points of each ordinate are joined by straight lines. Thus, the top profile of ground surface is obtained along the centre line of say road. (If the profile levelling is carried out for road work).
- The horizontal scale selected is usually same as the scale adopted for plan. The vertical scale used is usually ten times the horizontal scale.
- The object of choosing the enlarged scale is to make the surface irregularities of the ground more clear. The scales usually adopted for plotting are as follows.
  Horizontal scale – 1 in 1000 to 1 in 2500.
  Vertical scale – 1 in 100 to 1 in 250.

Fig. 1.25 shows a typical longitudinal section based on the reduced levels shown in Table 1.1.

1.10 SELECTION OF A FORMATION LINE FOR WORKING PROFILE

Usually, for a road work or railway alignment, when a longitudinal section is plotted, a working profile is prepared. The engineer can estimate the volume of earthwork involved, from the study of working profile. In order to prepare working profile, formation line is drawn with suitable gradients from the beginning of alignment to the end chainage of the longitudinal section. While drawing the formation line, it should be seen that the volume of cutting and the volume of filling should balance each other. Although this is a desirable condition, it should be seen that the longitudinal gradient chosen does not exceed the ruling gradient (maximum permissible value of gradient). In Fig. 1.25, it will be seen that the 'ab' and 'bc' are the formation lines with falling gradient of 1 in 45 and 1 in 150 respectively. Thus, it can be seen that the portion i.e. volume of cutting over formation line db is approximately equal to portion i.e. volume of filling under the line ad. Between the portion bf, there is a big depression indicating the bed of nalla and probable site of the culvert. Similarly, the portion i.e. volume of ground over the line fe in cutting is approximately equal to the portion i.e. volume of filling under the formation line etc.

1.11 CALCULATION OF FORMATION LEVELS

Once the formation line is drawn for a working profile, it is very easy to calculate the formation levels at each staff station. Refer to Fig. 1.25.

Let the formation level at 0 chainage be the same as the ground level at 0 chainage.

∴ Formation level at 0 chainage = 320.780.

For the line ab, the falling gradient provided is 1 in 45, hence there is a drop of 1 m for every 45 m chainage. Therefore, the formation level at 15 m chainage will be 320.780 − 0.33 = 320.45 m. Similarly, the formation level at 30 m chainage will be 320.78 − 0.66 = 320.12 m. Thus, ground profile above the formation line will obviously indicate the cutting whereas the ground profile below the formation line will indicate filling.

To find the depth of cutting or the height of embankment, the difference between the R.L. of formation and R.L. of ground is found out which gives the depth of cutting or height of filling as the case may be.

1.12 CROSS-SECTIONING

This can be defined as "the sections taken at right angles to the main alignment with a view to find the transverse nature of the ground surface". These are then plotted to obtain the outline of the ground surface at right angles to the centre line. Cross-sections are taken at 20 m or 30 m interval along the centre line. Cross-sections are set out by optical square or box sextant.

In Fig. 1.26, plan of the centre line of roads PQ and QR is shown. The cross-sections 1–1, 2–2, 3–3 etc. are laid at 30 in intervals. It is to be noted that where the direction of alignment changes, there are two cross-sections such as 6-6 perpendicular to line PQ and 7–7 perpendicular to line QR. The cross-sections may be laid to a distance of 30 m to 60 m on each side of the centre line in case of road work or the distance may be increased to 100 m to 200 m in the case of a railway line. The work of cross-sections is generally carried simultaneously with the longitudinal sectioning. The tabulation of readings is as shown in Table 1.2.

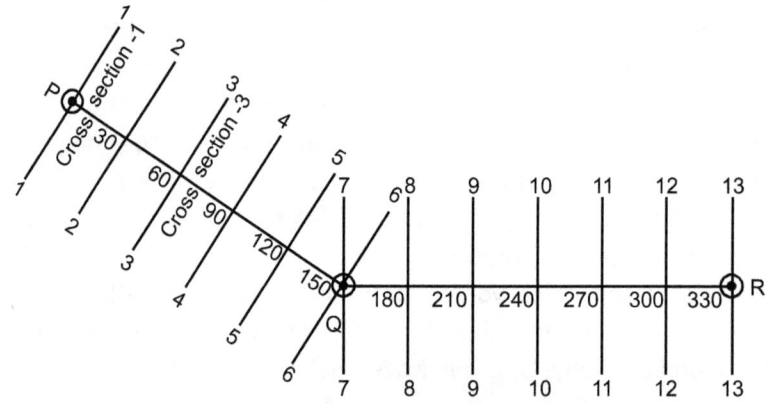

Fig. 1.26 : Cross-sections on the Lines PQ and QR

Table 1.2

Distance in m			B.S.	I.S.	F.S.	H.I.	R.L.	Remarks
Left	Centre	Right						
			1.180			113.800	112.620	T.B.M.
	0			1.450			112.350	
				1.315			112.485	
5				1.120			112.680	
10				1.050			112.750	
15				1.625			112.175	
		5		1.800			112.000	
		10		1.960			111.840	
		15		1.780			112.020	
	30			1.665			112.135	
5				1.410			112.390	
10				1.225			112.575	
15				1.940			111.860	
		5		1.855			111.945	
		10					111.460	
		15			2.340			
			1.180		2.340			

Arithmetic Check :

$$\Sigma \text{ B.S.} - \Sigma \text{ F.S.} = 1.180 - 2.340 = -1.160$$

Last R.L. − First R.L. = 111.460 − 112.620 = − 1.160 (Tallied).

While booking field notes, it can be seen from Table 1.2 that the only change is in the 'Distance Column' where additional column for distance measured to the left and to the right are introduced as compared to the tabulation of readings for profile levelling shown in Table 1.1.

1.13 PLOTTING THE CROSS-SECTIONS

The procedure for plotting the cross-sections is similar to the plotting of profile on ground. The only change is in the scales used for plotting. The scale used for plotting the horizontal and vertical distances is same. The reduced levels of the datum line may be different for different cross-sections. The horizontal and vertical scales used for plotting vary from 1 : 100 to 1 : 200. Fig. 1.27 shows a typical cross-section at chainage 30 m. The reduced levels for plotting are taken from Table 1.2.

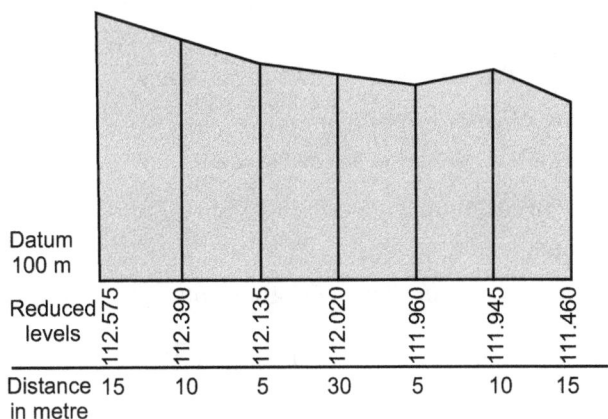

Fig. 1.27 : Typical Cross-section at Chainage 30 m

REVIEW QUESTIONS

(1) (a) State and define the fundamental axes of a Dumpy level.
 (b) How will you test whether the line of collimation is parallel to the axis of bubble tube ?

(2) (a) Describe with a neat sketch Tilting level.
 (b) In what respects, a Tilting level differs from the dumpy level ?

(3) (a) Explain the procedure of carrying out the profile levelling and cross sectioning by means of dumpy level and staff.

(b) How will you make the axis of the bubble tube perpendicular to the vertical axis?

(4) What are the circumstances under which reciprocal levelling is recommended? How?

(5) (a) What are the special features of an automatic level?

(b) Describe briefly the tilt compensator used in self alignment levels.

(6) (a) What are the effects of curvature of earth and atmospheric refraction on the levelling work? How the staff readings are affected?

(7) (a) Derive an expression for the correction for (i) curvature of earth and (ii) Refraction.

(b) State the advantages of reciprocal levelling and describe the method.

(8) Write short notes on:
(a) Folding staff.
(b) Fixing the formation line in L - section.
(c) Self-aligning level.

(9) (a) Describe briefly the Construction of a Laser Level.

(b) State the uses of Laser level.

(10) (a) Explain the construction of a Digital Level.

(b) Mention any five uses of Digital Level.

(11) State the advantages of Auto level.

(12) Define the terms 'Contour line', 'Contour interval', 'Horizontal equivalent' and 'Ridgeline'.

(13) Differentiate between:
1. Direct and indirect method of contouring
2. Contour interval and horizontal equivalent.

(14) Compare the following:
1. Contour interval and Horizontal equivalent.
2. Contour lines representing ridgeline and Valley line.

(15) Draw typical contours along with designating (R.L. values) for
(i) Lake (ii) Hill (iii) Ridge (iv) Uniformly slopping ground.

(16) State the different methods of interpolation of counters, Explain any one method in brief.

(17) Show the fallowing features in contour maps :
   (i) Steeply sloping and Gently sloping ground,
   (ii) Ridge line and Valley line.
(18) With neat sketch explain any four characteristics of contour lines.
(19) Explain in detail the direct method of locating contours and discuss its merits and demerits.
(20) Draw the contour lines showing the following characteristics.
   (1) Ridge lines (2) Valley lines (3) Overhanging diff. (4) Hill % Depression or pond.
(21) Write uses of contour maps.
(22) What are the methods of contouring ? Give relative merits and demerits of each.

EXAMPLES

(1) (a) In testing a Dumpy level, reciprocal levels are taken and the following results were obtained.

Instrument at	Staff reading in metres	
	P	Q
P	1.425	1.070
Q	1.060	0.735

Is the line of collimation in adjustment ? What should be the staff reading on P during the second set of the instrument to make the line of collimation truly horizontal ?

   [**Ans.** : (i) True difference of level = – 0.340 m.
   (ii) Line of collimation is inclined downwards by an amount 0.015 m.]

(2) (a) In a two peg method of Dumpy level, the following readings were observed.

Instrument at	Staff reading on		Remarks
	A	B	
(i) O (midway between A and B)	2.655	2.350	Horizontal distance between A and B is 100 m
(ii) A	2.425	2.115	

Find the staff reading on B so that the line of sight will be horizontal when the instrument is at A.

   [**Ans.** : Staff reading on B when the instrument is at A = 2.120].

(3) The following notes refer to reciprocal levels taken with one levelling instrument.

Instrument position	Staff readings in metres on		Remarks (Distance)
	P	Q	
Near P	1.600	2.750	PQ = 1000 m
'Near Q	2.700	1.550	R.L. of P = 125.000 m

Find :

(i) the R.L. of Q,

(ii) the combined correction of curvature and refraction, and

(iii) the collimation error.

[**Ans.** : R.L. of Q = 125.00 m and Collimation error 1.0827 m]

(4) A level is set up at a station O and the reading on the staff held at P 700 m away from O, is 1.470. The reading on the staff at Q 1500 m away is 2 865. Find the true difference in elevation between P and Q.

[**Ans.**: 1.277 m]

(5) Find the distance to the visible horizon from the top of a light house 35 m high. Take the diameter of earth as 12740 km. What is the dip of horizon ?

(Dist. to visible horizon = 22.80 km and dip of horizon = 12.30 minutes).

Unit - II

THEODOLITE

2.1 PRINCIPAL AXES AND TEMPORARY ADJUSTMENTS OF TRANSIT THEODOLITE

2.1.1 Study of Vernier Transit 20" Theodolite

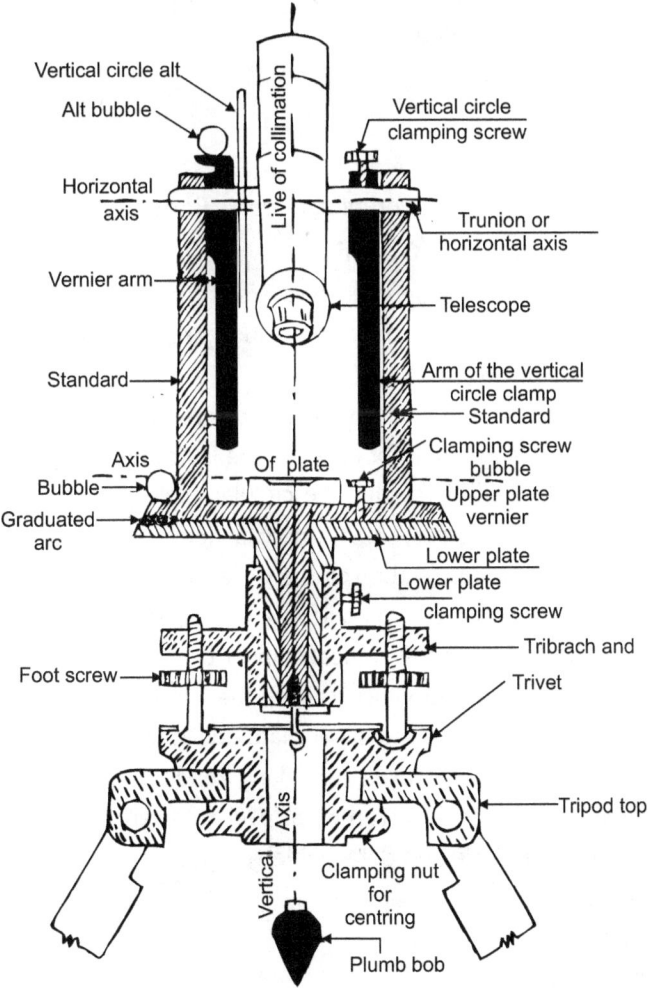

Fig. 2.1 : Transit Vernier Theodolite (Sectional Elevation)

Theodolite is a most accurate instrument used for measuring the horizontal and vertical angles. It can also be used for locating points on a line, prolonging survey lines, finding differences in deviations, setting out curves, grades, ranging curves etc.

2.1.2 Classification of Theodolite

Theodolites are primarily classified as,

(1) Transit

(2) Non-transit

A theodolite is called to be transit when its telescope can be transited i.e. revolved through a complete revolution about its horizontal axis in the vertical plane, whereas in non-transit type, the telescope cannot be transited. The non-transit Theodolites are inferior in utility and have now become obsolete.

Theodolites are also classified as :

(1) Vernier Theodolites.

(2) Micrometer Theodolites.

Depending upon where the vernier or micrometer is fitted to read the graduated circle.

2.1.3 Different Parts of a Theodolite

A transit vernier theodolite essentially consists of the following parts :

(1) Levelling head : This supports the main working parts of the instrument and screws onto a tripod. It comprises of two parts :

(i) Tribrach and trivet stage filled with levelling screws.

(ii) Centre shifting arrangement for centring the instrument quickly and accurately.

(2) Lower Circular Plate : This carries the circular scale graduated from 0 to 360° to degrees and half degrees or degrees and third of a degree and a tapered spindle which works in the outer conical bearing. To the spindle is fitted a well ribbed bracket, carrying on opposite side, the slow motion and clamping screws for upper plate and lower plate.

(3) Upper Plate : The centre of the vertical spindle of the lower plate is bored to form a bearing for an other vertical spindle which carries the upper circular horizontal plate. The upper plate can be rotated relative to the lower plate about this spindle as axis. It carries two verniers marked **A** and **B**, which are used for taking readings accurately upto 20" on two lower graduated circle. This plate also carries a level tube and two vertical standards for supporting telescope, vertical circle and detachable compass.

The compass may be :

(i) The circular box compass.

(ii) The trough compass.

(iii) The tubular compass.

(4) Telescope : The telescope of theodolite may be :
   (i) External focussing telescope.
   (ii) Internal focussing telescope.

The first type is used in older type of theodolites, while the later is used in modern instruments. It is mounted near its centre on a horizontal axis at right angles to the main longitudinal axis of the theodolite.

(5) Vertical Circle : The vertical circle is rigidly fixed to the horizontal axis of the telescope and moves with it. It is silvered and is usually divided into four quadrants. The graduations in each quadrant are numbered from 0° to 90° in opposite directions from the two zeros placed at ends of the horizontal diameter of the vertical circle so that the line joining the zeros is parallel to the line of collimation of the telescope when it is horizontal. The subdivisions on the vertical circle are similar to those of horizontal circle. A clamp and fine motion tangent screw are provided for the vertical circle.

(6) T Frame or Index Bar : It is T shaped and is centred on the horizontal axis of the telescope infront of the vertical circle. The two verniers C and D are provided on it at the ends of the horizontal called the *index arm*. A vertical leg, known as clipping arm is provided with a fork and two clipping screws at its lower extremity. The index and clipping arm together are known as T frame. At the top of this frame is attached a bubble tube which is called the altitude bubble tube.

(7) Plumb bob : A plumb bob is suspended from the hook fitted to the bottom of the vertical axis for centring the instrument exactly over the station point.

(8) Tripod Stand : The theodolite is supported on a tripod when in use. The tripod consists of three solid or framed legs and its head carries an external screw to which the internal screw of the instrument may be fitted. A cap should be provided on the external screw to protect it from injury when the tripod is not in use.

(9) Standards : Two standards each resembling letter A, are mounted on the upper plate and they support the horizontal axis of the telescope. The index frame and arm of the vertical circle clamp are also attached to the standards or A frames.

(10) Level Tubes : The upper surface of the upper plate carries two level tubes, also known as *plate levels*, at right angles to each other. One of the level tube is parallel to the horizontal axis. The level tubes are in the form of spirit levels and they are used for levelling the instrument.

(11) Optical Plumet : In modern theodolites, optical plumet is provided for centring of the theodolite. In the optical plumet, a small telescope is provided by adjusting the eyepiece at the end of the telescope, it is possible to see the image of station peg and the centring of the instrument can be easily done.

2.1.4 Various Definitions

(1) Transit : It is the operation of revolving the telescope in a vertical plane by 180° about the horizontal or trunion axis. It is also referred to as plunging or reversing.

(2) Face Right : When the vertical circle of a theodolite is on the right of the observer, the position is called face right and the observation made is called face right.

(3) Face Left : When the vertical circle of a theodolite is on left of the observer the position is called face left and the observation made is called face left observation.

(4) Axis of Level Tube : It is a straight line tangential to the longitudinal curve of the level tube at its centre. It is also known as the bubble line and it is horizontal when the bubble is central.

(5) Axis of Telescope : It is the line joining the optical centre of the object glass to the centre of the eye-piece.

(6) Centring : It is the operation carried out to ascertain the fact that the vertical axis of the instrument passes through the centre of the peg fixed at the required station point. It is carried out by suspending a plumb bob from the underside of the instrument.

(7) Swinging the Telescope : Revolving the telescope in the horizontal plane about its vertical axis is called swinging. A right swing means clockwise rotation of the telescope, whereas left swing means anticlockwise rotation of the telescope.

(8) Telescope Normal : The telescope is said to be normal or direct when its vertical circle is to the left of the observer and the bubble is up.

(9) Telescope Inverted : The telescope is said to be inverted when its vertical circle is to the right of the observer and the bubble is down.

(10) Horizontal Axis : It is the axis about which the telescope and the vertical circle rotate in a vertical plane. It is also known as trunion axis or transverse axis.

(11) Vertical Axis : It is the axis about which the telescope can be rotated in a horizontal plane.

(12) Line of Sight : It is an imaginary line joining the intersection of cross hairs to the optical centre of the objective and its continuation.

2.1.5 Principal Axes

(1) Vertical Axis : It is the axis about which the telescope can be rotated in a horizontal plane.

(2) Horizontal Axis : It is the axis about which the telescope and the vertical circle rotate in a vertical plane. It is also known as *trunion* axis or *transverse axis*.

(3) Axis of bubble tube : It is an imaginary straight line which is tangential to the longitudinal curvature of the bubble tube at its mid-point.

(4) **Axis of Telescope :** It is defined as the line joining the optical centre of the object glass to the centre of eye piece.

(5) **Line of collimation :** It is an imaginary line joining the intersection of the cross hairs of the diaphragm to the centre of the object glass and its continuation. It is also called as the *line of sight*.

2.1.6 Temporary Adjustments of Transit Theodolite

Theodolite must be adjusted at every set up of the instrument before making observations. These adjustments are therefore temporary. They include the following :

(1) Setting up the instrument over the station.
(2) Levelling of the instrument.
(3) Elimination of the parallax.

(1) Setting up the instrument over the station : The operation of setting up includes the centring of the theodolite over the ground station mark and approximate levelling of the instrument. The centring of the instrument is carried out in the following steps :

(1) Suspend the plumb bob with a string attached to the hook fitted to the bottom of the vertical axis.
(2) Place the theodolite over the station mark by spreading the legs of the tripod, well apart so that the telescope is at a convenient height.
(3) Do approximate centring by moving the legs radially and circumferentially till the plumb bob hangs within 1 cm horizontally of the station mark.
(4) Do finer centring by unclamping the centre-shifting arrangement.

Before centring the instrument over the station mark it should be ensured that the level of the tripod head is approximately levelled. In case, there is a considerable dislevelment, the centring will be disturbed, when levelling is done. The approximate levelling may be done with reference to a small circular bubble attached to the tribatch or by eye adjustment.

(2) Levelling of the Theodolite : The levelling operation is performed to make the vertical axis of the instrument truly vertical and pass through the ground station mark. The following steps are involved in the levelling operation. (See the Fig. 2.2 (i)).

(a) Turn the horizontal plate until the longitudinal axis of the plate level becomes parallel to the line joining any two levelling screws. (See the Fig. 2.2 (i) (a)).
(b) By turning the levelling screws simultaneously in opposite directions either inwards or outwards bring the bubble to the centre of its run.
(c) Turn the instrument through 180° in azimuth.
(d) If the bubble position is found different, move it by means of the same levelling screws to the approximate mean of the two positions.
(e) Turn the instrument through 90° in azimuth so that the plate level becomes perpendicular to the previous position. (Fig. 2.2 (i) (b)).

(f) Using the third levelling screw move the bubble to the approximate mean position already indicated.

(g) Repeat the above steps until the bubble retains the same position for every setting of the instrument in azimuth.

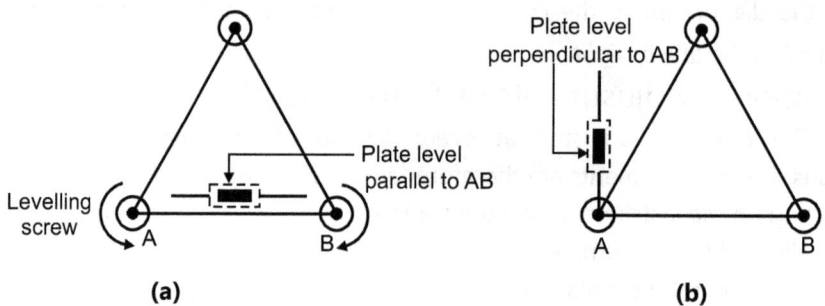

Fig. 2.2 (i) : Levelling of a Theodolite

(3) Elimination of Parallax :

(a) For making an observation first focus the eye piece for the observer's eye. This is most easily done by holding a white paper about 150 m infront of the objective and turning eye piece in or out until the cross-hairs are sharp and distinct. Then an object is selected and focussed and the image of the object is brought into the plane of the cross-hairs.

(b) This can be checked by moving the eye up and down or sideways a small amount to detect whether or not the cross-hairs appear to move with respect to the object sighted.

(c) If there is no relative movement, the focussing lens in the proper position and the telescope is properly focused (Fig. 2.2 (ii) (c)). If there is relative motion between the cross-hairs and the object sighted, the condition is called parallax and it exists between the image and the cross-hairs. This condition arises when the focussing lens is not in its proper position as shown in Fig. 2.2 (ii) (a) and (b) and the image is not formed in the plane of cross hairs. Refocussing brings the focussing lens in the proper position and the parallax is eliminated.

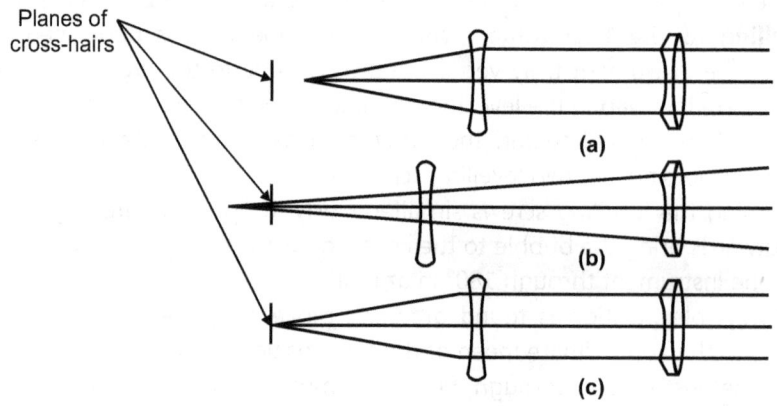

Fig. 2.2 (ii) : Parallax

2.2 USES OF THEODOLITE

Following are the various uses of Theodolite :
1. To carry out the traverse survey.
2. To establish the gradients.
3. To measure the horizontal and vertical angle.
4. To prolong the survey lines.
5. To lay out the curves.
6. To locate the point of intersection of two straight lines.
7. To measure deflection angles.
8. To measure direct angles.
9. To measure magnetic bearing of a line.
10. To run a straight line between two points.
11. Taking observations for the measurement of areas and volumes.

2.3 MEASUREMENT OF HORIZONTAL ANGLES BY USING THEODOLITE

Procedure :

To measure the horizontal angle AOB.

(1) Set the instrument over the station O and level it accurately.

(2) Set the vernier A to the zero (usually marked 360°) of the horizontal circle. To do this, loosen the upper clamp, turn the upper plate until the index (the arrow) of the vernier A nearly coincides with the zero of the horizontal circle. Clamp both plates together with the upper clamp and by turning the upper slow motion or tangent screw, bring the two zeros into exact coincidence. This may be judged by observing the divisions each side of the zero and noting that they are symmetrically placed with respect to the coinciding lines. Both plates being clamped, the instrument will now revolve upon the lower motion (the outer axis).

(3) Loosen the lower clamp. Turn the instrument and direct the telescope approximately to the left-hand signal A by sighting over the top of the telescope. Tighten the lower clamp and bisect A exactly by using the lower slow motion screw. The point of intersection of the horizontal and vertical cross-hairs should be brought into exact coincidence with the station mark whenever possible by means of the vertical circle clamp on a tangent screw. Otherwise the vertical cross-hair should be brought exactly on the lower portion of the arrow of the ranging rod making the station in order to minimize the error due to non-verticality of the signal.

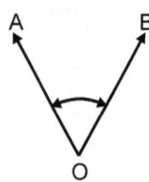 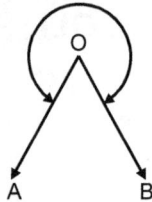

Fig. 2.3

(4) Check the setting of the vernier A to detect the error caused by turning the wrong tangent screw. Read the vernier B and record the readings.

(5) Unclamp the upper or vernier plate and turn the telescope clockwise until the line of sight is set nearly on the right hand signal 'B'. Tighten the upper clamp and by turning the upper tangent screw, bisect B exactly. It may be noted that during this movement of the telescope, the lower clamp and lower slow motion or tangent screw are untouched.

(6) Read both verniers. The reading of the vernier 'A' which was initially set at 360° gives the value of the angle AOB directly and the other vernier B by deducting 180°. The mean of the two vernier readings (after deducting 180° from the reading on vernier B) gives the value of the required angle AOB. Both verniers should always be read –

    (i)   to detect the mistake in readings of the vernier A, and

    (ii) to eliminate errors of eccentricity of centres and verniers.

(7) Change the face of the instrument and repeat the whole process. The mean of the two vernier readings gives the second value of the angle.

On all important work, face left and face right observations should be made to eliminate the errors due to imperfect adjustments of the instruments. The mean of the two observations gives the value of the required angle free from all instrument errors.

It may be noted that the vernier A is initially set to zero of the circle for convenience only. It may be set at any other reading which should be noted. The difference between the initial and final readings of the vernier A will then give the value of the required angle.

2.3.1 To Measure a Horizontal Angle by Method of Repetition

This method is used for very accurate work. In this method the angle is added several times mechanically and the value of the angle is obtained by dividing the accumulated drawings by the number of repetitions. In repeating the angle several times, the vernier A is kept clamped each time at the previous readings when the back sight is taken. The method of repetition consists in measuring the angle clockwise, any desired number of times (six) half of which are made with the telescope normal and the other half with the telescope inverted. By this means the angle can be determined to a finer degree of accuracy, than that obtained with the least count of the vernier.

Measurement of angle AOB is done as follows :
(1) Set up the instrument at the station point O and level it accurately. (The face of the instrument should be face left and telescope in normal position).
(2) Set the vernier A to 0° or 360° by using the upper clamp and its tangent screw. Then loosen the lower clamp, direct the telescope to the left hand object A and bisect A exactly by using the lower clamp and its tangent screw.
(3) Check the reading of the vernier A and B, if still it reads 0° at A and 180° at B.
(4) Loosen the upper clamp, turn the telescope clockwise and bisect the right hand object 'B' exactly by using the upper clamp and its tangent screw.
(5) Read both the verniers. The object of reading the vernier is to obtain the approximate value of the angle. (Suppose the main reading 40° 2').
(6) Loosen the lower clamp, turn the telescope clockwise until the object 'A' is sighted again. Bisect A accurately using the lower tangent screw. Check the vernier reading which must be the same as before.
(7) Loosen the upper clamp, turn the telescope clockwise and again sight towards B. Bisect B accurately by using the upper tangent screw. The vernier will now read twice the value of the angle (it should be approximately 80° 4').
(8) Repeat the process until the angle is repeated the required number of times (usually 3). Read both verniers. The final readings after n repetition should be approximately $n \times 40°\ 2'$. Divide the sum by the number of repetitions and the result thus obtained gives the correct value of the angle AOB.
(9) Change the face of the instrument (now the face will be right). Repeat exactly in the same manner and find another value of the angle AOB.
(10) The average of the two values of the angles thus obtained gives the required precise value of the angle AOB.

2.3.2 To Measure the Horizontal Angle on Horizontal Circle

The horizontal angles are measured with the vernier A and the vernier B of the horizontal circle. It is to be noted that the least count of vernier is as 20".

$$\text{Least count of vernier} = \frac{\text{Smallest division of main scale}}{\text{Total number of divisions on vernier scale}}$$

$$= \frac{20'}{60}$$

$$= \frac{20 \times 60 \text{ seconds}}{60}$$

$$= 20 \text{ seconds}$$

or Least count of vernier = 20"

(1) First see the index mark or zero of the vernier A is lying nearer to which main scale division. See Fig. 2.4, it is lying between 25° and 40' division of main scale, so reading of the main scale will be 25° 40'.

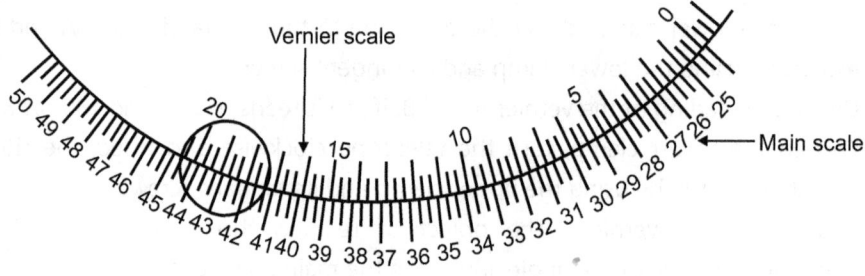

Fig. 2.4

(2) Then we see the division on the vernier scale that is joining the main scale i.e. 19' 20".

∴ The reading on the vernier A = 25° 0' 00"
                                                          0° 17' 20"
                                                         25° 17' 40"

∴ The reading on the vernier B = 25° 17' 40"

2.3.3 Reiteration Method

Reiteration is an another precise and comparatively less tedious method of measuring the horizontal angles. It is generally preferred when several angles are to be measured at a particular station. This method consists in measuring the several angles successively and finally closing the horizon at the starting point. The final reading of the vernier A should be the same as its initial reading. If not, the discrepancy is equally distributed among all the measured angles.

If suppose it is required to measure the angle AOB, BOC, COD, DOA, the method used is *Reiteration method*.

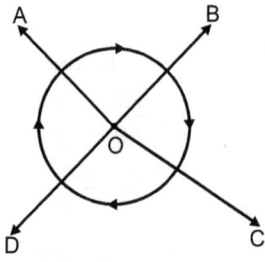

Fig. 2.5

Procedure :
(1) Set the instrument at the station O and level it accurately.
(2) Set the vernier A to 0 or 360° by using the upper clamp and its tangent screw.
(3) Direct the telescope to the station point A, which is known as reference object. Bisect it accurately by using the lower clamp and its tangent screw. Check the reading at vernier A which should be 0° or 360° and note the reading at the vernier B.
(4) Loosen the upper clam and turn the telescope clockwise until the point B is exactly sighted by using the upper tangent screw. Read both verniers. The mean of the vernier readings (after deducting 180° from the reading at vernier B) will give the value of the angle AOB.
(5) Similarly bisect CD successively, read both verniers at each bisection, find the values of the angles BOC and COD.
(6) Finally close the horizon by slighting towards station point A.
(7) The vernier at A should now read 360°. If not, note down the error. This error occurs due to slip etc.
(8) If the error is small, it is equally distributed among the several observed angles. If the error is large, the readings should be discarded and a new set of readings be taken.
(9) Now, change the face of instrument.
(10) Set the vernier A to a reading other than 0°, say 60° or 90°. This is done to avoid the errors of graduation.
(11) Again measure all the angles in the same manner by turning the telescope, this time in the counter clockwise direction to compensate of slip and errors due to twisting of the instrument.
(12) Close the horizon and apply the necessary correction to all the angles as before.
(13) Take the main value of the two angles as a true value.

2.4 MEASUREMENT OF A VERTICAL ANGLE

(i) Definition : Vertical Angle : The angle made between the inclined line of sight and the horizontal line of collimation is known as the vertical angle.

(ii) Angle of Elevation : If the point is above the horizontal plane, it is called the angle of elevation.

To measure the vertical angle of an object A procedure is as follows :
(1) Set up the theodolite at station point O and level it accurately.
(2) The zero of the vertical vernier is exactly set to zero of the vertical circle by using the vertical clamps and tangent screw.

(3) Bring the bubble of the altitude level in the central position by using the clip screw. The line of sight is thus made horizontal, while the vernier reads zero.
(4) Loosen the vertical circle clamp screw and direct the telescope towards the object A and sight it exactly by using the vertical circle tangent screw.
(5) Read both verniers on the vertical circle. The mean of the two vernier readings gives the value of the required angle.
(6) Change the face of the instrument and repeat the process. The mean of the two vernier readings gives the second value of the required angle.
(7) The average of the two values of the angle thus obtained, is the required value of the angle free from instrumental errors.

2.4.1 To Measure the Vertical Angle Between the Two Points A and B

(1) Sight A as before and take the mean of the two vernier readings at the vertical circle. It is taken as α.
(2) Similarly sight B and take the mean of the two vernier readings at the vertical circle. It is taken as β.
(3) The sum or difference of these readings will give the value of the vertical angle between A and B. Accordingly as one of the points is above and the other below the horizontal plane. (Fig. 2.6) and both the points are on the same side of the horizontal plane.

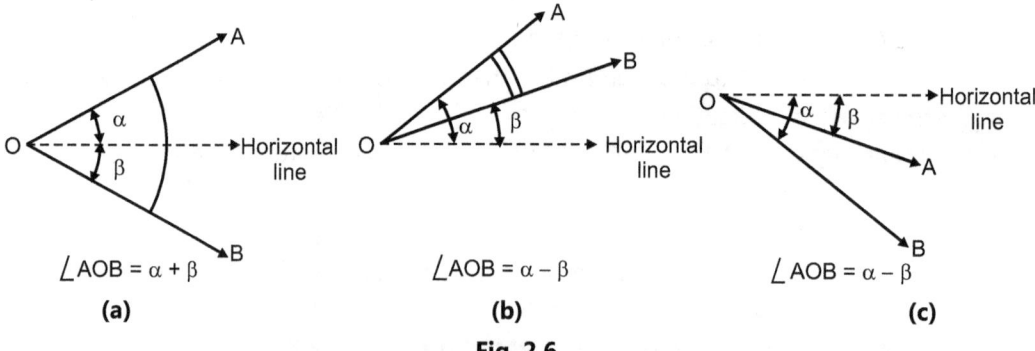

Fig. 2.6

2.5 MEASUREMENT OF MAGNETIC BEARINGS

The measurement of a magnetic bearing of a line can be considered of a horizontal angle between the reference direction i.e. magnetic north and the given line i.e. AB as shown in (Fig. 2.7). A trough compass or tubular compass is attached to the A frame of the theodolite to know the reference meridian (i.e. Magnetic North).

Procedure :
(1) Set up the theodolite at A and level it accurately.
(2) Set the vernier A to the zero of the horizontal circle.

(3) Release the magnetic needle and loosen the lower clamp.
(4) Rotate the instrument in the horizontal plane until the magnetic needle takes the normal position, i.e. the zeros of the small scales in the trough compass or the N and S graduations in the circular box compass, or the index mark in the tubular compass are opposite to the ends of the needle. Tighten the lower clamp and use its tangent screw for the exact coincidence. The line of sight is now parallel to magnetic meridian and the vernier A reads zero.
(5) Loosen the upper clamp. Turn the telescope and sight the object B. Bisect B exactly by using the upper tangent screw.
(6) Read both the verniers on the horizontal scale. The mean of the two vernier readings gives the magnetic bearing of the line AB.
(7) If greater accuracy is desired, change the face, take a second reading and record the mean of the two.

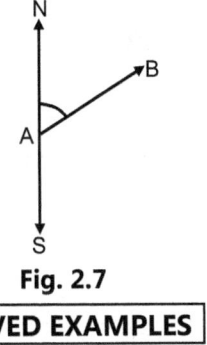

Fig. 2.7

SOLVED EXAMPLES

Example 2.1 : A theodolite was set up at point P and a staff was kept at station Q. The distance PQ was 3000 m. If the angle of elevation to a vane 4 m above the foot of the staff is 8° 59′, determine the reduced level of Q. The elevation of the instrument axis was 120.80 m.

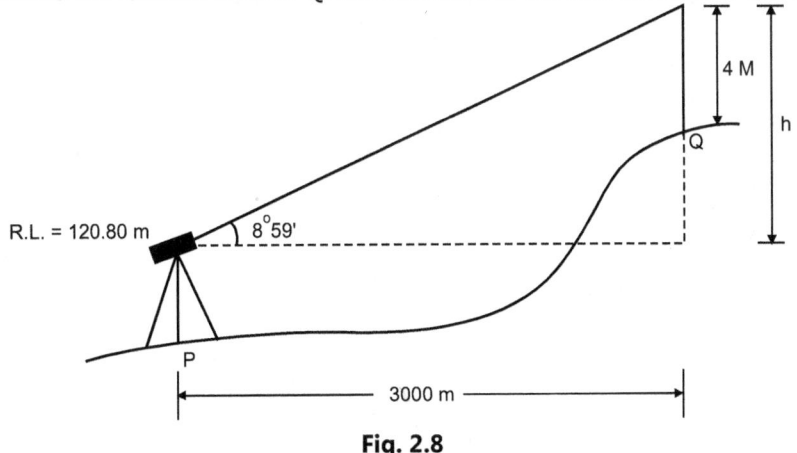

Fig. 2.8

Solution : Height of the vane above the instrument axis is given by,

$$h = D \tan \alpha = 3000 \times \tan 8° 59'$$
$$= 474.258 \text{ m}$$

and the combined correction for earth curvature and atmosphere is given by,

$$C_{cr} = 0.06735 \, D^2 = 0.06735 \times (3000)^2 = 0.606 \text{ m}$$

The correct difference in elevation between the vane and the instrument axis.

$$H = h + C_{cr} = 474.258 + 0.606 \text{ m}$$
$$\boxed{H = 474.864 \text{ m}}$$

R.L. of vane = R.L. of instrument axis + H
= 120.80 + 474.864
= 595.664 m

∴ R.L. of Q = R.L. of vane − 4
∴ R.L. of Q = 595.664 − 4
∴ $\boxed{\text{R.L. of Q} = 591.664 \text{ m}}$

Example 2.2 : An instrument was set up at A and the angle of elevation of the top of a tower BC was 29° 15'. The horizontal distance AB_1 B being the foot of the tower, was 820 m. Determine the R.L. of the top of the tower if the staff reading held on a station P of R.L. 120 m, 2.455 m with the telescope normal.

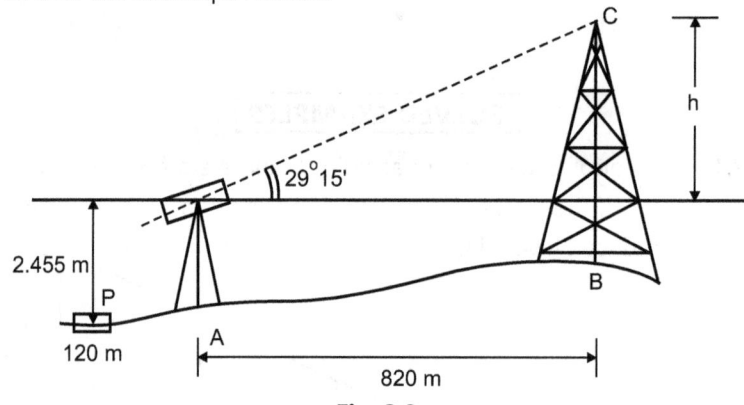

Fig. 2.9

Solution : Height of C above the instrument axis,

$$h = 820 \times \tan 29° 15'$$
$$h = 820 \times 0.560$$
$$h = 459.22 \text{ m}$$

R.L. of C = R.L. of P + B.S. (2.455) + h
= 120 + 2.455 + 459.22
$\boxed{\text{R.L. of C} = 581.677 \text{ m}}$

Example 2.3 : The observations were made on the top A of flag AB on a hill from two instrument stations P and Q, 100 m apart, the stations P and Q being in the line with A. The angles of elevation of A at P and Q, are 29° 25' and 18° 55' respectively. The staff reading upon the BM (R.L. 325, 40 m) were respectively 2.570 m and 3.915 m when the instrument was at P and Q. The telescope being horizontal determine the elevation of the foot B of the flag if AB is 3.55 m.

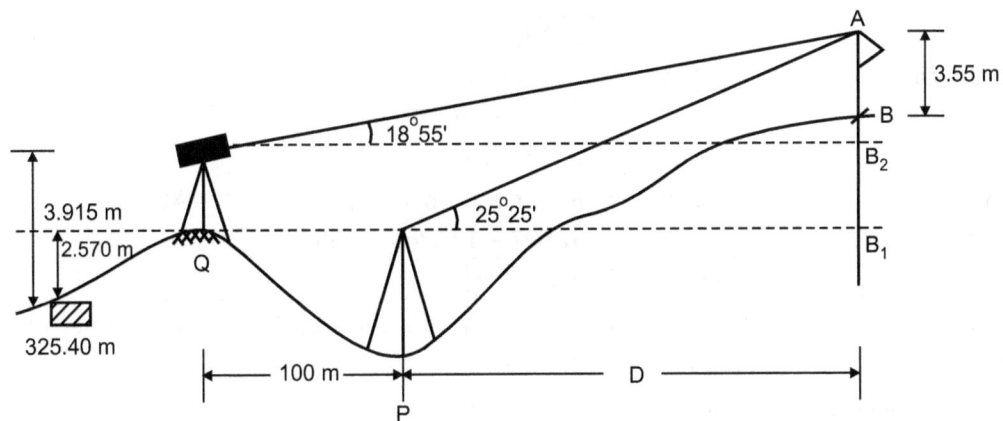

Fig. 2.10

Solution :

R.L. of instrument axis at P = R.L. of BM + B.S. on BM
= 325.40 + 2.570

∴ R.L. of instrument axis at P = 327.97 m

R.L. of instrument axis at Q = R.L. of BM + B.S. on BM
= 325.40 + 3.915

R.L. of instrument axis at Q = 329.315 m

Difference in level of the instrument axis,

S = 329.315 − 327.97

S = 1.345 m

If D is the horizontal distance between P and B.

∴ AB_1 = D tan 25° 25'

AB_2 = (100 + D) × tan 18° 35'

But we have,

B_1B_2 = $AB_1 − AB_2$

D × tan 25° 25' − (100 + D) × tan 18° 35' = S = 1.345 m

D × tan 25° 25' − 100 tan 18° 55' − D tan 18° 55' = 1.345

$$D (\tan 25° 25' - \tan 18° 55') = 1.345 + 100 \tan 18° 55'$$

$$D = \frac{1.345 + 100 \tan 18° 55'}{(\tan 25° 25' - \tan 18° 55')}$$

∴ $$D = \frac{1.345 + 34.270}{(0.47519 - 0.34270)}$$

∴ $$D = \frac{35.615}{0.13248}$$

∴ $$\boxed{D = 268.83 \text{ m}}$$

We have,
$$AB_1 = D \times \tan 25° 25'$$
$$= 268.83 \times \tan 25° 25'$$

∴ $$\boxed{AB_1 = 127.745 \text{ m}}$$

∴ R.L. of B = R.L. of instrument axis at P + AB_1 − AB
$$= 327.97 + 127.745 - 3.55$$

∴ $$\boxed{\text{R.L. of B} = 452.165 \text{ m}}$$

Example 2.4 : To find the elevation of the top of a chimney, the following observations were made from two stations P and Q apart 50 m.

Horizontal angle at station P, between chimney and Q = 60°.
Horizontal angle at station Q, between chimney and P = 50°.
Angle of elevation from P to the top of chimney = 30°.
Angle of elevation from Q to the top of chimney = 29°.
R.L. of the line of collimation at P = 22.5 m.
R.L. of the line of collimation at Q = 20.5 m.
Determine the elevation of the top of the chimney.

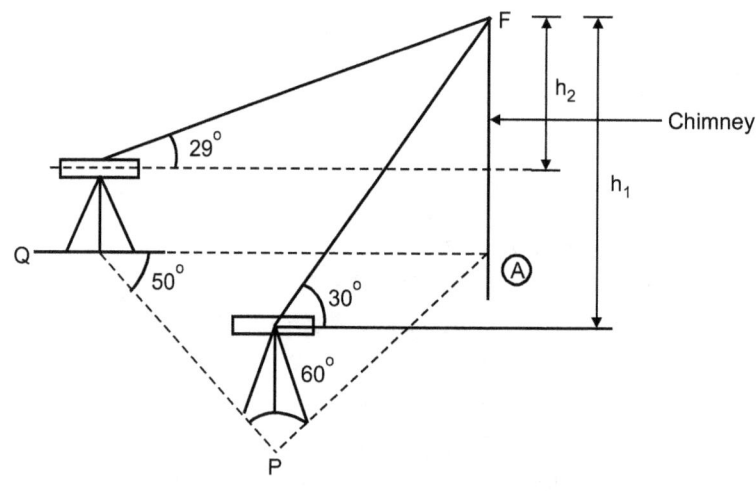

Fig. 2.11

Solution : Refer to Fig. 2.11.

Let P and Q be the instrument stations and F be the top of the chimney.

In △ APQ, ∠ APQ = 60° and ∠ AQP = 50°

∴ ∠ PAQ = 180° − (50° + 60°) = 70°

Applying sine rule,

$$\frac{PA}{\sin 50°} = \frac{QA}{\sin 60°} = \frac{PQ}{\sin 70°}$$

or $PA = 50\left(\dfrac{\sin 50°}{\sin 70°}\right) = 40.76$ m

and $QA = 50\left(\dfrac{\sin 60°}{\sin 70°}\right) = 46.08$ m

h_1 = PA tan α = 40.76 tan 30° = 22.533 m

h_2 = QA tan α = 46.08 tan 29° = 25.543 m

Hence, R.L. of chimney top = R.L. of line of collimation + h_1 or h_2

R.L. of F from observation at P = 22.5 + 22.533 = 45.033 m

and R.L. of F from observation at Q = 20.5 + 20.543 = 45.043 m

Hence, elevation of F = $\dfrac{(45.033 + 46.043)}{2}$ = $\boxed{45.538 \text{ m}}$

Example 2.5 : An instrument was set up at O and the angle of elevation to a vane 4 m above the foot of the staff held at Q was 9° 30′. The horizontal distance between the instrument and the staff was 2 km. Determine the R.L. of the staff station O. The R.L. of the line of collimation was 2650 m.

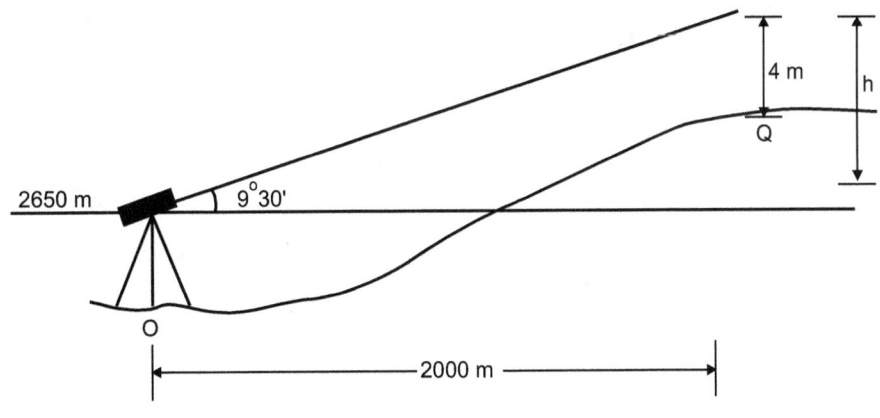

Fig. 2.12

Solution : Height of the vane above the instrument axes is given by,

$$h = D \tan \alpha$$

∴ $\quad h = 2000 \times \tan 9° 30'$

∴ $\quad \boxed{h = 334.685 \text{ m}}$

and the combined correction for earth curvature and atmosphere is given by,

$$C_{cr} = 0.06735 \, D^2 = 0.06735 \times \left(\frac{2000}{1000}\right)^2$$

∴ $\quad C_{cr} = 0.1347 \text{ m}$

The correct difference in elevation between the vane and the instrument axis is,

$$H = h + C_{cr} = 334.685 + 0.1347$$

$$\boxed{H = 334.8197 \text{ m}}$$

R.L. of vane = R.L. of Instrument axis + h

$\quad\quad\quad\quad\quad = 2650 + 334.8197$

$\boxed{\text{R.L. of vane} = 2984.819 \text{ m}}$

R.L. of Q = R.L. of vane − 4

$\quad\quad\quad = 2984.819 − 4$

$\boxed{\text{R.L. of Q} = 2980.819 \text{ m}}$

2.6 MEASUREMENT OF DEFLECTION ANGLES

Definition : It is an angle made by a survey line with the prolongation of the preceding line. When the angle is measured in the clockwise sense i.e. to the right, it is termed as deflection angle R (Right). Similarly, when the deflection angle is measured in the anticlockwise sense i.e. to the left, it is termed as deflection angle L (Left). In Fig. 2.13, ∠ Q_1QR is deflection angle to the right which is measured as $\theta_1 R$. Similarly, ∠ R_1RS is measured to the left and hence it is denoted as $\theta_2 L$.

Setting of deflection angles is used in locating points in case of road or railway curves.

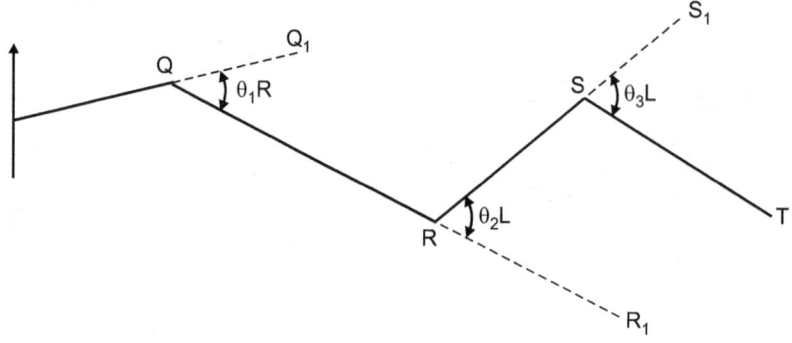

Fig. 2.13

Procedure :

1. Set up the theodolite at Q. Level it carefully.
2. Clamping both the plates and with reading on vernier 'A' as 0° 0' 0", take back sight on P.
3. Transit the telescope and it will be directed along QQ_1. Loosen the upper clamp, turn telescope clockwise and bisect R accurately using upper clamp and upper tangent screw. Read both the verniers. The mean of the two vernier readings will give the value of deflection angle $θ_1$.
4. Loosen the lower clamp screw and rotate the telescope horizontally and back sight on P again. The reading on the vernier will be same as obtained in step (3).
5. Plunge the telescope and loosen the upper clamp and rotate the telescope clockwise to accurately bisect station R by upper tangent screw.
6. Read both the verniers and find the mean of the final readings. One half of the mean value of readings will give the value of deflection angle at Q. Errors of eccentricity of the centres and verniers are eliminated since both the verniers are read.

2.6.1 Traversing by Measurement of Deflection Angles

The deflection angle is one which a survey line makes with the prolongation of preceding line. In Fig. 2.14, Q'QR or R'RS are the deflection angles. In the case of survey work for roads, railways and drainage or water supply pipe lines, this method is very useful.

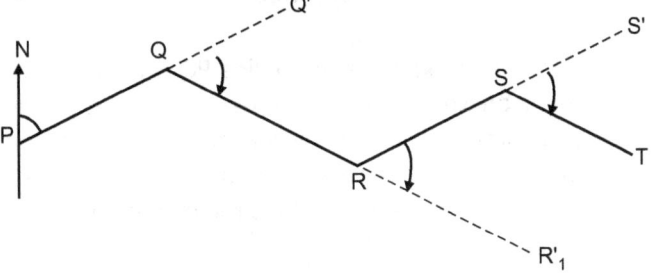

Fig. 2.14

Procedure : Suppose it is required to run an open traverse PQRST as shown in Fig. 2.14. Initially, the theodolite is set up at P and the fore bearing of PQ is observed by attaching a trough compass to the theodolite. The theodolite is then shifted to station Q and reading on vernier A is set to zero. Then point P is bisected. The telescope is transited and by releasing the upper clamp, it is turned in clockwise direction till R is roughly bisected. Upper clamp is tightened and accurate bisection of R is done by upper tangent screw. Reading on both verniers (A and B) is taken and mean of these readings gives the deflection angle Q'QR to the right. Then theodolite is shifted to station R. Point Q is backlighted with reading on vernier A as 0° 0' 0", and ∠ R'RS is measured as explained earlier. Since this angle is measured to the left from the prolongation of line QR, this is deflection angle to the left. In the same way, the deflection angle S'ST to the right is measured and recorded in the field book. Measurement of the length of survey lines and location of adjoining details are done by taking offsets in the usual way.

2.6.2 Traverse Survey by the Measurement of Direct Angles

These are called as angles to the right. Direct angle can be defined as "the angle measured clockwise from the preceding line to the next one". These angles are measured twice, once with telescope direct and then with telescope inverted, to eliminate the instrumental errors.

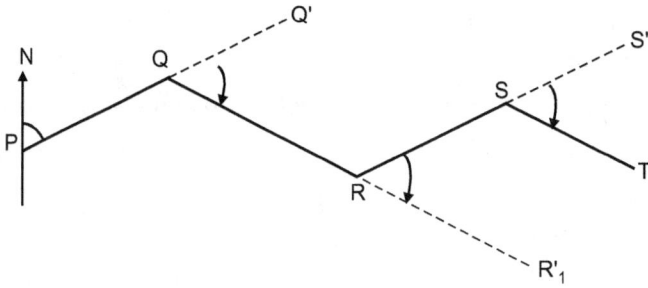

Fig. 2.15

Procedure :

The theodolite is set up at P and the bearing of line PQ is measured. Then the theodolite is shifted to Q and reading on vernier A is coincided to 0° 0' 0". Preceding station P is bisected. The telescope is turned clockwise by loosening upper clamp and station R is bisected. Reading on both the verniers is taken. The mean value of the angle is found out which is the required value of ∠ PQR. Here, ∠ PQR is the exterior angle. In the same manner, ∠ QRS, ∠ RST etc. are measured (See Fig. 3.38).

The lengths of the lines PQ, QR, RS etc. are measured and the adjoining details along the survey line are located by means of offsets.

2.7 THEODOLITE TRAVERSING

The theodolite traversing is carried out more or less in similar way as the compass traversing and the relative directions of the lines of a traverse are determined by the following methods :

(I) By direct observations of angles.

(II) By fast needle method.

(I) By Direct Observations of Angles :

In this method, the angles between successive lines are measured directly by the theodolite and the bearing of the initial line is observed. The bearing of the remaining lines are then computed from the observed bearing and the measured angles. This method is adopted for long traverses requiring high precision. The angles measured at different stations may either be included angles or deflection angles and accordingly, the process can be carried out in one of the following two ways.

(a) Traversing by Included Angles :
Procedure :

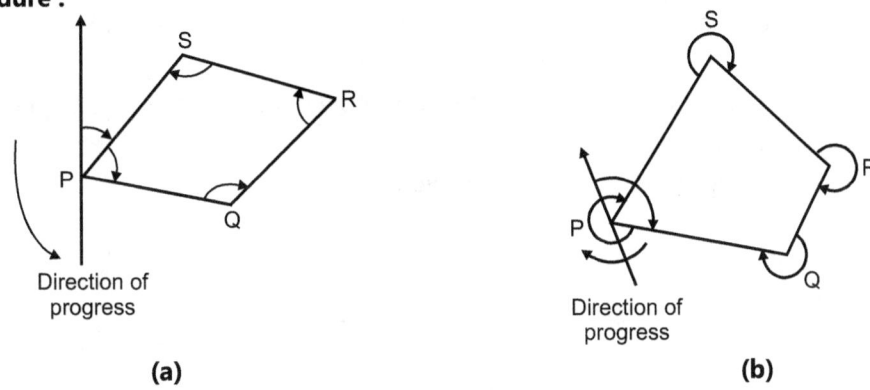

Fig. 2.16 : Traversing by Included Angles

(1) The process consists of measuring included angles by conducting the traverse in anticlockwise or clockwise direction as shown in (Fig. 2.16 (a)) and (Fig. 2.16 (b)) respectively.

(2) It merely consists of measuring a back sight on the preceding station and a foresight on the forward station.

(3) It is adopted in land surveying of a closed traverse and great accuracy can be achieved by adopting repetition method for getting an accurate included angle.

(4) If the direction of progress is anticlockwise, as shown in Fig 2.16 (a), the angles measured will be the interior angles and if it is clockwise as shown in (Fig. 2.16 (b)), the angles measured will be exterior angles.

(b) Traversing by the Method of Direct Angles :
Procedure :

(1) This method is commonly used for open traverse. In running the traverse as shown in (Fig. 2.17), set up the station at the starting station A and observe the bearing of line AB.

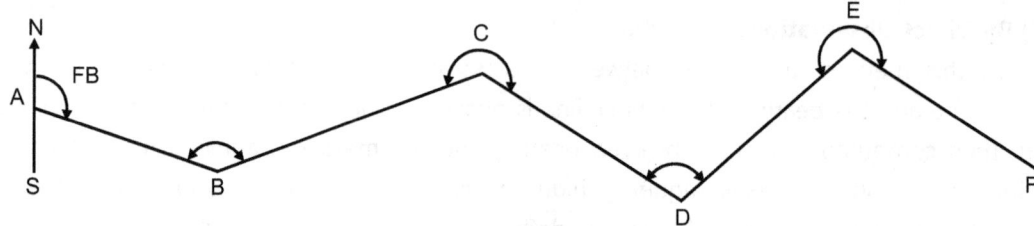

Fig. 2.17

(2) Shift the theodolite to B. Set the vernier to A to 0° or 360°, take back sight on the preceding station A. Unclamp the upper plate, turn the telescope clockwise, take a fore sight on the following station C and read both the vernier readings.

(3) The mean of the two vernier readings is the required direct angle ABC. Take other angles in the similar manner. Chain the lines AB, BC, CD etc. and take the necessary offsets in the usual way.

(c) Traversing by the Method of Deflection Angles :

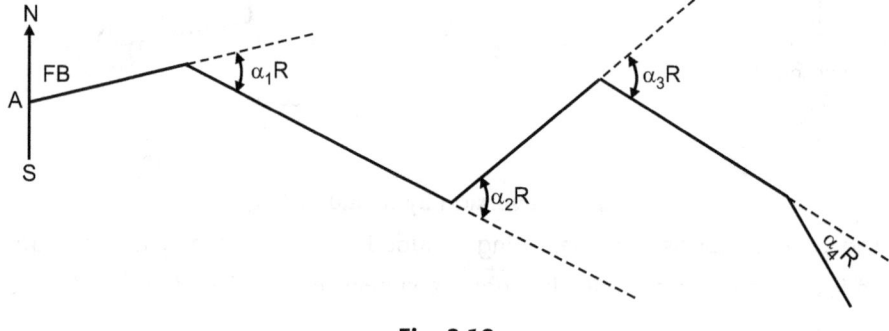

Fig. 2.18

Procedure :

(1) This method is used for open traverse. This is much suitable when the survey lines make small deflection angles with each other as in case of surveys for roads, railways, pipeline etc.

(2) In running a traverse as in (Fig. 2.18), set up the theodolite at A and observe the bearing of line AB.

(3) Shift the instrument to station B, set the vernier A to zero and take a back sight on A. Then transit the telescope, loosen the upper clamp, turn the telescope clockwise and take a fore sight on C.

(4) Read both verniers, mean of these readings is the required deflection angle of BC from AB. Also note down its direction. In this case, it is taken as (α_1R i.e. α_1 Right). Then set up the theodolite at each of the successive stations C, D, E etc. and observe the deflecting angles and record them in the field book chaining and offsetting is done in the usual manner.

2.7.1 Theodolite Traversing by Direct Observation of Bearings

This method is also called as Fast Needle Method. There are the three methods of observing bearing directly in the field.

(I) Direct Method in which the telescope is transited.

(II) Direct Method in which the telescope is not transited.

(III) Back bearing Method.

(I) Direct Method in Which the Telescope is Transited :

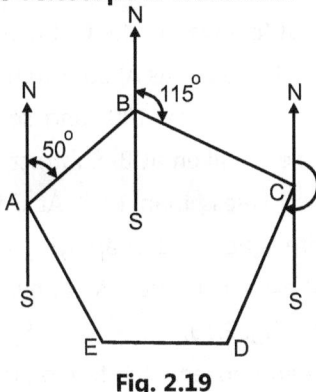

Fig. 2.19

(1) Set up the instrument at A and level it accurately. Set the vernier A to zero. Point the telescope to the magnetic north as indicated by the magnetic needle attached to the transit by using the lower lamp and tangent screw.

(2) Loosen the upper clamp and bisect B exactly by using the upper clamp and its tangent screw. Head the vernier A which gives the bearing of AB say 50°. If the traverse closed on one, then observe also the back bearing of the last line (E, A). This will serve as a check.

(3) Shift the instrument and set it up at B. Check weather the vernier A still reads the bearing of AB i.e. 50°. If due to slip the readings differs, correct it with the help of upper tangent screw.

(4) Using the lower clamp and tangent screws, back sight on A.

(5) Transit the telescope. The line of sight is thus directed towards AB produced and the vernier A still reads the bearing of AB. Loosen the upper clamp, turn the telescope and bisect C exactly by using the upper clamp and tangent screw.

(6) Read vernier A, which now gives the bearing of line BC, say 115°.

(7) With the vernier A clamped at 115° transfer the instrument to C and repeat the process.

(8) To take a check upon the accuracy of work in a closed traverse, the back bearing of the last line (EA) observed in step (2) at the first station A and its fore bearing taken at the last station (E) must differ exactly by 180°.

The telescope is transited to alternate back and fore bearing in this method.

(II) Direct Method in Which the Telescope is Not Transited :

This method is preferable in the case of non-transit instrument or in the case of transit instruments having poor adjustment. (Refer above Fig. 2.19).

(1) The process is similar to that followed in the first method except that the telescope at B is not transited after the back sight is taken as A, but rotated in a horizontal plane to C.

(2) The orientation thus becomes out by 180° and so a correction of 180° has to be applied to the reading of the vernier A taken at B. Subtract 180° if the reading is more than 180° and add it 180° if the reading is less than 180°. At C the orientation becomes out by 360° and is therefore correct. There is no need of applying the correction of 180°. Therefore, this correction is necessary only at even instrument station i.e. 2nd, 4th, 6th and so on.

(III) Back Bearing Method : (Refer Fig. 2.19).

(1) Set up the instrument at A and observe the fore bearing of line AB.

(2) Shift the instrument and set it up at B.

(3) Set the vernier A to back bearing of AB.

(4) With the vernier A kept clamped at the same reading, back sight on A by using the lower clamp and its tangent screw. As the vernier A is set to the back bearing of AB and the line of sight is directed towards BA, the instrument is in correct orientation.

(5) Unclamp the upper plate and turn the telescope until C is sighted. Bisect C exactly by using the upper clamp and its tangent screw.

(6) Read the vernier A which gives the bearing of BC.

(7) Repeat the process at each of the subsequent stations.

2.8 COMPUTATION OF CONSECUTIVE AND INDEPENDENT CO-ORDINATES

In theodolite traversing, the positions of different stations are plotted with reference to two lines, one of which is parallel to the magnetic meridian towards magnetic North-South direction and the other one at right angles to magnetic meridian towards East-West direction. Thus, the intersection of N-S line and E-W line forms the origin, and the position of any survey station is determined by its distance with reference to axes of reference i.e. North-South line and East-West line.

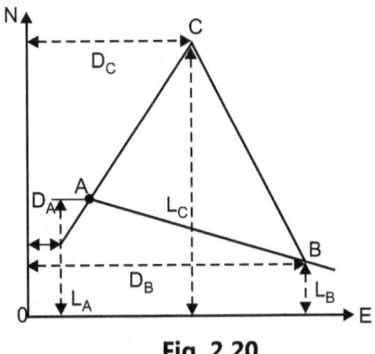

Fig. 2.20

Latitude : When the distance is measured parallel to N-S line (perpendicular to East-West line), it is called latitude.

The distance measured towards North line is termed Northing and is positive. Similarly, the distance measured towards South direction is termed Southing and is negative.

Departure : When the distance is measured parallel to East-West line (perpendicular to North-South line), it is called departure. The distance measured towards East direction is called Easting and is positive. The distance measured towards West is called **Westing** and is negative.

Consecutive Co-ordinates : The knowledge of co-ordinates is necessary for plotting purposes. In this system, the co-ordinates of a station are worked out with reference to the preceding station, considering it as origin. Thus, the co-ordinates of station B are worked out with respect to preceding station A. Similarly, the co-ordinates of station C are worked out with respect to station B. The co-ordinates worked out in this fashion are called Consecutive Co-ordinates.

Independent Co-ordinates : The use of consecutive co-ordinates is not so convenient from the point of view of plotting. Hence, it is possible to reduce these co-ordinates to only one reference axis i.e. North and East axis. Thus, when the co-ordinates of a station are worked from the common origin, they are called as Independent co-ordinates or Total latitude and Total departure. Thus, in Fig. 3.23, the independent co-ordinates of stations A, B and C of the traverse ABC are given by A (L_A, D_A), B (L_B, D_B) and C (L_C, D_C).

2.8.1 Calculation of Consecutive Co-ordinates

While working out the consecutive co-ordinates of the stations, each line AB, BC and CA is considered separately, its measured length and the reduced bearing are obtained and its components towards North or South and towards East or West direction are worked out.

Latitude = $l \cos \theta$, where θ is the reduced bearing and l is the length of the line. Either Northing or Southing will be obtained.

Departure = $l \sin \theta$, where θ is the reduced bearing and l is the length of the line. Either Easting or Westing is obtained.

Depending on the quadrant in which the line lies; the calculation of co-ordinates is explained in the paragraphs below. The sign of the latitude and departure depends upon the reduced bearing of the line.

(i)

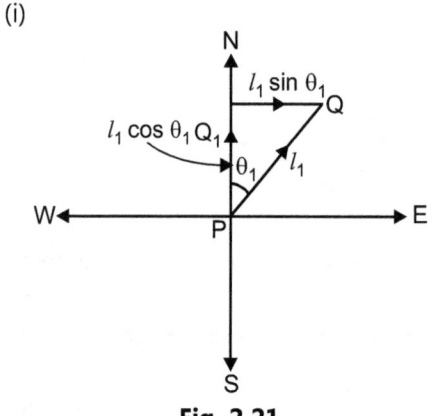

Fig. 2.21

If line PQ is in the first quadrant (N, E), and its length is l_1 and reduced bearing is $N\theta_1 E$, its components $l_1 \cos \theta_1$ (PN) along North direction and $l_1 \sin \theta_1$ (NQ) along East direction are Northing and Easting respectively and both of them are positive. (See Fig. 2.21) Thus, in the calculations of consecutive co-ordinates, it is to be borne in mind that to obtain co-ordinates of Q, length of PQ is considered and its reduced bearing is used in finding $l_1 \cos \theta_1$ and $l_1 \sin \theta_1$ components.

(ii)

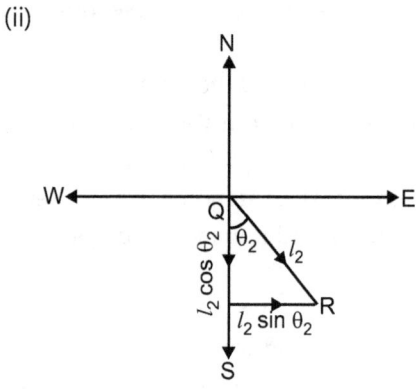

Fig. 2.22

If line QR is in the second quadrant (S, E) and its length is l_2 and reduced bearing $S\theta_2 E$, the component $l_2 \cos \theta_2$ (QS) along South direction and $l_2 \sin \theta_2$ (SR) along East direction are its Southing and Easting respectively. The Southing is negative while Easting is positive. (See Fig. 2.22).

(iii)

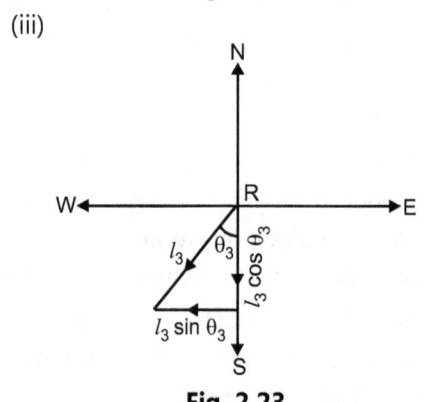

Fig. 2.23

Similarly, if line RT is in the third quadrant (S, W) and its length is l_3 and reduced bearing is $S\theta_3 W$, the component $l_3 \cos \theta_3$ (RS) and $l_3 \sin \theta_3$ (ST) along South and West directions are its Southing and Westing respectively. Both the Southing and Westing are negative. (See Fig. 2.23).

(iv)

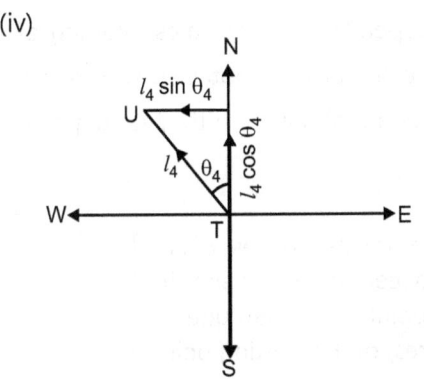

Lastly if line TU is in the IVth quadrant (N, W) and its length is l_4 and reduced bearing is $N\theta_4W$, the components $l_4 \cos \theta_4$ (TN) and $l_4 \sin \theta_4$ (NU) along North and West directions are its Northing and Westing respectively. Here, Northing is positive while Westing is negative. (See Fig. 2.24).

Fig. 2.24

In actual practice, we measure the lengths and calculate the whole circle bearings of all sides of a closed traverse, knowing the whole circle bearing of any one side and the corrected included angles of the closed traverse. These whole circle bearings are then converted into reduced bearings and from the lengths of the sides of the traverse and their corresponding reduced bearings, consecutive co-ordinates are worked out. The following Table 2.1 can be used to determine the signs of latitudes and departures.

Table 2.1

	W.C.B.	Quadrant		Latitude	Departure
Between	0 to 90°	I.	N.E.	+	+
Between	90° to 180°	II.	S.E.	−	+
Between	180° to 270°	III.	S.W.	−	−
Between	270° to 360°	IV.	N.W.	+	−

2.8.2 Calculation of Independent Co-ordinates from Consecutive Co-ordinates

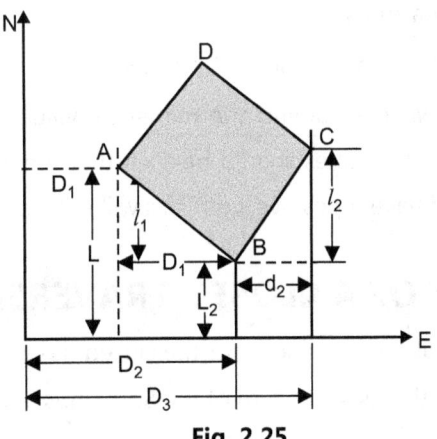

Fig. 2.25

If consecutive co-ordinates are converted to independent co-ordinates, plotting of the traverse becomes easier as the co-ordinates of all the stations are obtained with respect to the same origin. Usually the independent co-ordinates are obtained in the first quadrant i.e. w.r.t. North and East directions.

Rule :

$$\begin{bmatrix} \text{Total latitude or departure} \\ \text{of any point of a traverse} \end{bmatrix} = \begin{bmatrix} \text{The latitudes (or departures) of all} \\ \text{the lines between that point and the} \\ \text{starting point + Total latitude} \\ \text{(or departures) of the starting point} \end{bmatrix}$$

Fig. 2.25 shows the consecutive co-ordinates of station B with respect to station A $(-l_1, d_1)$, consecutive co-ordinates of station 'C' with respect to station 'B' (l_2, d_2).

If independent co-ordinates of station A are assumed as L_1, D_1, then the independent co-ordinates of B will be,

$$L_2 = L_1 - l_1 \text{ and } D_2 = D_1 + d_1$$

Independent co-ordinates of station C will be

$$L_3 = L_2 + l_2 = L_1 - l_1 + l_2$$

and, $D_3 = D_2 + d_2 = D_1 + d_1 + d_2$

This proves the rule stated in the beginning.

In a closed traverse,

Algebraic sum of latitudes = 0

i.e. Sum of Northings = Sum of Southings and

Algebraic sum of departures = 0

i.e. Sum of Eastings = Sum of Westings

It is to be noted that while assuming the numerical values of Total latitude and Total departure of the first point, the values should be such that the independent co-ordinates of the remaining points would have a positive sign. This will ensure that the traverse would lie in the first quadrant.

2.9 ADJUSTMENT OF A CLOSED TRAVERSE

We have seen above that the conditions for the closed traverse are :

(i) the sum of the Northings = the sum of the Southings and,

(ii) the sum of the Eastings = the sum of the Westings.

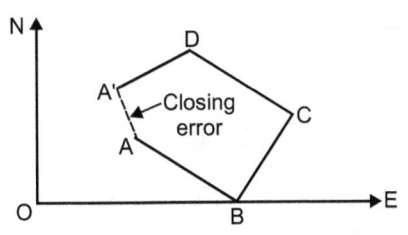

Fig. 2.26 : Closing Error in a Closed Traverse

Due to the errors in the field measurements of the closed traverse the above two conditions are not satisfied and therefore after plotting the traverse from the field measurements, the last station will not coincide with the first station of the traverse. The distance by which the last station fails to coincide with the first station of the closed traverse is called the *closing error*.

In Fig. 2.26, A'A is called the closing error or error of closure.

If we consider (L_1, D_1) as the independent co-ordinates of station A and $(-l_1, d_1)$, (l_2, d_2), $(l_3, -d_3)$ and $(-l_4, -d_4)$ as the consecutive co-ordinates of the stations B, C, D and A' respectively, then according to the theory explained in Article 3.19, the independent co-ordinates of the station A' will be $L_1 + \Sigma l$ and $D_1 + \Sigma d$ where Σl and Σd are the algebraic sum of the latitudes and departures respectively while the independent co-ordinates of station A are (L_1, D_1).

∴ Length of the closing error A'A $= e = \sqrt{(L_1 + \Sigma l - L_1)^2 + (D_1 + \Sigma d - D_1)^2}$

$$\boxed{e = \sqrt{(\Sigma l)^2 + (\Sigma d)^2}}$$

Here, it is understood that the latitudes l_1, l_2, l_3 and l_4 and departures d_1, d_2, d_3 and d_4 may be positive or negative, depending upon the quadrants in which the sides AB, BC, CD and DA' lie.

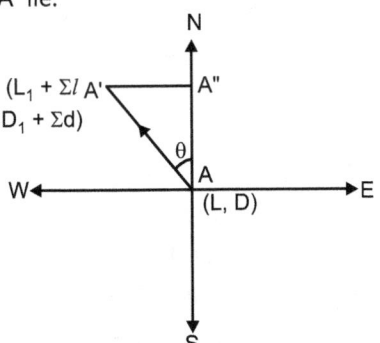

Direction of a closing error can be obtained from the direction AA' i.e. the quadrant in which the closing error AA' lies. In Fig. 2.27 the closing error AA' lies in the IVth quadrant (N.W.). Departure of closing error = AA' sin θ (A'A") and latitude of closing error = AA' cos θ (AA").

Fig. 2.27 : Direction of a Closing Error

where, θ is the reduced bearing of the closing error and its value can be found out by the relation,

$$\tan\theta = \frac{AA'\sin\theta}{AA'\cos\theta} = \frac{A'A''}{AA''}$$

$$= \frac{[D_1 + \Sigma d - D_1]}{[L_1 + \Sigma l - L_1]} = \frac{\Sigma d}{\Sigma l}, \quad \boxed{\tan\theta = \frac{\Sigma d}{\Sigma l}}$$

where, Σd = algebraic sum of the departures, and
Σl = algebraic sum of the latitudes worked out from the consecutive co-ordinates of the stations B, C, D and A'.

Relative Error of Closure : "It is the ratio of the length of closing error (e) to the perimeter of the traverse (P) expressed with numerator as a unity".

$$\boxed{\text{Thus, relative error of closure} = \frac{e}{P} = \frac{1}{\frac{P}{(e)}}}, \text{ where, closing error and perimeter are in the}$$

same units, usually in metres.

The permissible linear error of closure in theodolite traverse survey is given by the formula –

$$\boxed{E = \frac{P}{1000}\sqrt{1 + \frac{e'^2 N}{12}}}$$

where, E = the closing error in m,
P = perimeter of the traverse in m,
N = the number of sides of the traverse, and
e' = the permissible error per angle (commonly 1').

Angular Error of Closure : In a closed traverse theoretically the sum of the interior angles should be (2N – 4) right angles, where N is the number of sides. If the actual sum of the measured angles is not equal to (2N – 4) right angles, then the difference between the sum of measured angles and the theoretical sum of the interior angles is called the *angular error of closure*. Thus, in a closed traverse of 5 sides, the theoretical sum of the angles = (2 × 5 – 4) right angles i.e. 6 right angles = 6 × 90 = 540°.

If the sum of the measured angles is 539° 59' the angular error of closure is (539° 59') – 540° = – 1'. If all the angles are measured with equal precision, then the error of closure will be equally distributed in all the angles and the correction per angle of opposite sign will be applied to all the measured angles. Thus, in the above example assuming that all the angles are measured with equal precision, error per angle is $\frac{-1'}{5} = \frac{-60''}{5} = 12''$ and the correction per angle = + 12 seconds, which is applied to each measured angle and the corrected interior angles are found out.

Correcting the Fore Bearings of Sides :

After correcting the interior angles, the correct fore bearings of the sides are computed from the fore bearings of the side which is observed accurately by the theodolite, using the relation :

$$\begin{bmatrix} \text{Fore bearing of the next side} \\ \text{of the closed traverse} \end{bmatrix} = \begin{bmatrix} \text{Fore bearing of the preceding line + next} \\ \text{included angle} \pm 180° \end{bmatrix}$$

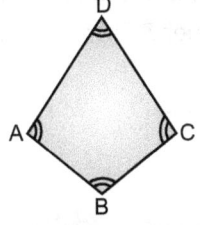

If the sum of the F.B. of preceding side and next included angle is greater than 180°, subtract 180° to obtain the F.B. of next side. If the sum is less than 180° then add 180° to the sum to obtain F.B. of the next side.

Fig. 2.28 : Computing Bearings of the Closed Traverse

Check : The fore bearing of the last side + Last interior angle should be equal to first observed bearing.

Let fore bearing of side AB be measured accurately.

Then,   F.B. of BC = F.B. of AB + interior ∠ B ± 180°
Similarly,   F.B. of CD = F.B. of BC + interior ∠ C ± 180°
             F.B. of DA = F.B. of CD + interior ∠ D ± 180°
and   F.B. of AB = F.B. of DA + interior ∠ A ± 180°

180° are to be added when the sum of first two quantities is less than 180° and 180° are to be subtracted if the sum of first two quantities exceeds 180°.

Reduced Bearings of Sides : After the fore bearings of the sides are computed, these are converted into reduced bearings and the quadrants in which sides AB, BC, CD and DA lie, will decide the consecutive co-ordinates of each point B, C, D, A etc.

Working Out the Consecutive Co-ordinates : From the measured sides of the closed traverse and the reduced bearing of each side, the latitudes and departures are worked out by the relation : latitude = length of side × cosine of reduced bearing and departure = length of side × sine of reduced bearing of that side; which gives the values of Northings, Southings, Eastings and Westings of all the stations.

Finding Out the Closing Error and Relative Error of Closure : The sum of the Northings is compared with the sum of the Southings and the sum of the Eastings is compared with the sum of the Westings.

If the field measurements are correct, the sum of the Northings will be equal to the sum of Southings. Similarly, the sum of the Eastings will be equal to the sum of the Westings. However, if the field measurements are not accurate, the difference between the sum of Northings and sum of Southings will be worked out and called Σl. Σl will be positive or negative depending on whether Σ Northings is greater or less than Σ Southings.

Similarly, the difference between the sum of the Eastings and Westings is found out and called Σd. Σd will be positive or negative depending on whether Σ Eastings is greater or less than Σ Westings.

The magnitude of the closing error is obtained by the relation :

Closing error $\qquad e = \sqrt{(\Sigma l)^2 + (\Sigma d)^2}$

The direction of closing error is given by the relation

$$\tan \theta = \frac{\Sigma d}{\Sigma l}$$ where θ is the reduced bearing of the closing error.

Depending upon the signs of Σd and Σl, the quadrant in which the closing error lies can be found out. If Σd and Σl are both positive, closing error is in the quadrant NE, if Σd is +ve and Σl is −ve, closing error is in the quadrant SE, if Σd is −ve and Σl is positive, closing error is in the quadrant NW and if both Σl and Σd are negative, the closing error lies in the quadrant SW.

The relative error of closure is found out by the relation $= \dfrac{1}{\dfrac{P}{e}}$

where, $\qquad$ P = perimeter of the traverse in m

and $\qquad$ e = closing error of the traverse in m.

2.10 GALE'S TRAVERSE BY CO-ORDINATE METHOD

The traverse computations described above are entered in the tabular form called Gale's traverse table.

The steps in traverse computations are summarized below in sequence.

1. Add all the included angles of the traverse and compare the sum of measured angles with the theoretical sum of the angles given by the formula. Theoretical sum of all the interior angles of a closed traverse = (2N — 4) right angles. Where, N = No. of sides of the traverse.
2. If sum of measured included (interior) angles is not equal to theoretical sum of the interior angles, the included angles are corrected so that their sum agrees to the theoretical sum of the interior angle.
3. Calculate the corrected whole circle bearings of all the sides from the observed bearings of the first line and the corrected included angles.

Check : Starting from the bearing of first line, the bearings of all the sides are worked out and by adding the next included angle the bearing of the first line should be calculated from the bearing worked out for the last line and adding the first included angle to it which should agree with the observed bearing of first line.

4. From the corrected whole circle bearings, find out the reduced bearings of the sides of the traverse.
5. From the measured lengths of the sides and the reduced bearings, work out the consecutive co-ordinates of each station, of the traverse and enter them in proper column.
6. Find out the sum of all the Northings, Southings, Eastings and Westings and the difference between sum of Northings and sum of Southings. Similarly, find out the difference between sum of Eastings and sum of Westings.
7. Apply the corrections to the latitudes and departures of each station so that sum of Northings equals to sum of Southings and sum of Eastings equals to sum of Westings.
8. From the corrected consecutive co-ordinates, independent co-ordinates are obtained by choosing the co-ordinates of the first point of such value that the independent co-ordinates of all the stations lie in the first quadrant (N.E.).
9. The closing error, relative error of closure and the direction of closing error are also found out.

Gale's traverse table is prepared for a closed traverse ABCD and is shown in Table 3.3. All the lengths, included angles and bearing of one side as measured are tabulated.

2.10.1 Correction by Bowditch's Rule

Table 2.2 : Gale's Traverse Table

In St.	Angles (measured) ° ′ ″	Corr. (–ve) ′ ″	Corrected angle ° ′ ″	W.C. bearings ° ′ ″	Reduced bearings ° ′ ″	Quadrant	Line length
1	2	3	4	5	6	7	8
A	80 41 10	–1 4	80 40 6				AB 15.20 m
				87 53 30	87 53 30	NE - I	
B	96 32 30	–1 4	96 31 26				BC 21.40 m
				4 24 56	4 24 56	NE - I	
C	87 2 20	–1 4	87 1 16				CD 13.90 m
				271 26 12	88 33 48	NW- IV	
D	95 48 16	–1 4	95 47 12				DA 22.60 m
				187 13 24	7 13 24	SW - III	
Tot.	360 4 16	4 16	360 0 0				P = 73.10

In. St.	Consecutive co-ordinates				Corrections			
	Latitude		Departure		Latitude		Departure	
	N	S	E	W	N	S	E	W
9	10	11	12	13	14	15	16	17
A		22.421		2.842		– 0.0546		+ 0.0309
B	0.559		15.190		+ 0.0367		– 0.0208	
C	21.336		1.648		+ 0.0517		– 0.0293	
D	0.349			13.896	+ 0.0336			+ 0.0190
Tot.	22.244	22.421	16.838	16.738	+ 0.1220	– 0.0546	– 0.0501	+ 0.0499

In. St.	Corrected consecutive co-ordinates				Independent Co-ordinates		Remarks
	N	S	E	W	N	S	
	18	19	20	21	22	23	24
A		22.366		2.872	30.000	20.000	1. Angles were measured by repetition method
B	0.596		15.169		30.596	35.169	2. The traverse was run in anticlockwise direction
C	21.388		1.618		51.984	36.787	3. F.B. of AB was observed
D	0.382			13.915	52.366	22.872	
Tot.	22.366	22.366	16.787	16.787			

Calculations for length of closing error, its direction and relative error of closure :

$$\Sigma l = -22.421 + 22.244 = -0.177$$
$$\Sigma d = 16.838 - 16.738 = +0.100$$
$$\text{Closing error length} = \sqrt{-(0.117)^2 + (0.100)^2}$$
$$= \sqrt{0.041329} = 0.2033 \text{ m}$$

Reduced bearing of error,

$$\tan\theta = \frac{0.100}{0.177} = 0.5648$$

$$\therefore \theta = S\ 29.46522\ E = S\ 29°\ 27'\ 54''\ E$$

$$\text{Relative error of closure} = \frac{1}{P} = \frac{1}{\frac{73.10}{0.2033}} = \frac{1}{359.567}$$

2.10.2 Correction by Transit Rule

Table 2.3 : Gale's Traverse Table

In. St	Angles (measured) ° ' "	Corr. (–ve) ' "	Corrected angle ° ' "	W.C. bearings ° ' "	Reduced bearings ° ' "	Quadrant	Line length
1	2	3	4	5	6	7	8
A	80 41 10	–1 4	80 40 6				AB
				87 53 30	87 53 30	NE - I	15.20 m
B	96 32 30	–1 4	96 31 26				BC
				4 24 56	4 24 56	NE - I	21.40 m
C	87 2 20	–1 4	87 1 16				CD
				271 26 12	88 33 48	NW-IV	13.90 m
D	95 48 16	–1 4	95 47 12				DA
				187 13 24	7 13 24	SW - III	22.60 m
Tot.	360 4 16	4 16	360 0 0				P = 73.10

In. St	Consecutive co-ordinates				Corrections			
	Latitude		Departure		Latitude		Departure	
	N	S	E	W	N	S	E	W
9	10	11	12	13	14	15	16	17
A		22.421		2.842		– 0.0886		+0.0085
B	0.559		15.190		+ 0.0022		– 0.0452	
C	21.336		1.648		+ 0.0846		– 0.0049	
D	0.349			13.896	+ 0.0014			+ 0.0414
Tot.	22.244	22.421	16.838	16.738	+ 0.0882	– 0.0886	– 0.0501	+ 0.0499

In. St.	Corrected consecutive co-ordinates				Independent Co-ordinates		Remarks
	N 18	S 19	E 20	W 21	N 22	S 23	24
A		22.332		2.850	30.000	20.000	1. Angles were measured by repetition method
B	0.561		15.144		30.561	35.144	2. The traverse was run in anticlockwise direction
C	21.421		1.643		51.982	36.787	3. F.B. of AB was observed
D	0.350			13.937	30.000	22.000	
Tot.	22.332	22.332	16.787	16.787			

2.10.3 Correction by Modified Transit Rule

Table 2.4 : Gale's Traverse Table

In. St	Angles (measured) ° ′ ″	Corr. (-ve) ′ ″	Corrected angle ° ′ ″	W.C. bearings ° ′ ″	Reduced bearings ° ′ ″	Quad-rant	Line length
1	2	3	4	5	6	7	8
A	80 41 10	−1 4	80 40 6				AB 15.20 m
				87 53 30	87 53 30	NE - I	
B	96 32 30	−1 4	96 31 26				BC 21.40 m
				4 24 56	4 24 56	NE - I	
C	87 2 20	−1 4	87 1 16				CD 13.90 m
				271 26 12	88 33 48	NW - IV	
D	95 48 16	−1 4	95 47 12				DA 22.60 m
				187 13 24	7 13 24	SW - III	
Tot.	360 4 16	4 16	360 0 0				P = 73.10

In. St.	Consecutive co-ordinates				Corrections			
	Latitude		Departure		Latitude		Departure	
	N	S	E	W	N	S	E	W
9	10	11	12	13	14	15	16	17
A		22.421		2.842		– 0.0882		+ 0.0085
B	0.559		15.190		+ 0.0022		– 0.0451	
C	21.336		1.648		+ 0.0846		– 0.0049	
D	0.349			13.896	+ 0.0014			+ 0.0415
Tot.	22.244	22.421	16.838	16.738	+ 0.0882	– 0.0882	– 0.0500	+ 0.0500

In. St.	Corrected consecutive co-ordinates				Independent Co-ordinates		Remarks
	N	S	E	W	N	E	
	18	19	20	21	22	23	24
A		22.332		2.850	30.000	20.000	1. Angles were measured by repetition method
B	0.561		15.145		30.561	35.145	2. The traverse was run in anticlockwise direction
C	21.421		1.642		51.982	36.787	3. F.B. of AB was observed
D	0.350			13.937	52.332	22.850	
Tot.	22.332	22.332	16.787	16.787			

Explanation :

Let us see step by step the procedure how the Gale's traverse table is prepared.

Column 1 : Shows the instrument stations from where the included angles were measured.

Column 2 : Shows the values of measured included angles. Sum of the included angles of the traverse 360° 04' 16".

Theoretical sum should be (2 x 4 – 4) right $\angle$ s = 360°.

∴ Total error is 4' 16" for which correction per angle works out to be $\dfrac{4' 16"}{4}$ = 1' 4".

Assuming all the angles were measured with same precision.

Column 3 : Shows the correction per angle.

Column 4 : Shows the corrected included angles which give the correct sum of the angles = 360°.

Column 5 : Shows the W.C. bearings of sides AB, BC, CD and DA.

Actually only one F.B. of line AB was observed and the other bearings were calculated by the formula F.B. of the line + Next included angle ± 180° = F.B. of the next line.

Thus, F.B. of BC = F.B. of AB + incl. $\angle$ B ± 180°.

F.B. of AB + incl. $\angle$ B = 87° 53' 30" + 96° 31' 26"
= 184° 24' 56"

The sum is more than 180°, therefore 180° is to be subtracted to find the F.B. of BC.

Hence, F.B. of BC = 184° 24' 56" – 180°
= 4° 24' 56"

Column 6 : Indicates reduced bearings of AB, BC, CD and DA.

Column 7 : Shows the quadrant of every line.

For example : Whole circle bearing of line CD = 271° – 26' 12" which is in the North-West quadrant.

Column 8 : Shows the measured lengths of sides AB, BC, CD and DA.

Columns 10, 11, 12 and 13 : Shows the consecutive co-ordinates of each side.

For example : Latitude of station B is obtained from the length of side AB and its reduced bearing,

= 15.20 (cos 87° 53' 30")
= 0.559 (Northing)

and Departure of station B = 15.20 (sin 87° 52' 30") = 15.190 (Easting because line AB lies in the first quadrant (N.E.)

Now, Σ Northings is not equal to Σ Southings.

Difference of Σ Northing and Σ Southing
= 22.244 – 22.421 = Σl = – 0.177

Similarly, difference of Σ Eastings and Σ Westings = 16.838 – 16.738
Σd = 0.100

The calculations for closing error and its direction and relative error of closure, have already been shown in the Gale's traverse table (Table 3.5). Length of closing error = 0.2033 m, reduced bearing of closing error is given by the formula $\tan \theta = \frac{\Sigma d}{\Sigma l}$.

Now, Σd is positive and Σl is negative.

∴ Quadrant in which closing error lies is S.E.

Columns 14, 15, 16 and 17 shows the corrections for latitudes and departures by each method explained below.

1. Bowditch's Rule :

$$\begin{bmatrix} \text{The correction to latitude} \\ \text{or departure of any station} \end{bmatrix} = \begin{bmatrix} \text{Total error} \\ \text{in latitude} \end{bmatrix} \times \frac{\text{Latitude of that side}}{\text{Arithmetical sum of all latitudes}}$$

For station B,

$$\text{Correction to latitude (Northing)} = 0.177 \times \frac{\text{Length of side AB}}{\text{Perimeter of the closed traverse}}$$

$$= \frac{0.177 \times 15.20}{73.10} = +0.0367$$

and Correction to departure (Easting) $= \frac{0.100 \times 15.20}{73.10} = -0.0208$

Correction to latitude (Northing) is plus because Σ Northings is less than Σ Southings while correction to departure (Easting) is minus, because sum of Eastings is more than sum of Westings.

2. Transit Rule :

$$\begin{bmatrix} \text{The correction to latitude} \\ \text{or departure of any station} \end{bmatrix} = \begin{bmatrix} \text{Total error in} \\ \text{latitude or departure} \end{bmatrix} \times \begin{bmatrix} \text{Latitude or departure of} \\ \text{the station} \\ \overline{\text{Arithmetical sum of all}} \\ \text{the latitudes or departures} \\ \text{of the station} \end{bmatrix}$$

To find corrections for latitude and departure for station B :

Total error in latitude = 0.177
Total error in departure = 0.100
Arithmetic sum of latitudes = 22.244 + 22.421 = 44.665

∴ The correction to latitude (Northing) $= \frac{0.177 \times 0.559}{44.665}$

$= 0.0022 \ (+)$

Arithmetic sum of departures = 16.838 + 16.738 = 33.576

Correction to departure (Eastings) $= \frac{0.100 \times 15.190}{33.576}$

$= 0.0452 \ (-)$

3. Modified Transit Rule :

$$\begin{bmatrix} \text{Correction to Northing or} \\ \text{Southing of the station} \end{bmatrix} = \frac{1}{2} \begin{bmatrix} \text{Total error} \\ \text{in latitude} \end{bmatrix} \times \begin{bmatrix} \dfrac{\text{Northing or Southing of that station}}{\text{Sum of Northings or Southings of the respective stations}} \end{bmatrix}$$

Similarly,

$$\begin{bmatrix} \text{Correction to Easting or} \\ \text{Westing of the station} \end{bmatrix} = \frac{1}{2} \begin{bmatrix} \text{Total error} \\ \text{in departure} \end{bmatrix} \times \begin{bmatrix} \dfrac{\text{Easting or Westing of that station}}{\text{Sum of Eastings or Westings of the respective stations}} \end{bmatrix}$$

Total error in latitude = 0.177
Total error in departure = 0.100
Northing of B = 0.559
and Easting of B = 15.190
Sum of all Northings = 22.244

Correction to Northing of station B = $\dfrac{0.177}{2} \times \dfrac{0.559}{22.244}$ = + 0.0022

Correction to Easting of station B :
Sum of all Eastings = 16.838

Correction to Easting of station B = $\dfrac{0.100}{2} \times \dfrac{15.190}{16.838}$ = − 0.0451

Columns 18, 19, 20, 21 are for corrected consecutive co-ordinates.
Thus, where Bowditch's rule is applied for correction,
Corrected latitude of B = 0.559 + 0.0367 = 0.596 (upto 3 decimals)
Similarly, corrected departure of B = 15.190 − 0.0208 = 15.169 (upto 3 decimals)
The same procedure is also used for calculating the corrected co-ordinates by transit and third rule method.

Columns 22 and 23 : The independent co-ordinates of the first station A are taken of such values in the first quadrant (N.E.), that after adding algebraically the consecutive co-ordinates successively, the co-ordinates of all other stations still remain in N.E. quadrant.

Thus, independent co-ordinates of station A are assumed as

N	E
30.000	20.000

∴ Independent co-ordinates of station B can be calculated as follows :

Independent latitude of B (Bowditch's rule) = Independent latitude of A + Corrected latitude of station B
= 30.000 + 0.596 = 30.596 (N)

Independent departure of B = Independent departure of A +
(Bowditch's rule)   Corrected departure of station B

= 20.000 + 15.169
= 35.169

Column 24 : Remarks column, explains –
1. The method of measurement of included angles.
2. Direction of running of traverse whether clockwise or anticlockwise.
3. The bearing of which side was observed in the field, and
4. Which rule was used for applying corrections to the consecutive co-ordinates.

After obtaining the independent co-ordinates of the stations, the final work is that of plotting. For this, the North and East axis are chosen. Choosing suitable scale for co-ordinates, the co-ordinates of all stations are marked and then these points are joined to get the final outline of corrected traverse ABCD Fig. 3.32 shows the plotting of the final traverse as obtained from the independent co-ordinates in the illustrative example.

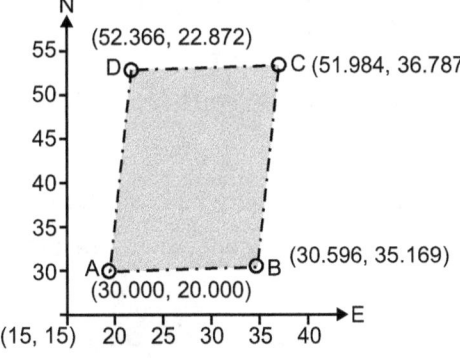

Fig. 2.29 : Plotting of a Closed Traverse

SOLVED EXAMPLES

Example 2.6 : In a closed traverse ABCDEA carried out with a transit vernier theodolite, the following is the part of a Gale's Traverse Table.

Line	Length in m	Reduced Bearing
AB	28.21	N 15° 16' 15" E
BC	21.25	N 23° 10' 20" W
CD	29.80	N 82° 15'41" W
DE	34.10	S 14° 16'21" W
EA	42.90	S 65° 19' 55" E

Compute the length and reduced bearing of a linear error of closure.

Solution : The consecutive co-ordinates of different points will be calculated and tabulated as under.

Line	Length in m	Reduced Bearing	Point	Northing	Southing	Easting	Westing
AB	28.21	N 15° 16' 15" E	B	27.213	–	7.430	–
BC	21.25	N 23° 10' 20" W	C	19.535	–	–	8.361
CD	29.80	N 82° 15' 41" W	D	4.012	–	–	29.528
DE	34.10	S 14° 16' 21" W	E	–	33.047	–	8.406
EA	42.90	S 65° 19' 55" E	A	–	17.904	38.984	–
		Σ		50.760	50.951	46.414	46.295

Sum of latitudes = ΣL = 50.760 − 50.951 = − 0.191 m

Sum of departures = ΣD = 46.414 − 46.295 = 0.119 m

Length of closing error = $\sqrt{(\Sigma l)^2 + (\Sigma d)^2}$

$= \sqrt{(-0.191)^2 + (0.119)^2}$

= 0.225 m

Reduced bearing of closing error = $\dfrac{\Sigma D}{\Sigma L}$

$\tan \theta = \dfrac{0.119}{0.191} = 0.623$

θ = S 31° 55' 27" E

Calculation of Co-ordinates : Illustration for co-ordinates of 'B'.

Co-ordinates of B (i.e. Northing and Easting of B) are obtained by using length and reduced bearing of AB.

Northing of B = $l \cos \theta$ = 28.21 cos 15° 16' 15" = 27.213 m

Easting of B = $l \sin \theta$ = 28.21 sin 15° 16' 15" = 7.430 m

Example 2.7 : In a closed traverse. PQRSTP, the following are the corrected consecutive co-ordinates in metres.

Station	N	S (−)	E (+)	W (−)
P	–	17.87	38.94	
Q	27.26	–	7.42	–
R	19.57			8.37
S	4.03	–		29.57
T	–	32.99		8.42

Compute the independent co-ordinates and the area of the traverse in sq. metres by co-ordinate method. To start with, assume independent co-ordinates of station P as N = 00.00 and E = 50.00.

Solution : The assumed co-ordinates of P are N = 00.00 and E = 50.00.

The independent co-ordinates of Q = Northing of P + Northing of Q
Northing of Q = 00.00 + 27.26 = 27.26
Easting of Q = Easting of P + Easting of Q
= 50.00 + 7.42 = 57.42
Northing of R = Northing of Q + Northing of R
= 27.26 + 19.57 = 46.83
Easting of R = Easting of Q − Westing of R
= 57.42 − 8.37 = 49.05

Similarly,
Northing of S = 46.83 + 4.03 = 50.86
Easting of S = 49.05 − 29.57 = 19.48
Northing of T = 50.86 − 32.99 = 17.87
Easting of T = 19.48 − 8.42 = 11.06

As a check −
Northing of P = 17.87 − 17.87 = 0.00
Easting of P = 11.06 + 38.94 = 50.00

The independent co-ordinates are tabulated as under :

Station	Northing	Easting
P	00.00	50.00
Q	27.26	57.42
R	46.83	49.05
S	50.86	19.48
T	17.87	11.06
P	00.00	50.00

To find the area of traverse :

Arranging the independent co-ordinates in the determinant form −

A	00.00	27.26	46.83	50.86	17.87	00.00
B	50.00	57.42	49.05	19.48	11.06	50.00

ΣA = {00.00 (57.42) + 27.26 (49.05) + 46.83 (19.48) + 50.86 (11.06) + 17.87 (50.00)}
= {0 + 1337.103 + 912.248 + 562.511 + 893.5)}
= 3705.262 sq.m.

ΣB = {50 (27.26) + 57.42 (46.83) + 49.05 (50.86) + 19.48 (17.87) + 11.06 (00.00)}
= {1363 + 2688.978 + 2494.683 + 348.107 + 00.00}
= 6894.768 sq.m.

Twice area = $\Sigma A - \Sigma B$ = 3189.406 (positive difference)

∴ Area of the traverse = 1594.703 sq. m.

REVIEW QUESTIONS

(1) (a) State the uses of theodolite.
(b) Explain how you will measure a horizontal angle with the theodolite.

(2) (a) Define the fundamental axes of a transit theodolite.
(b) State the relationship between the fundamental lines of a transit theodolite.

(3) (a) What are the methods of measurement of horizontal angles by a transit theodolite ? Describe any one method.
(b) State the advantages of the method of repetition.

(4) (a) How will you measure the magnetic bearing of a line by theodolite?
(b) How will you obtain the prolongation of a line by theodolite ?

(5) Write short notes on :
(a) Temporary adjustments.
(b) Internal focussing and External focussing telescope.
(c) Latitudes and Departures.
(d) Consecutive and Independent co-ordinates.

(6) (a) How will you find out the constants of the instrument in the field tacheometric survey ?
(b) Derive an expression for the horizontal distance of a vertically held staff from a tacheometer when the line of sight is inclined.

(7) (a) State the various permanent adjustments of a transit theodolite, in the order in which they are carried out.
(b) Describe how you would test and adjust the line of collimation of a transit theodolite so as to make it coincide with the axis of the telescope.

(8) (a) Explain the use of anallatic lens in a tacheometer.
(b) Explain Bowditch's rule of traverse adjustments.
(c) What is trigonometrical levelling ? What are the different cases of plane trigonometrical levelling ?

(9) (a) What are the methods of carrying out the theodolite traverse survey ?
(b) Describe any one : How will you find whether the traverse is closing or not? State, how you will find the magnitude of closing error.

(10) (a) If there is a closing error in the traverse, what are the methods of applying corrections ?
(b) What are the sources of error in theodolite traversing ?

(11) (a) Explain how will you test and adjust the transit theodolite to ensure that the horizontal axis is perpendicular to the vertical axis.

(b) How will you make the line of collimation perpendicular to the horizontal axis ?

(12) Define the following terms :
   (i) Closing error of a traverse.
   (ii) Independent co-ordinates.
   (iii) Open and closed traverse.

(13) Describe the various methods of traversing with a theodolite and discuss their merits and demerits.

(14) Bowditch's rule, is more suitable for a compass traverse than a theodolite traverse". Comment.

(15) Distinguish clearly between the following :
   (i) Latitude and Departure.
   (ii) Bowditch's rule and Transit rule.
   (iii) Face left and Face right observations.

EXAMPLES

(1) (a) In a closed traverse PQRSP, the following measurements were recorded :

   Sum of Northings = 440.00,   Sum of Eastings = 644.90
   Sum of Southings = 438.00,   Sum of Westings = 646.20

Find the error of closure of a traverse. If the relative error of closure of the traverse is 1 in 1000, what is the perimeter of the traverse ?

[**Ans.** : Error of closure = 2.385 m, perimeter = 2385 m]

(2) During a theodolite traverse, the following observations were recorded in the field.

Line	Length in metres	Whole circle bearing
AB	161.20 m	121° 30'
BC	141.38 m	18° 09'
CD	201.39 m	218° 31'

Calculate the length and bearing of DA and obtain the co-ordinates of the stations B, C and D, if the co-ordinates of the station A are (700 N, 500E).

[**Ans.** : (DA = 121.205 m, Bearing of DA = 332° 27' Co-ord. of B ≡ (615.773, 637.446), C ≡ (750.119, 681.487), D ≡ (592.546, 556.073)]

(3) Two points A and D are connected by a traverse survey ABCD and the following records are obtained.

   AB = 267 m, BC = 208 m, CD 300 m

(Clockwise ∠ ABC = 118° 30', Clockwise ∠ BCD = 108° 30'). Assuming as the meridian, calculate :

(i) Co-ordinates of D, if those of A are (500, 450).

(ii) Length AD.   (iii) Angle BAD.

[**Ans.** : Co-ord. of D ≡ (661.649, 47.800), AD = 433.47 m, ∠ BAD = 680 6' 15"]

(4) The following lengths and bearings were recorded in running a theodolite traverse ABCD. There are. obstacles which prevent direct measurement of the bearing and length of line DA

Line	Length in Metres	Whole Circle Bearing
AB	485 m	341° 15'
BC	1725 m	16° 30'
CD	1050 m	142° 00'

Compute the length and bearing of line DA.

[**Ans.** : DA = 1616.985 m, Bearing of DA = 217° 19' 35"]

Unit - III

TACHOMETRY

3.1 INTRODUCTION

Tachometry is a branch of surveying in which the horizontal and vertical distances are determined from angular observations by a tachometer. The chaining operations being altogether eliminated, tachometer is not as accurate as in chaining, but it is far more rapid, in rough and difficult country where levelling is tedious and chaining is both inaccurate and slow. Thus, it is best suited when obstacles such as steep and broken ground, deep varines, stretches of water or swaraps are met with. Tachometry is mainly used while preparing contour plans and traversing and it is also suitable for hydrographic surveys, location surveys of roads, railways etc. It is also sometimes employed for small surveys in which elevations are not determined.

3.1.1 Instruments Used in Tacheometer

The various instruments used in tacheometer are as follows :
(1) Tacheometer
(2) Levelling or Stadia Rod

(1) Tacheometer : A tacheometer in general sense is a transit theodolite having a telescope fitted with a stadia diaphragm i.e. a telescope equipped with two horizontal hairs called stadia hairs in addition to the usual central hair. The additional lines are equipped from the central one and are also known as stadia lines. The types of stadia diaphragm is shown in Fig. 3.1. Usually the arrangement shown in (Fig. 3.1 (i) (a) is provided.

(2) Stadia Rod : Specially designed graduated rod known as stadia rod is used in tacheometer. The stadia rod is transparent. It may be folding or telescopic. It is 3 to 5 m long and 5 cm to 15 cm wide. The graduations are bold and clear with a least count usually less than the least count of an ordinary levelling staff. The stadia rod should be as light as possible. (See the Fig. 3.1).

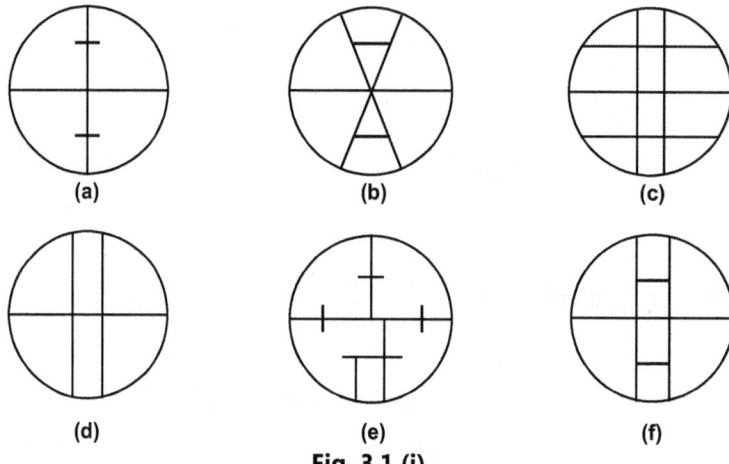

Fig. 3.1 (i)

An ordinary levelling staff can be used if the sights are short but in tacheometry since the sights are usually of much greater length, an ordinary levelling staff cannot serve the purpose.

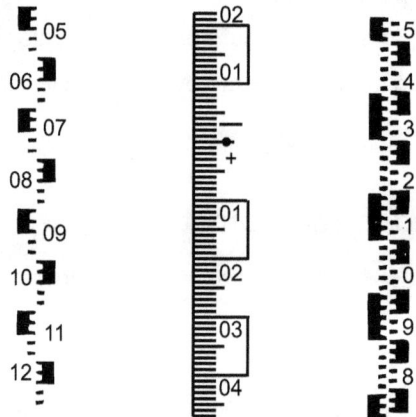

Fig. 3.1 (ii) : Various Patterns of Stadia Rod

3.2 PRINCIPLE OF STADIA TACHEOMETRY

The general principle of stadia tacheometry is explained as follows :

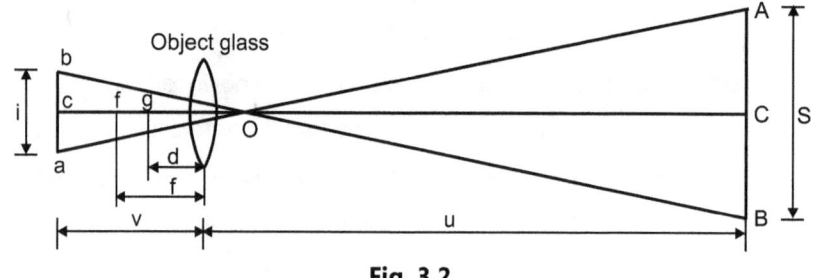

Fig. 3.2

Let, O be the optical centre of the object glass.

a, b and c the bottom, top and central hairs at diapharm.

A, B and C the points on the staff out by three lines.

∴ a, b = i, the interval between stadia lines.

(ab is the length of the image of AB)

AB = S = the staff intercept (the difference of the stadia hair readings)

f = the focal length of object glass i.e. the distance between the optical centre O to the principal focus (f_1) of the lens.

u = the horizontal distance from the optical centre (O) to the staff.

v = the horizontal distance from the optical centre (O) to the image of the staff, u and v being called the conjugate focal length of the lens.

d = the horizontal distance from optical centre (O) to the vertical axis of the tacheometer.

D = the horizontal distance from the vertical axis of the instrument to the staff.

The $\triangle$ AOB and $\triangle$ aOb are similar triangles.

$$\frac{i}{S} = \frac{v}{u}$$

∴ $$v = \frac{iu}{S} \quad \ldots (3.1)$$

We know the property of a lens,

$$\frac{1}{v} + \frac{1}{u} = \frac{1}{f} \quad \ldots (3.2)$$

Substituting the value of V from equation (5.1) in (5.2) we have,

$$\frac{1}{\frac{iu}{S}} + \frac{1}{u} = \frac{1}{f}$$

We have,

$$\frac{S}{iu} + \frac{1}{u} = \frac{1}{f}$$

or

$$\frac{1}{u}\left(\frac{S}{i} + 1\right) = \frac{1}{f}$$

$$\left(\frac{S}{i} + 1\right) = \frac{u}{f}$$

∴ $$u = \left(\frac{S}{i} + i\right)f$$

∴ $$\left(u = \frac{Sf}{i} + f\right)$$

But $\quad D = u + d$

∴ $\quad D = \left(\dfrac{Sf}{i} + f\right) + d$

∴ $\quad D = \left(\dfrac{f}{i}\right)S + (f + d)$

The quantities $\left(\dfrac{f}{i}\right)$ and $(f + d)$ are called the *constants of the instrument.*

The constant $\left(\dfrac{f}{i}\right)$ is called *multiple constant* and its value is taken as 100. While the constant $(f + d)$ is called the *additive constant* and its value varies from 30 cm to 60 cm in case of external focussing. It is very small ranging from 10 cm to 20 cm and is therefore ignored. To make the additive constant zero, an additional convex lens, known as anallactic lens, is provided in the telescope between the object glass and eye-piece at a fixed distance from former. By this arrangement the calculation is reduced.

In general we can write the equation as,

$$D = mS + c$$

where, $\quad m = \dfrac{f}{i}$ is multiplying constant

$\quad c = (f + d)$ is additive constant

and $\quad S =$ staff intercept

3.3 FIXED HAIR METHOD OF STADIA TACHEOMETRY

While finding the horizontal distance between an instrument station and a point and the elevation of a point with respect to the instrument station, the line of sight may be horizontal or inclined depending upon their position in the vertical plane.

CASE – I : When the line of sight is horizontal and the staff is held vertical.

In this case, the horizontal distance from the axis of the instrument to the staff station is given by the equation,

∴ $\quad D = \left(\dfrac{f}{i}\right)S + f + d$

$\quad D = mS + c$

In this case, R.L. of staff station = R.L. of instrument, Axis – Staff reading on the central hair i.e axial hair reading

CASE – II : When the line of sight is inclined to the horizontal and the staff is held vertical.

When the ground is rough and horizontal sights are not possible, inclined sights have to be taken. In this case, the staff may be either vertical or normal to the line of sight. In general, the method of holding the staff vertically is easy and the formulate involved are simpler.

When the Staff is Held Vertical.

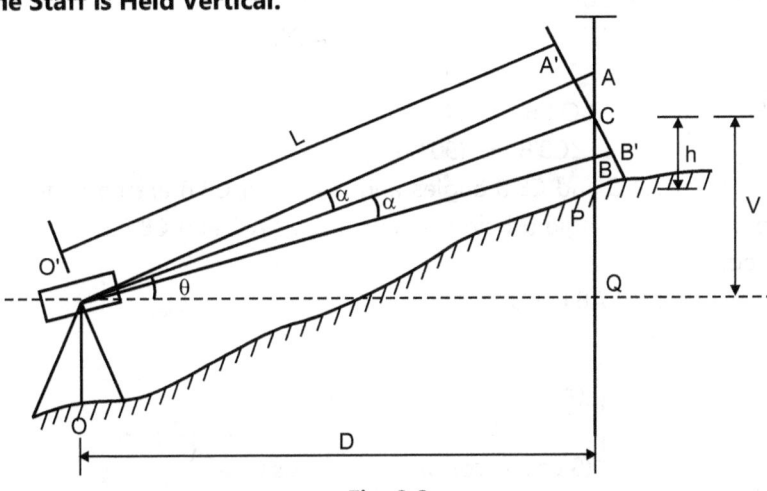

Fig. 3.3

O = The instrument station.
O' = The position of the instrument axis.
P = The staff station.
A, C, B = The points on the staff cut by the hairs of the diaphragm.
∠ CO'Q = The inclination to the line of the sight to the horizontal.
AB = S, the staff intercept.
PC = h, the reading with the central hair i.e the axial reading.
O'C = L = the inclined distance along the line of sight from the instrument axis to the staff station P.
QC = V = the vertical distance from the instrument axis to the point C.

Through C, draw AB perpendicular to OC cutting OA and OB at A' and B' respectively.

The inclined distance $L = \frac{f}{i}(A'B') + (f + d)$ as the line of sight and AB are perpendicular to each other (case – I).

From Δ O'CQ the required horizontal distance

$$P = L \cos\theta = \frac{f}{i}(A'B')\cos\theta + (f + d)\cos\theta$$

The nature of D can be obtained by expressing AB in terms in the staff intercept AB (i.e. S)

In ΔO'CQ;   ∠CQO' = (90° − θ)
            ∠ BCB' = ∠ A'CA = θ
Let   ∠AO'C = ∠ CO'B = α

The exterior angle AA'C of A'O'C
$$= \angle ACO + \angle A'O'C$$
$$= (90° + \alpha)$$
In $\Delta O'CB'$; $\angle O'CB' = 90°$
$$\angle CB'B = (90° - \alpha)$$

Thus, in triangles AA'C and CB'B angles and AA'C and CB'B are equal to (90° + α) and (90° – α) respectively. The angle α being small, angles AA'C and CB'B may be considered to be practically equal to 90°.

∴   A'B' = AB cos θ
P = L cos θ

∴ $D = \dfrac{f}{i} (A'B') \cos \theta + (f + d) \cos \theta$

∴ $D = \dfrac{f}{i} (S \cos \theta \cdot \cos \theta) + (f + d) \cos \theta$

where   A'B' = S cos θ

$$\boxed{D = \dfrac{f}{i} (S \cdot \cos^2 \theta) + (f + d) \cos \theta} \quad \ldots (3.3)$$

Now, $V = L \sin \theta = \dfrac{f}{i} S \sin \theta \cdot \cos \theta + (f + d) \sin \theta$

∴ $V = \dfrac{f}{i} \sin \dfrac{2\theta}{2} (S) + (f + d) \sin \theta$

∴ $\boxed{V = D \cdot \tan \theta} \quad \ldots (3.4)$

Knowing the values of V, the elevation of staff station P may be determined as follows:
(a) When the observed angle i.e. vertical angle is an angle of elevation of angle.

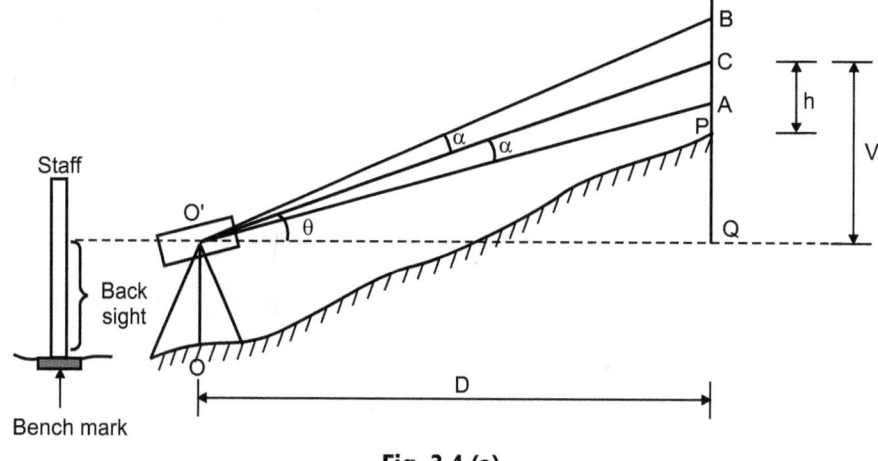

Fig. 3.4 (a)

(1) Elevation or R.L. of instrument axis = Elevation of BM + Back sight.
(2) Elevation or R.L. of staff station = R.L. of instrument axis + V − h.

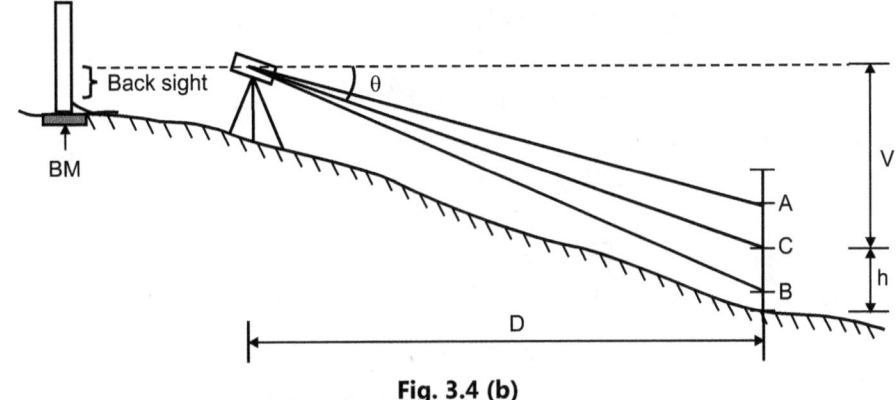

Fig. 3.4 (b)

(1) Elevation or R.L. of instrument axis = Elevation of BM + Back sight.
(2) Elevation or R.L. of staff station = R.L. of instrument axis − V − h.

SOLVED EXAMPLES

Example 3.1 : In order to determine the constants of a tacheometer two distances 250 m and 421 m were accurately measured from the instrument and readings on a stadia rod on the upper and lower wires were taken as follows :

Sr. No.	Distances in m	Reading at	
		Lower stadia	Upper stadia
1	250	2.50	5.50 m
2	421	0.50	3.50 m

Determine value of the constants and find the distance when the readings of the wire are 1.5 and 4.5 m, the line of sight being horizontal in all cases.

Solution : We know the equation,

$$D = \left(\frac{f}{i}\right)S + f + d$$

or

$$D = mS + c$$

In first case, we have, $D = 250$ m
Staff intercept $S = 4.50 - 2.50 = 2.00$ m
∴ We have, $250 = m \cdot 2 + c$ ... (I)

In second case, we have, $D = 421$
Staff intercept $S = 3.50 - 0.50 = 3$ m
∴ We have, $421 = m \cdot 3 + c$ ... (II)

Solving (I) and (II),

$$2m + c = 250$$
$$3m \pm c = \pm 421$$
$$\overline{-m + 0 = -171}$$
$$m = -171 \text{ i.e. } f/i$$

Put this value in equation (I)
We have,
$$250 = 2m + c$$
$$\therefore 250 = 2 \times 171 + c$$
$$\therefore 250 = 342 + c$$
$$\therefore c = 250/342 = 0.730 \text{ i.e. } (f + d)$$

(b) We know,
$$D = \frac{f}{i}S + (f + d)$$
$$\therefore D = 171 \times S + (0.730) \text{ i.e. } (f/i) = 171 \text{ and } (f + d) = 0.730$$
$$\therefore S = 4.5 - 1.5 = 3.00 \text{ m}$$
$$\therefore D = 171 \times 3 + 0.730$$
$$D = 513 + 0.730$$

∴ Distance is $D = 513.730$ m

Example 3.2 : To determine the tacheometric constants of a transit fitted with stadia hairs. The following observations were taken on a staff held vertically at distance measured from the instrument.

Horizontal distance (m)	50	100	150
Staff interval (m)	0.495	0.998	1.500

The line of sight was kept horizontal. The focal length of the object is 15 cm and the distance of the objective glass from the trunion axis of the instrument is 10 cm. Determine the values of m and c.

We know the equation,
$$D = \left(\frac{f}{i}\right)S + f + d$$
$$D = mS + c$$
$$\therefore c = f + d$$
$$c = 15 + 10 = 25 \text{ cm} = \boxed{0.25 \text{ m}}$$
$$D = mS + c$$
$$\therefore m = \frac{D - c}{S} \text{ where } c = 0.25 \text{ m}$$

(1) For $D = 50$ m and $S = 0.495$ m
$$m = \frac{50 - 0.25}{0.495} = 100.50$$

(2) For D = 100 m and S = 0.998

$$m = \frac{100 - 0.25}{0.998} = 99.74$$

(3) For D = 150 m and S = 1.50 m

$$m = \frac{150 - 0.25}{1.50} = 99.83$$

∴ Mean value of m $= \frac{1}{3}(100.50 + 99.74 + 99.83)$

$$= \frac{300.07}{3}$$

m = 100.02

Example 3.3 : Two horizontal distances of 50 and 80 metre were accurately measured and the intercepts on the staff between the outer stadia wires were 0.496 m and 0.796 m respectively. Calculate the tacheometric constants.

Solution : Given :

Horizontal distance	50 m	80 m
Staff intercepts	0.496 m	0.796 m

We have the equation,

D = m.S + c

(1) For D = 50 m and S = 0.496 m

∴ 50 = m (0.496) + c

∴ 50 = 0.496 m + c   ... (I)

(2) For D = 80 m and S = 0.796 m

D = m.S + c

80 = m(0.796) + c

∴ 80 = 0.796 m + c   ... (II)

∴ Solving two simultaneous equations we have,

  80 = 0.796 m + c   ... (II)
 −50 = ±0.496 m ± c   ... (I)
 ─────────────────
  30 = 0.3 m + 0

∴ 0.3 m = 30

∴ m = 30/0.3 = 100

Put this value in equation (II),

80 = 0.796 m + c

80 = 0.796 (100) + c

∴ 　　　　　　　　　　80 = 79.6 + c
∴ 　　　　　　　　　　 c = 80 − 79.6
∴ 　　　　　　　　　　 c = 0.4
∴ Multiplying constant　m = $\left(\dfrac{f}{i}\right)$ = 100
∴ Additive constant　　 c = f + d = 0.4

Example 3.4 : Calculate the tacheometric constants from the following readings with a tacheometer onto a vertical staff.

Sr. No.	Horizontal Distance Between Instrument and Staff	Staff Reading m		
(1)	66.3	0.770	1.100	1.430
(2)	75.3	1.680	2.055	2.430

Solution : We have the equation,

Where　　　　　　　　$D = \left(\dfrac{f}{i}\right) S + f + d$

or　　　　　　　　　　 D = mS + c

For set (1), D = 66.3 and staff intercept = 1.430 − 0.770 = 0.66
∴　　　　　　　　　　 D = m (0.66) + c
∴　　　　　　　　　　66.3 = 0.66 m + c　　　　　　　　　　… (I)

For set (2), D = 75.3 and staff intercept = 2.430 − 1.680 = 0.75
　　　　　　　　　　　D = m.S + c
　　　　　　　　　　　75.3 = m (0.75) + c
∴　　　　　　　　　　75.3 = 0.75 m + c　　　　　　　　　　… (II)

Solving the two simultaneous equations, we have,

　　　　　　　　　　　75.3 = 0.75 m + c　　　　　　　　　　… (II)
　　　　　　　　　　 − 66.3 = ±0.66 m ± c　　　　　　　　　 … (I)
　　　　　　　　　　　―――――――――――
　　　　　　　　　　　　9 = 0.09 m + 0

∴　　　　　　　　　　 m = $\dfrac{9}{0.09}$ = 100

Put in equation (I) we have,

　　　　　　　　　　　66.3 = 0.66 × 100 + c
∴　　　　　　　　　　 c = 1.004

Example 3.5 : The stadia readings with horizontal sight on a vertical staff 100 m from a tacheometer 1.385 and 1.880. The focal length of the object glass was 20 cm. The distance between the object glass and the vertical axis of the tacheometer was 15 cm. Calculate the stadia interval.

Solution : We know,

$$D = mS + c$$
$$D = \left(\frac{f}{i}\right)S + f + d$$
$$\therefore c = f + d = 20 + 15 = 35 \text{ cm} = 0.35 \text{ m}$$
$$S = 1.880 - 1.385 = 0.495$$
$$D = \left(\frac{f}{i}\right)S + f + d$$
$$\therefore D = \left(\frac{0.2}{i}\right)0.495 + 0.35 \text{ m}$$
$$\therefore 100 - 0.35 = \frac{0.2}{i}(0.495)$$
$$\therefore 99.65 = \frac{0.099}{i}$$
$$i = \frac{0.099}{99.65}$$
$$i = 9.93 \times 10^{-4} \text{ m}$$

Example 3.6 : A tacheometer reads 1.274 m and 1.770 m corresponding to the stadia hairs on a vertical staff 50 m away. The distance between the object glass and the trunion axis was found to be 146 mm. If the focal length of the object glass is 356 mm. Compute the value of the multiplying constant.

Solution : Staff intercept = 1.770 − 1.274 = 0.496 m.
Distance between the object and the station is 50 m = D

$$d = 146 \text{ mm}$$
$$f = 356 \text{ m}$$

We have the formula,
$$D = \left(\frac{f}{i}\right)S + (f + d)$$
$$\therefore 100 = mS + c$$
$$\therefore c = f + d$$
$$= 356 + 146$$
$$c = 0.502 \text{ m}$$
$$\therefore 50 = m(0.496) + 0.502$$
$$\therefore 50 - 0.502 = m(0.496)$$
$$\frac{49.498}{0.496} = m$$
$$\therefore m = 99.794$$

Example 3.7 : To determine the distance between two points A and B and the R.L. of Q. The following observations were made –

Height of a Tacheometer   A = 1.480 m
Vertical angle   B = 5°20'
Staff reading = 0.545, 0.905, 1.265
     R.L. of P = 150. 00 m

Solution :   m = 100.00
     c = 0.00 m
     θ = 5° 20'

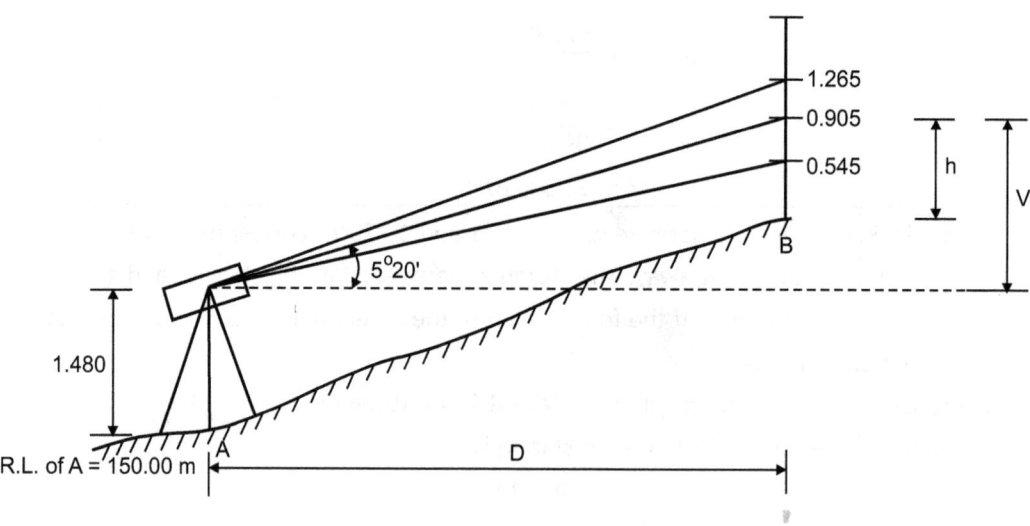

Fig. 3.5

Staff intercept = 1.2675 – 0.545 = 0.720 m

We have by the formula

$$D = 100 \, S \cos^2 \theta$$
$$D = 100 \times 0.720 \times \cos^2 (5°20')$$
$$\boxed{D = 71.378 \text{ m}}$$

∴

R.L. of B = R.L. of axis + V – h

We have, V = D tan θ

$$\boxed{V = 71.378 \times \tan (5° 20') = 6.663 \text{ m}}$$

R.L. of B = (150 + 1.480) + 6.663 – 0.9015
$$\boxed{\text{R.L. of B} = 137.238 \text{ m}}$$

Example 3.8 : Determine the gradiant from point A to point B from the following observations made with a tacheometer fitted with an anallactic lens. The constant of the instrument was 100 and the staff was held vertically.

Instrument station	Staff station	Bearing	Vertical angle	Stadia reading
P	A	134°	+ 10° 32'	1.360, 1.915, 2.470
P	B	224°	+ 5° 6'	1.065, 1.885, 2.750

Solution : Assuming that the staff is held vertically.

From P to A →

$$PA = D_1 = 100\ S \cos^2 \theta$$
$$= 100 (2.470 - 1.360) \cos^2 (10° 32')$$
∴ $D_1 = 107.290$
and $V = D_1 \tan \theta = 107.290 \times \tan(10° 32')$
∴ $V = 19.9495$ m

From P to B →

$$PB = D_2 = 100\ S \cos^2 \theta$$
$$D_2 = 100 (2.750 - 1.065) \times \cos^2 (5°6')$$
∴ $D_2 = 167.108$ m
and $V = D_2 \tan (5° 6')$
∴ $V = 167.168 \times \tan 5° 6'$
∴ $V = 14.919$ m

The gradient from P to Q can be calculated as follows :

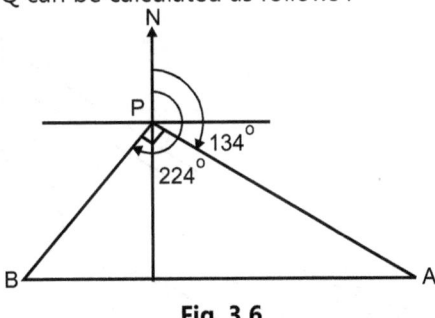

Fig. 3.6

The bearings are given,
∴ $\angle APB = 90°$
∴ The distance $AB^2 = BP^2 + AP^2$
$AB = \sqrt{BP^2 + AP^2}$
∴ $AB = \sqrt{167.168^2 + 107.290^2}$
$AB = 198.63$ m

Difference in elevations between A and Instrument axis
$$= 19.949 - 1.915$$
$$= 18.034 \text{ m}$$
Difference in elevation between B and Instrument axis
$$= 14.919 - 1.885 = 13.034$$
Difference in elevation between A and B $= 18.034 - 13.034 = 5$

∴ Gradient from A to B $= \dfrac{5}{198.63}$

∴ The gradient is 1 : 39.726

Example 3.9 : Determine the gradient from a point P to point Q from the following observations carried out with a tacheometer fitted with anallactic lens.

Instrument	Staff point	Bearing	Vertical angle	Staff reading
0	P	345°	+ 15°	0.750 1.435 2.120
	Q	75°	+ 10°	0.625 1.835 3.050

Assume that the staff is held vertically and that the multiplying constant of that instrument is 100.

(1) From O to P :
$$OP = D_1 = 100 \cdot S \cdot \cos^2 \theta$$
$$= 100 (2.120 - 0.750) \cdot \cos^2 (15°)$$
$$D_1 = 127.82 \text{ m}$$

Now, $V = D_1 \tan \theta$
$V = (127.82) \tan 15°$
∴ $V = 34.25 \text{ m}$

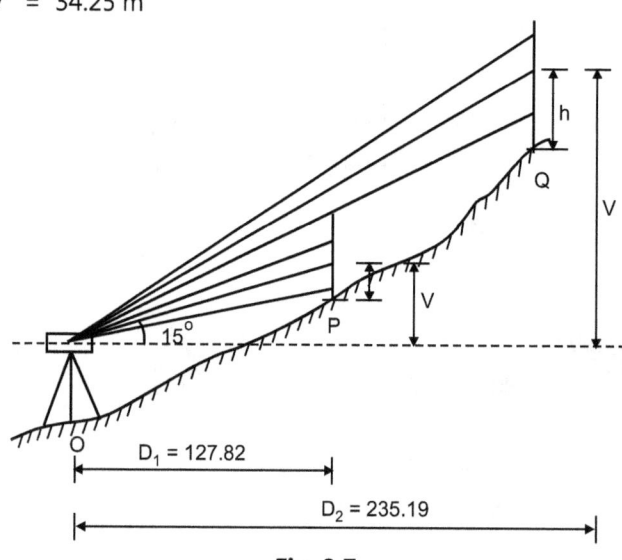

Fig. 3.7

(2) From O to Q :

$$D_2 = 100 \cdot S \cdot \cos^2 \theta$$
$$= 100(3.050 - 0.625) \times \cos^2(10°)$$
$$\boxed{D_2 = 235.19 \text{ m}}$$

$$V = D_2 \tan \theta$$
$$V = 235.19 \times \tan(10°)$$
$$\boxed{V = 41.47 \text{ m}}$$

We have the bearings

∴   ∠POQ = 360° − 345° + 75°
∴   ∠POQ = 90° [in right angle △ POQ]
∴ $PQ^2 = OP^2 + OQ^2$

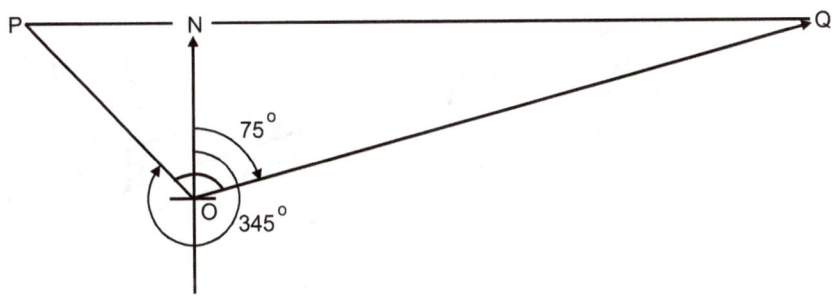

Fig. 3.8

∴ $PQ = \sqrt{OP^2 + OQ^2} = \sqrt{(127.32)^2 + (235.19)^2}$
∴ $\boxed{PQ = 267.68 \text{ m}}$

R.L. of staff station at P = R.L. of instrument axis + V − h

∴   = 00 + 34.25 − 1.435 = 32.815 m

∴ R.L. of staff station at Q = R.L. of instrument axis + V − h
         = 0 + 41.47 − 1.835
         = 39.635 m

Difference in elevation between P and Q
         = 39.635 − 32.815
         = 6.82 m (Q is heigher than P)

∴ Gradient from P to Q $= \dfrac{6.82}{l(PQ)} = \dfrac{6.82}{267.68}$

∴ Gradient from P to Q is $\boxed{1 : 39.25 \text{ rising}}$

Example 3.10 : Determine the distance between the points P and Q from the data.
R.L. of tacheometer axis P = 190.300 m
Vertical angle at P = – 6° 20'
Staff reading at Q = 1.540, 0.800, 0.260
Also determine the R.L. of Q if the staff is held vertical and m = 100 and c = 0.00 m.

Solution : Given : Instrument station P.
Staff at Q.

$$\begin{aligned}
\text{R.L. of tacheometer axis} &= 190.300 \text{ m.} \\
\text{Vertical angle at P} &= -6°20' \text{ (depression)} \\
\text{Staff reading at Q} &= 1.540, 0.800, 0.260 \\
\text{Staff intercept} &= 1.540 - 0.260 = 1.28 \text{ m} = S.
\end{aligned}$$

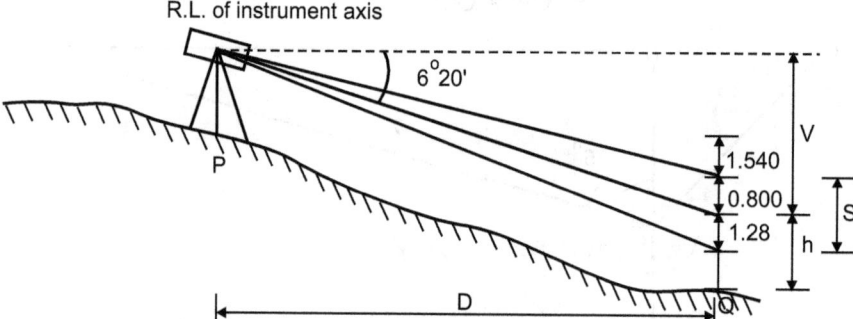

Fig. 3.9

We have the formula,

R.L. of staff station (Q) = R.L. of instrument axis = V – h

We have, R.L. of instrument axis = 190.300 m.

∴ $V = D . \tan \theta$
∴ $D = 100.S \cos^2 \theta$
   $D = 100 . (1.28) . \cos^2 (6°20')$
∴ $\boxed{D = 126.44 \text{ m}}$

Now, $V = D . \tan \theta$
∴ $V = 126.44 \times \tan (6° 20')$
∴ $\boxed{V = 14.033 \text{ m}}$

∴ R.L. of staff station = 190.300 – 14.033 – 0.800
   $\boxed{\text{R.L. of staff station} = 175.466 \text{ m}}$

Example 3.11 : A tacheometer with multiplying constant 100 and additive constant 0.3 was setup at a station O and the following results were obtained by keeping the staff vertical. Calculate the horizontal distance between O and P and the reduced level of P.

Instrument station	Staff station	Major reading	Vertical angle	Remarks
O	BM – O	1.875, 2.150, 2.425	+ 6°00'00"	R.L. of BM
	P	1.650, 1.800, 1.950	– 10°30'00'	132.600

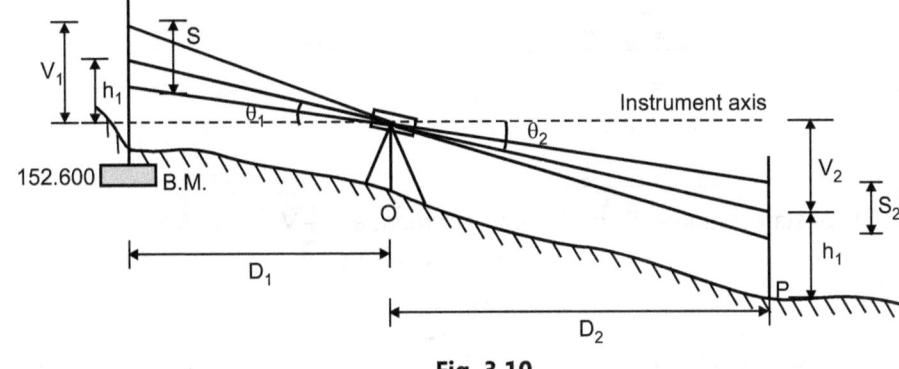

Fig. 3.10

We have,

Given : Multiplying constant, $m = 100$ i.e. $= \frac{f}{i}$; R.L. of staff station = 152.60

Additive constant, $(f + d) = 0.3$

For the angle of Elevation (see the Fig. 3.11).

We have the formula,

$$D = \frac{f}{i} S \cos^2 \theta + (f + d) \cos \theta \quad \ldots \text{(I)}$$

$$V = \frac{f}{i} \sin \frac{2\theta}{2} (S) + (f + d) \sin \theta \quad \ldots \text{(II)}$$

By using the formula from Fixed hair method of stadia tacheometry.

∴ $D_1 = 100 \cdot S \cdot \cos^2 \theta_1 + 0.3 \cos \theta_1$

$D_1 = 100 (2.425 - 1.875) \cdot \cos^2 (16°) + 0.3 \cdot \cos (6°)$.

$D_1 = 54.39 + 0.298$

∴ $D_1 = 54.69$ m

∴ $V_1 = D_1 \cdot \tan \theta_1$

∴ $V_1 = 54.69 \times \tan (6°)$

∴ $\boxed{V_1 = 5.749 \text{ m}}$

∴ R.L. of staff station = R.L. of instrument axis + $V_1 - h_1$

∴ R.L. of instrument axis = R.L. of staff station − $V_1 + h_1$
= 152.60 − 5.749 + 2.150
R.L. of instrument axis = 149.001 m

Case II : For the angle of depression (see the Fig. 5.19)
$D_2 = 100\ S \cdot \cos^2 \theta_2 + 0.3 \cos \theta_2$
∴ $D_2 = 100\ (1.950 − 1.650) \cos^2 (10° 30') + 0.3 \cos (10° 30')$
∴ $D_2 = 29.003 + 0.295$
∴ $D_2 = 29.297$ m

and $V_2 = D_2 \tan \theta_2$
$V_2 = 29.297 \cdot \tan (10° 30')$
$V_2 = 5.429$ m

R.L. of staff station at P = R.L. of instrument axis − $V_2 − h_2$
= 149.001 − 5.429 − 1.800
P = 141.772 m

Example 3.12 : To determine the distance between two stations A and B. A tacheometer was set up at point P on the line AB and the following observations were made.

(a) When the staff was held at A.
 Staff reading = 2.225, 2.605, 2.985
 Vertical angle = + 8°24'

(b) When the staff was held at B.
 Staff reading = 1.640, 1.920, 2.200
 Vertical angle = − 1°06'

Also determine the R.L. of B if the R.L. of A is 315.67 m.
where, (k = 100.00 ; c = 0.00)

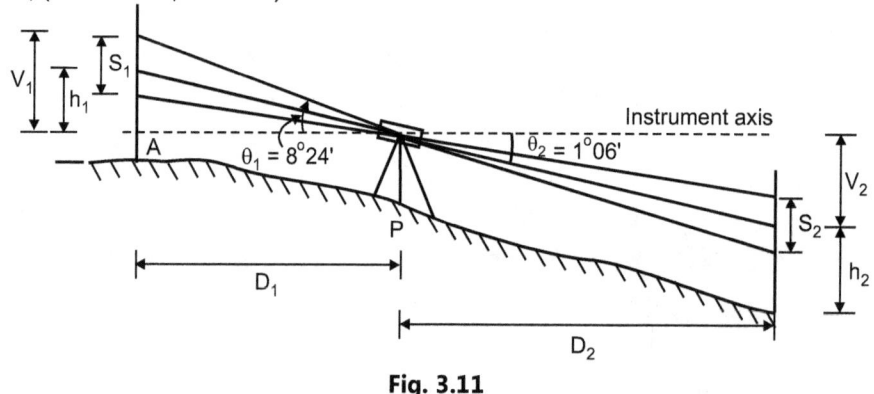

Fig. 3.11

Solution:

Given: Multiplying constant = 100; additive constant = 0.

$\boxed{\text{R.L. of A} = 315.677 \text{ m}}$

We have
$S_1 = 2.985 - 2.225 = 0.760 \text{ m}$
$S_2 = 2.200 - 1.640 = 0.560 \text{ m}$
$h_1 = 2.605$
$h_2 = 1.905$
$\theta_1 = 8° 24'$
$\theta_2 = -1° 06'$
$D_1 = 100 \cdot S_1 \cos^2 \theta_1$
$= 100 \times 0.760 \times \cos^2 (8° 24') = 74.378 \text{ m}$
$D_2 = 100 \times S_2 \cdot \cos^2 \theta_2$
∴ $D_2 = 100 \times 0.560 \times \cos^2 1°06' = 55.979 \text{ m}$

∴ Distance AB = $D_1 + D_2$ = 74.378 + 55.979 = 130.357 m

$V = D_2 \tan \theta_1$
∴ $V = 74.378 \tan 8° 24'$
∴ $\boxed{V_1 = 1.074 \text{ m}}$

∴ $V_2 = D_2 \tan \theta_2$
∴ $V_2 = 55.979 \times \tan 1°06$
$\boxed{V_1 = 1.074 \text{ m}}$

R.L. of instrument axis = R.L. of A − V_1 + h_1
= 315.67 − 10.983 + 2.605

$\boxed{\text{R.L. of instrument axis} = 307.292 \text{ m}}$

R.L. of B is = R.L. of instrument axis − V_2 − h_2
= 307.292 − 1.074 − 1.905

$\boxed{\text{R.L. of B} = 304.313 \text{ m}}$

$D_2 = 100 \, S_2 \cos^2 \theta_2$
$= 100 \times 2.150 \times \cos^2 (5° 30')$
∴ $\boxed{D_2 = 214.010 \text{ m}}$

Now
$V_2 = D \tan \theta_2$
$V_2 = 214.010 \times \tan (5° 30)$
$\boxed{V_2 = 20.606 \text{ m}}$

∴ R.L. of Instrument axis = R.L. of A − V_1 + h_1
= 150.50 − 38.387 + 1.910

∴ R.L. of instrument axis = 114.023 m

R.L. of B = R.L. of instrument axis − V_2 − h_2
= 114.023 − 20.606 − 1.750

R.L. of B = 91.667 m

∴ Distance between A to B,
AB = D_1 + D_2
= 223.40 + 214.010

AB = 437.41 m

Example 3.13 : A tacheometer was set up at an intermediate point on a line AB and the following observations were made on a vertically held staff.

Staff at	Vertical angle	Central hair reading (m)	Staff interval
A	9°45′	1.910	2.300
B	5°30′	1.750	2.150

The instrument is fitted with an anallactic lens and the multiplying constant is 100. Determine the length AB and the R.L. of B if the R.L. of A is 150.50 m.

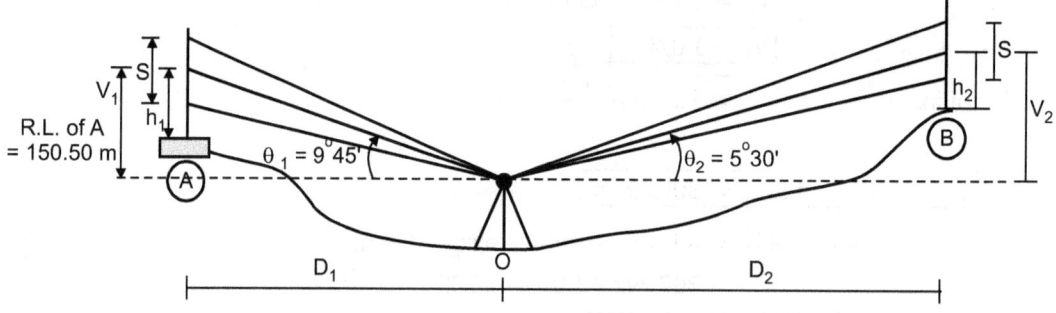

Fig. 3.12

Solution : Given : R.L. of A = 150.50
θ_1 = 9° 45′
θ_2 = 5° 30′
S_1 = 2.30
S_2 = 2.150
h_1 = 1.910
h_2 = 1.750

For the anallactic lens
(m = 100; (f + d) = 0)

We have $D_1 = 100 \cdot S_1 \cos^2 \theta_1$

∴ $D_1 = 100 \times 2.30 \times \cos^2 (9° 45')$

$\boxed{D_1 = 223.40 \text{ m}}$

Now $V_1 = D_1 \tan \theta_1$

∴ $V_1 = 223.40 \times \tan (9° 45')$

∴ $\boxed{V_1 = 38.387 \text{ m}}$

Example 3.14 : A line was levelled tacheometrically with tacheometer fitted with an anallactic lens, the value of the multiplying constant being 100. The following observation were made, the staff having been held vertically.

Instrument station	Height of instrument axis	Station at	Vertical angle	Staff reading		
				Bottom	Centre	Top
P	1.40	BM	−1° 35'	1.120	2.330	3.540
P	1.40	Q	+ 2° 54'	1.210	2.380	3.550
Q	1.38	R	+ 3° 12'	0.865	2.425	3.985

R.L. of BM = 583.66 m; Compute of R.L.'s of P, Q and R.

Solution : Given :

R.L. of BM = 583.66 m

S_1 = 3.540 − 1.120 = 2.420 m

h_1 = 2.330 m

θ_1 = − 1° 35'

S_2 = 3.550 − 1.210 = 2.340 m

h_2 = 2.380 m

θ_2 = 2° 54'

S_3 = 3.985 − 0.865 = 3.120 m

h_3 = 2.425

θ_3 = 3° 12'

For the anallactic lens multiplying constant is 100; additive constant i.e. (f + d) = 0

We have the equation

$D = 100 \, S \cdot \cos^2 \theta$

∴ $D_1 = 100 \, S_1 \cos^2 \theta_1$

∴ $D_1 = 100 \times 2.420 \times \cos^2 (1° 35')$ = 241.815 m

Similarly, $D_2 = 100 \times 2.340 \times \cos^2 (2° 54')$ = 233.401 m

$D_3 = 100 \times 3.120 \times \cos^2 (3° 12')$ = 311.028 m

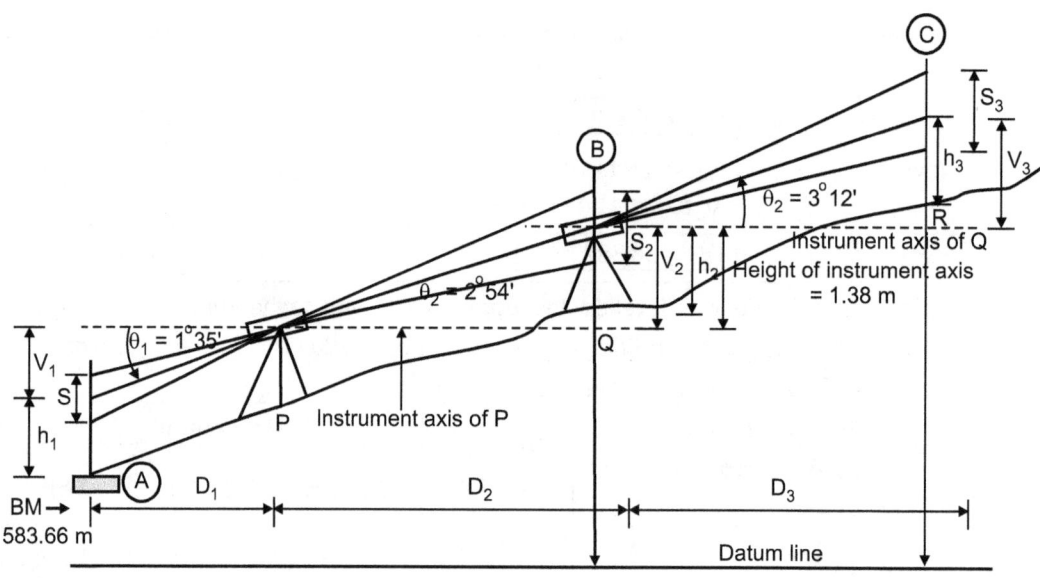

Fig. 3.13

Now, $V_1 = D_1 \tan \theta = 1$

∴ $V_1 = 241.815 \times \tan(1° 35') = 6.68$ m

$V_2 = D_2 \tan \theta_2 = 233.401 \times \tan(2° 54') = 11.82$ m

$V_3 = D_3 \tan \theta_3 = 311.028 \times \tan(3° 12') = 17.389$ m

$P = $ BM at A $+ V_1 + h_1$

$P = 583.66 + 6.08 + 2.330$

The instrument axis at P = 592.67 m

and R.L. of Q = Instrument axis at P $+ V_2 - h_2$

= 592.07 + 11.82 − 2.380

R.L. of Q = 602.118 m

R.L. of C = R.L. of Q + Height of instrument axis $+ V_3 - h_3$

= 602.118 + 1.38 + 17.389 − 2.425

R.L. of C = 618.46 m

3.4 USE OF TACHOMETRY IN SURVEYING

(1) **Differential Levelling :** By keeping the staff intercepts equal, the back sight distance and the fore sight distance can be easily balanced by a tacheometer in the differential levelling.

(2) **Photographic Mapping :** The tacheometer is an useful instrument for the field completion surveys required for the photographic mapping.

(3) **Plane Table :** The stadia observations can be made with a telescopic alidade with a modified form of a tacheometer. Thus, in plane table surveying, the horizontal distances and difference in elevation are computed in the field and the points are plotted directly.

(4) **Profile Levelling :** The distances from the instrument to the various points can be easily found by a tacheometer in the process of profile levelling.

(5) **Topographic Surveying :** The tacheometry is extremely useful for the topographic surveying because the relative location of points in the horizontal plane and the elevations of the points can be easily determined simultaneously.

(6) **Traverse of Low Accuracy :** The tacheometric method is more rapid than taping and hence, it can be used for the traverse of low accuracy where only horizontal angles and distances are required.

(7) **Trigonometric Levelling :** The tacheometric method of surveying proves to be more rapid than any other method for the indirect trigonometric levelling.

(8) **Contour Maps :** The main application of tacheometer is in the preparation of contour map of an area particularly when it is a rough and an even surface.

(9) **Location Survey :** The method may be employed very conveniently in case of location survey.

3.5 CONTOUR

Contour : A contour is defined as "imaginary line joining points of equal elevations".
For example, the line of intersection of the water surface of still lake or pond with the surrounding ground represents a counter line.

Contour Interval : It is the difference in elevation between two consecutive contour lines. For a contour map, the contour interval is always constant.

Fig. 3.14 (a) shows contour interval of 1 m whereas Fig. 3.14 (b) shows 10 m.

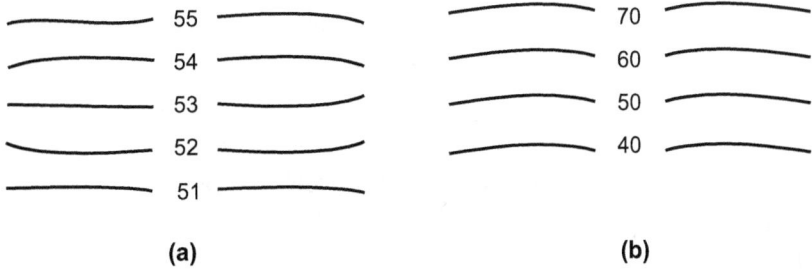

Fig. 3.14 : Contour Lines Showing Contour Method

The choice of suitable computer interval in a map depends upon four principal considerations. These are :
- Nature of the terrain.
- Scale of the map.
- Accuracy.
- Time of cost.

Horizontal Equivalent :

The horizontal distance between two points on two consecutive contour lines for a given slope is known as *horizontal equivalent*.

Horizontal equivalent depends upon the slope of the ground and required grade for construction of a road, canal and contour interval.

3.5.1 Characteristics of Contour

The principal characteristics of contour lines which help in plotting or reading a contour map are as follows :

1. All the points on a contour line have the same elevation.
2. Two contour lines do not intersect each other except in the case of an overhanging cliff (Fig. 3.15) or a cause penetrating a hill side.

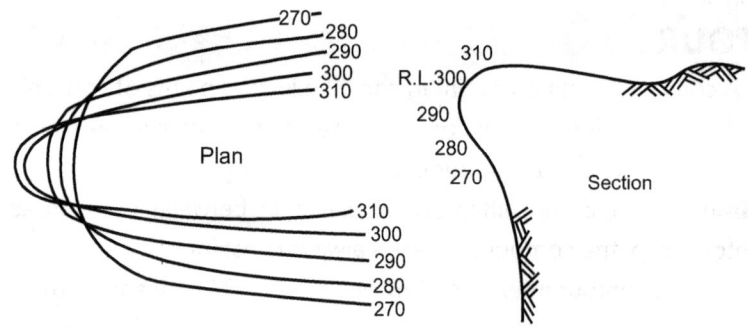

Fig. 3.15 : Overhanging Cliff

3. A contour line always closes either inside the boundary of maps or outside it.
4. Spacing between contour lines indicate the nature of ground. (See Fig. 3.16).

(a) **Closely spaced :** Steep slope.

(b) **Wide part :** Gentle or Flat slope.

(c) **Equally spaced :** Uniform slope.

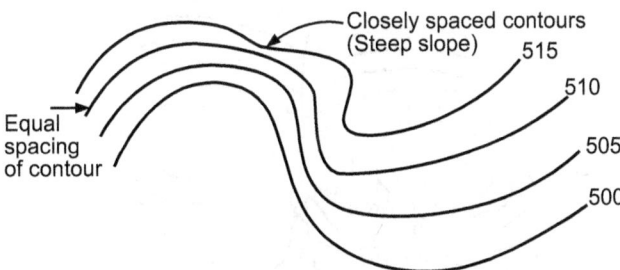

Fig. 3.16

5. A set of close contours with higher elevations inside and lower elevations outside indicate a hillock. Whereas in the case of depressions, lakes etc. the higher elevations are outside and lower elevations are inside.

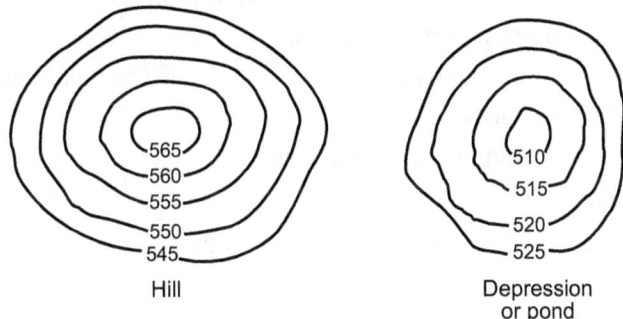

Fig. 3.17

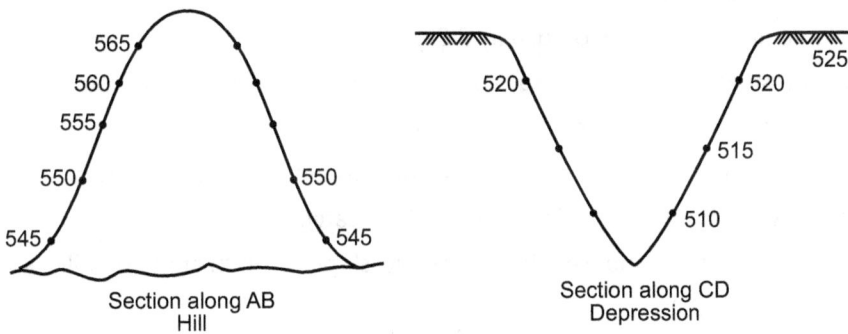

Fig. 3.18

6. Contour lines, cross ridge lines and valley lines are at right angles. For ridge line the higher elevation contours are inside the loop. Valley line is indicated by higher elevation contours outside the loop. Valley lines indicate streams or rivers.

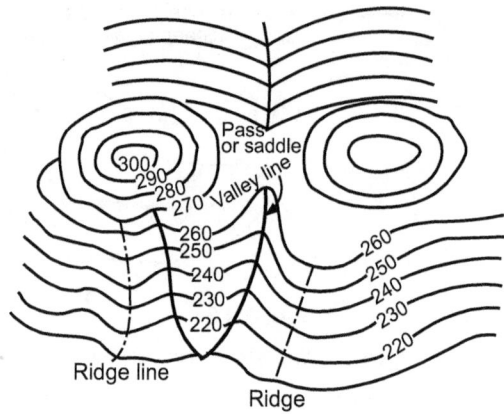

Fig. 3.19 : Ridge and Valley Lines

7. Irregular contours represent uneven ground.
8. Contours do not pass through permanent structures such as buildings.
9. Contours do not have sharp turnings.
10. Contour lines cannot begin or end on the plan.

3.5.2 Uses of Contour Map

1. From a contour map it can be ascertained whether two points are indivisible or not. (Fig. 3.20)
2. The extent of drainage area may be estimated on a contour map by locating the ridge line around the watershed. (Fig. 3.21)
3. The contour map is very useful to study the possible location of a dam and the volume of water to be stored. (Fig. 3.22)
4. The most economical and suitable side for structures such as buildings, bridges, dams etc. can be found from large scale contour maps.
5. By inspecting a contour map the most suitable site for a road, railways, canal etc. can be selected and also alignment can be located.
6. The nature of ground i.e. flat, uniformly sloping, undulating or hilly etc. can be known. (Fig. 3.23)
7. Estimation of volume of earthwork in cutting and embankment can be done by using contour maps.
8. Military operations can be planned with the help of contour maps.
9. A line of given gradient (contour gradient) can be traced on contour map. (Fig. 3.24)

10. The cross-section along any line can be drawn from the contour map. (Fig. 3.25)

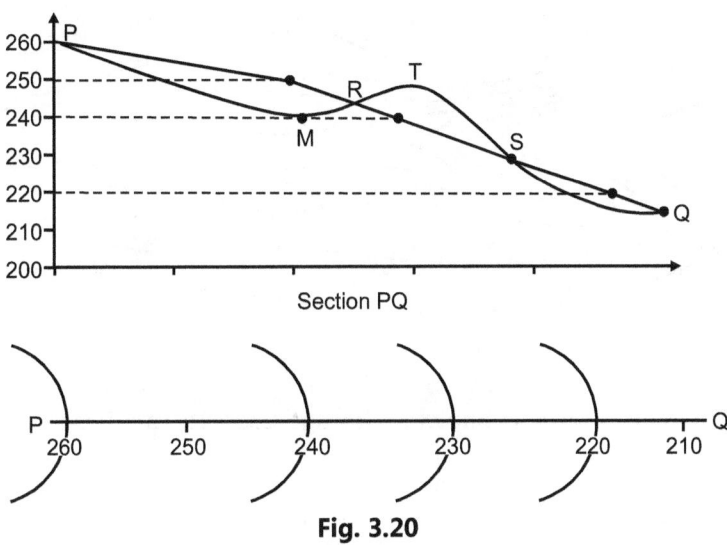

Fig. 3.20

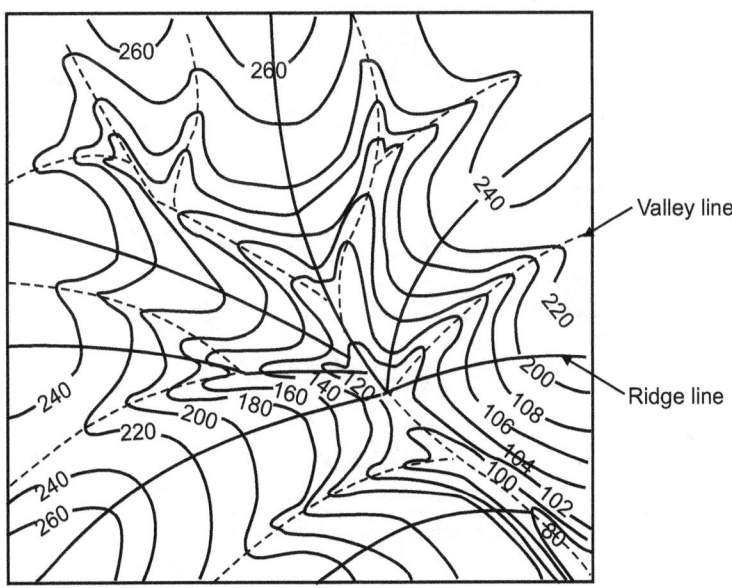

Fig. 3.21 : Shaded Portion Shows Catchment Area of a River

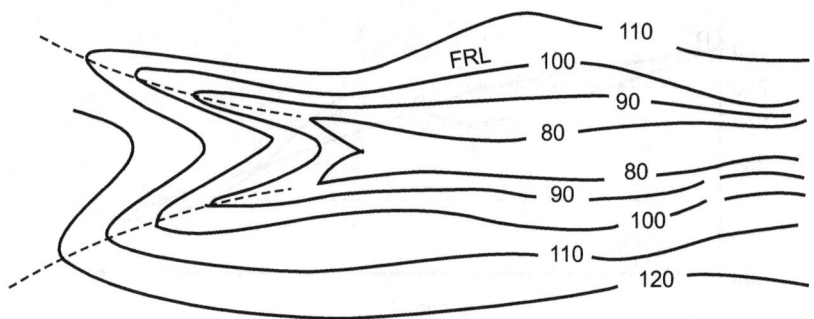

Fig. 3.22 : Contours Showing Storage Capacity of a Reservoir

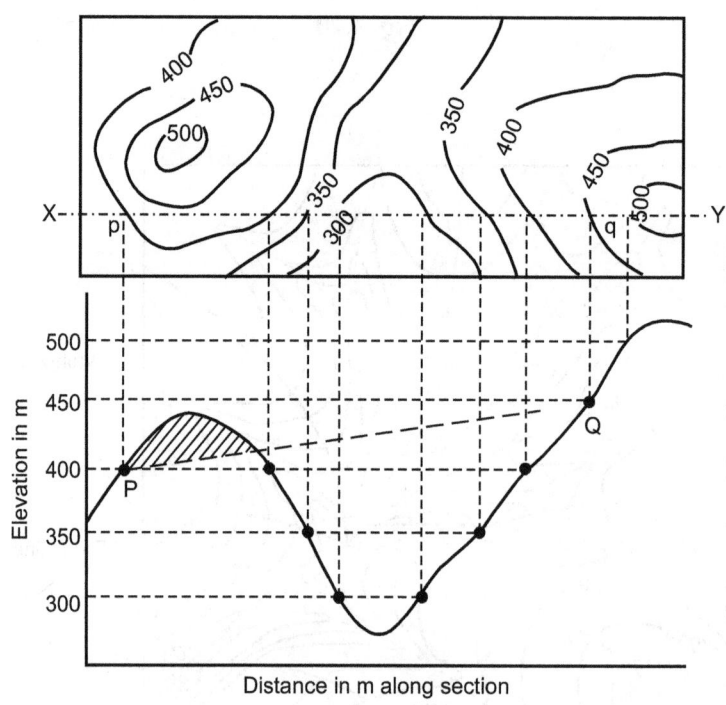

Fig. 3.23 : Nature of Terrain from Contour Map

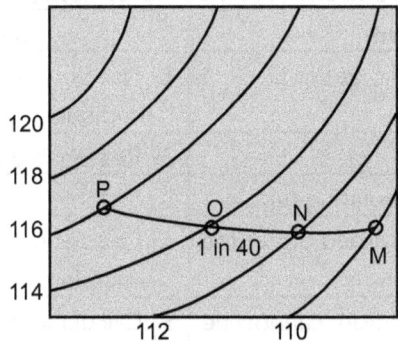

Fig. 3.24 : Tracing a Contour Gradient

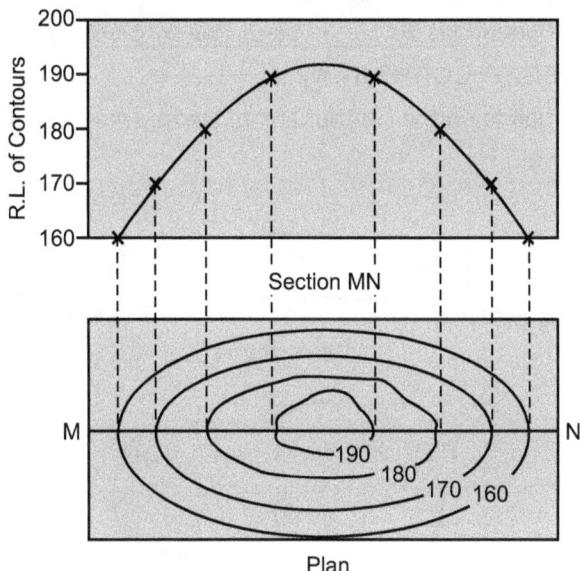

Fig. 3.25

3.5.3 Methods of Locating Contours

The method of locating contours on a plan or map is known as *contouring*. In general, the field materials of contouring may be divided into two classes.

(A) Direct Method :
   (i) By level and staff   (ii) By hand level.

(B) Indirect Method :
   (i) Method of squares   (ii) Method of cross-sections
   (iii) Tacheometric method   (iv) Plane table method.

Comparison between Direct and Indirect Method of Contouring

Direct Method	Indirect Method
1. Very accurate but slow and tedious.	1. Not very accurate but quicker and less tedious.
2. Expensive	2. Reasonable cost.
3. More suitable for low undulating terrain.	3. Suitable for hilly region.
4. Calculations need to be carried out in the field.	4. Calculation in the field is not mandatory.
5. After contouring, calculation cannot be checked.	5. Calculations can be checked as when needed.
6. Appropriate for small projects requiring high accuracy. E.g. layout of building, factory, structural foundations etc.	6. Suitable for large project requiring moderate to low accuracy. E.g. layout of highway, railway, canal etc.

3.5.4 Direct Method of Contouring

In this method, the points on the contour are located by marking points of that elevation on each contour by a level.

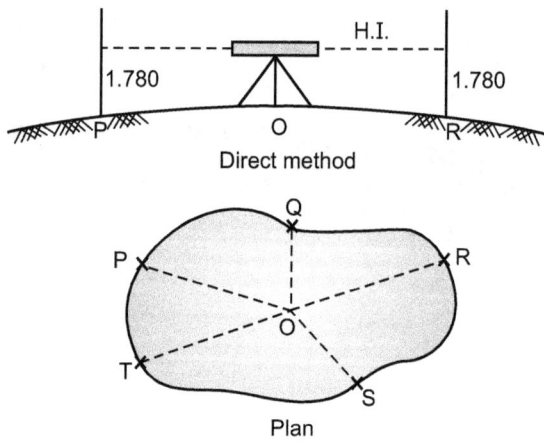

Fig. 3.26

Procedure :

- The dumpy level is set up in a commanding position say at O and accurately levelled. (See Fig. 3.26).
- The H.I. of level is found out by taking back sight on nearest Bench Mark.
- Knowing the R.L. of contour to be located and H.I. of level, the required staff reading to fix points on the contour is determined.

- Suppose H.I. of level is 106.780 m and if contour of R.L. 105.00 is to be located, the required staff reading will be 1.780 m. So the points where the staff reading of 1.780 m is obtained will lie on contour of R.L. 105.00 m.
- The staff is held at an estimated position and person operating the level directs the staffman to move forward or backward till the reading of 1.780 m is obtained.
- The point (P) is marked by a white cross on the ground. In the same way, other points Q, R, S, T are marked on the ground.
- These marks when joined, give a contour of R.L. 105.00 m. The positions of points P, Q, R, S, T are determined by suitable methods of surveying and noted in the field book.
- These points are plotted on the plan to a suitable scale and the contour lines are obtained by joining those points.
- The method is used for locating contours in small areas where great accuracy is desired. This method is tedious and time consuming.
- Instead of locating points in random directions, the points can be located in radial direction by drawing rays in radial direction with suitable angular interval. Ofcourse, the instrument to be used for keeping the desired angular interval will be theodolite or compass.

3.5.5 Indirect Methods of Contouring

There are three indirect methods of contouring (i) Method of squares, (ii) Method of cross-sections, (iii) Tacheometric method; which are described below.

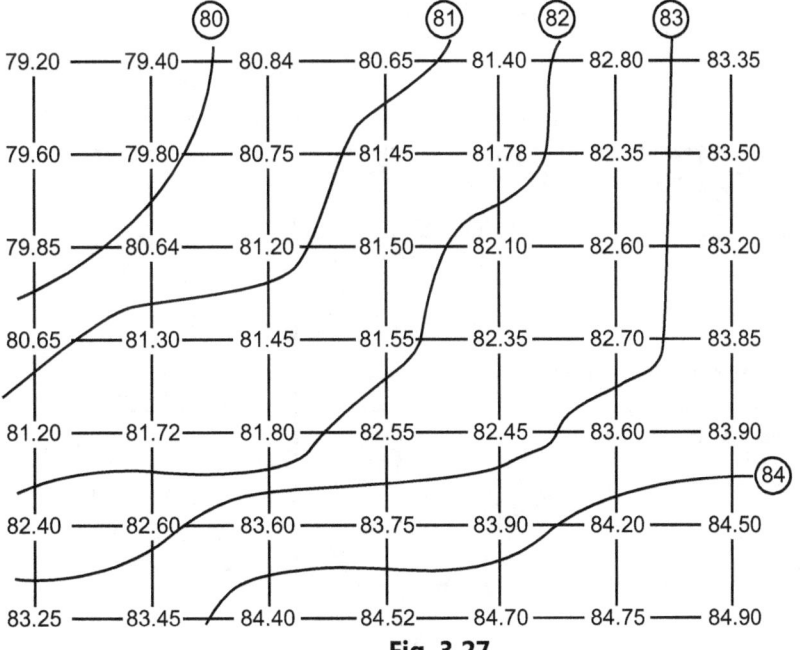

Fig. 3.27

(i) Method of Squares : The method is also called as *grid method*. The area is divided into a number of squares of size varying from 5 m to 20 m side. The size of the square depends upon the nature of ground and contour interval. The corners of the squares are marked with white or are pegged out. A theodolite may be used to lay the lines at right angles to each other or a tape and cross staff may be used. A level is set up in a commanding position and after finding the H.I. of the level, the reduced levels of the corners of the squares are found out and noted. The squares may vary in sizes depending on the character of the ground. If necessary, the level may be shifted and new height of instrument determined and the levelling carried further. After obtaining R.Ls. at all the corners of squares, the survey is plotted to a suitable scale and the elevations at each corners are written and the points on the contour are located by interpolation and the Contour lines are drawn. (Refer Fig. 3.27).

(ii) Method of Cross-sections : This method is employed when it is desired to know the nature of ground in route surveys such as in fixing the alignment of road, railway, canal or pipeline. Cross-sections are laid perpendicular to the proposed alignment of road, railway at regular intervals. The spacing of cross-sections may change with the nature of ground and contour interval. The cross-sections may be at closer intervals when there is sudden change in the slope of ground.

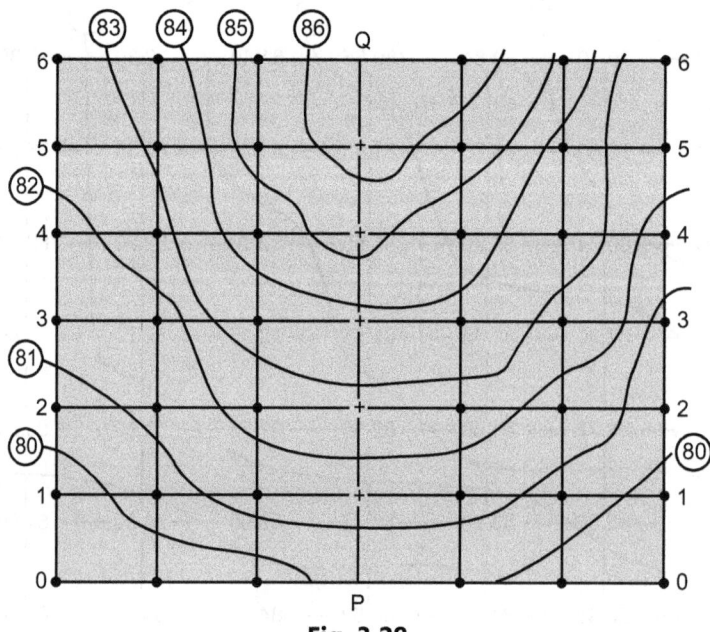

Fig. 3.28

The cross-section line may not be always perpendicular to the alignment but may be taken on a line at some other inclination. The reduced levels along the cross-section lines as well as along the centre of alignment are determined. The plotting of centre line and the cross-sections are drawn and the elevations of all the intersection points are written and the points of the contour are interpolated and the contour points are joined smoothly.

In Fig. 3.28, PQ is the centre line of proposed road. The centre line chainages are marked along the line PQ. The chainage interval may be 15 m or 20 m (depending on the nature of ground). The cross-section lines such as 1-1, 2-2, 3-3 etc. are laid perpendicular to the line PQ and to the left and right of PQ. Depending on the area to be covered by cross sections, the uniform distances are marked on the cross-sections to the left and to the right of line PQ. After the contour lines are plotted, the value of R.L. of each contour is written in circle at the end of contour as shown in figure.

(iii) Tacheometric Method : When the ground is steep, the tacheometer is set up in commanding position and the rays are drawn at regular intervals and R.Ls. of points along these rays are determined by tacheometry. These rays and reduced levels of point along the rays are plotted to a suitable scale and contours are interpolated by usual methods. This method is described in detail in Tacheometric Surveying.

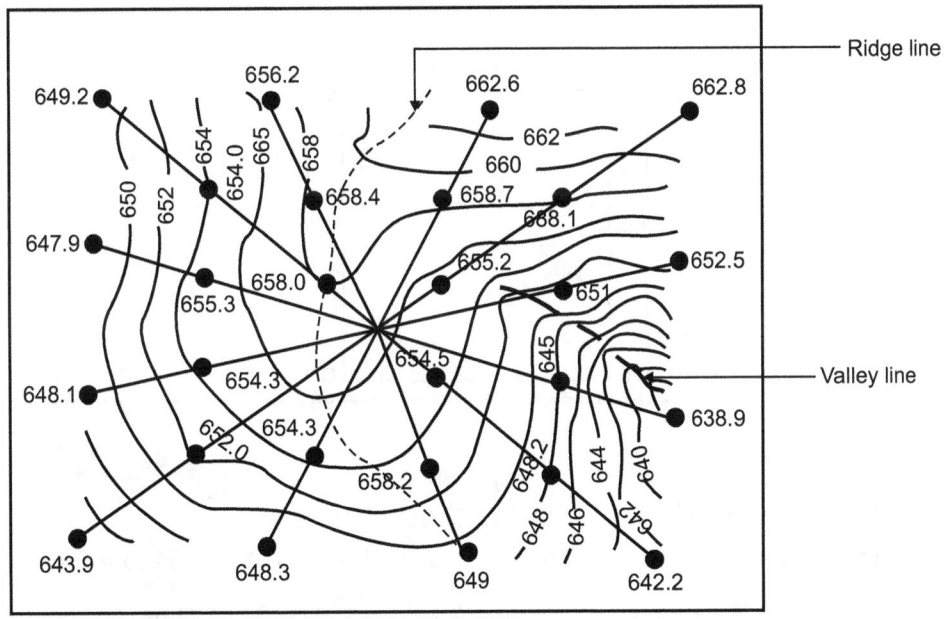

Fig. 3.29 : Contouring by Radial Line Method

3.5.6 Interpolation of Contours

Interpolation of contours can be defined as "the process of spacing the contours proportionately between the ground points."

Interpolation becomes necessary for indirect methods of contouring. The basic assumption made in interpolation is that ground is uniformly sloping between any two adjacent points.

The methods of interpolation are :
(i) By estimation.
(ii) By Arithmetical calculations.
(iii) By Graphical method.

(i) By Estimation : The location of contour points between the grid point are estimated by judgement and these points are marked on paper. These points are joined to obtain the required contour line. The method is very rough and is used for small scale maps.

(ii) By Arithmetical Calculation : In this method, the distance of the contour point from the corner point is found by arithmetical calculation. Let us say that interpolation of contour points in a rectangle ABCD of size 15 m × 20 m (on ground) with the elevations given is to be done. Now, if the contour interval is 1 m, between A and B, the contours of 95 and 96 can be located.

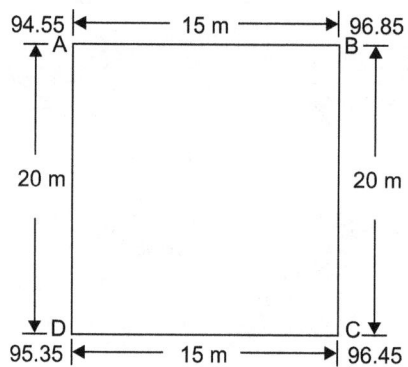

Fig. 3.30

Total difference between A and B = 96.65 – 94.55 = 2.10 m

The difference of level between 95 m contour and R.L. at A is 95.00 – 94.55 = 0.45 m

∴ The distance of 95 m contour point from A will be $\dfrac{0.45}{2.10} \times 15 = 3.21$ m

Similarly, the distance of 9.6 m contour from A will be $\dfrac{1.45}{2.10} \times 15 = 10.35$ m

The distances of 3.21 m and 10.35 m will be measured to the scale of plan from point A and plotted. On trio line AD, only contour of 95 m will lie. It's distance from point A will be $\frac{0.45}{0.80} \times 20 = 11.25$ m. Likewise on the line DC, only contour of 96 m will be located and its distance from point D will be $\frac{0.65 \times 15}{1.10} = 8.86$ m.

Though this meted is accurate, it is time consuming.

(iii) By Graphical Method : Mainly there are two graphical methods.

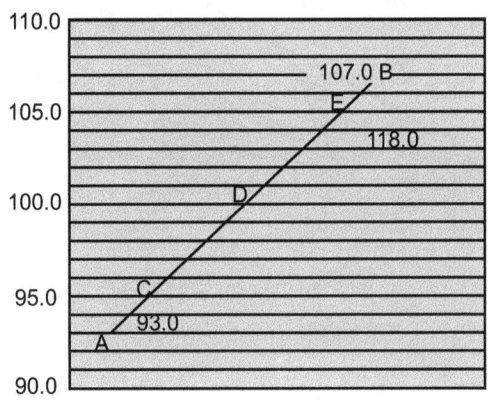

Fig. 3.31

(a) In this method, number of parallel lines are drawn at uniform spacing on a tracing paper say to represent 1.0 m interval. Every fifth line is made thicker to represent 5 m. Suppose it is required to locate 5 m contours between points A and B of R.L.s. 93.0 m and 107 m. If the bottom line represents R.L. of 90 m and the successive thicker lines represent 95 m, 100 m, 105 m, 110 m etc., point A will be on the third line (R.L. 93.0 m).

Rotate the tracing paper about A such that the point B lies on the seventeenth line from bottom to represent an elevation of 107 m. Find the points of intersection of C, D and E on the line AB to represent contour points 95 m, 100 m and 105 m. These contour points are then pricked on the bottom plan. Thus, contour points are located.

(b) Second Method : Draw a vertical line MN and divide it into number of equal parts, say 20. Now, bisect MN at P and draw a perpendicular OP to MN; selecting the point O. Draw guidelines 1-1', 2-2', 3-3' parallel to MN. Lines 1-1', 2-2', 3-3' are equally divided by radial lines. Let us presume that the lowest radial line represents an elevation of 90 m. Thick lines representing 95 m, 100 m, 105 m, 110 in etc. will be shown. The tracing paper is moved on the plan so that point A lies on the radial line representing R.L. of 93.0 m. Similarly, R.L. of

107 m will be located on ray. The tracing paper is moved such that line is parallel to MN. Prick the points of intersection of thick lines with the line AB to locate points C, D and E representing contours of 95 m, 100 m, 105 m. The method is simple, quick and gives fairly accurate results.

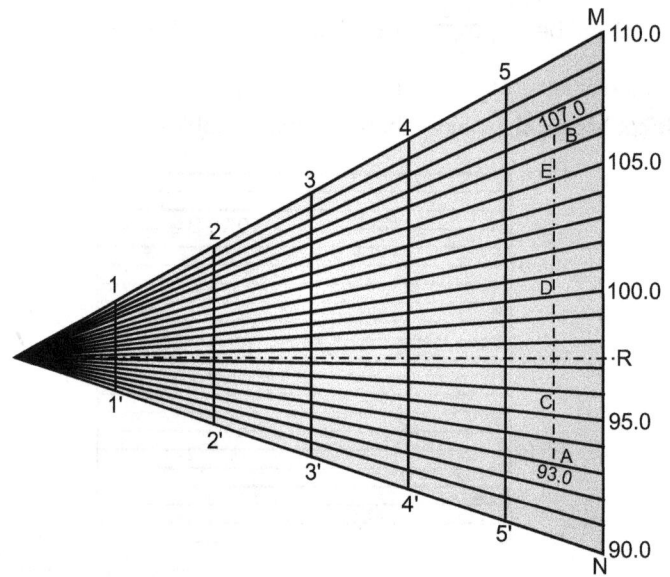

Fig. 3.32

3.6 TACHEOMETRIC CONTOUR SURVEY

1. The instrument is set up over the station A selected by the surveyor. It is centred and levelled accurately first with reference to plate levels and then with reference to altitude bubble.
2. The vertical angle is adjusted to zero and the height of instrument i.e. the vertical distance from the top of peg to the centre of trunnion axis is measured with a tape.
3. The instrument is correctly oriented at the first station A of a traverse to the North by adjusting zero of the vernier to the zero of the main scale and rotating the instrument around the outer axis until the north end of the needle of the trough compass (attached to the tacheometer), points towards the magnetic north.
4. The staff is held on the nearest bench mark with line of sight horizontal or inclined and observations of (i) the vertical angle, (ii) the magnetic bearing and (iii) staff readings of three hairs (top, axial and bottom) are taken. If the bench mark is not nearby, it is established by running fly levels from the G.T.S. or permanent bench mark available within that locality.

5. All the representative points around the station and within the range of instrument are located by taking observations on the staff kept over these points at uniform angular interval. Observations to the staff stations can be taken more easily and quickly if staff stations are placed on the radial line through the station, the angular interval being 30° or so. For example, over the ray A - 1 - staff is kept at points a, b, c, d, e. (Refer Fig. 3.33 b).
6. A foresight on the second traverse station B is taken (i) the fore bearing of AB, (ii) the vertical angle and (iii) the staff readings on station B of the three wires are observed to staff station B.
7. The instrument is transferred to the next station B, centred and levelled.
8. The height of the instrument (H.I.) is measured.
9. The staff held on the first station A is sighted and
    (i) the back bearing of line AB
    (ii) the vertical angle to the staff station A
    (iii) the staff readings of the three wires at station A are observed.

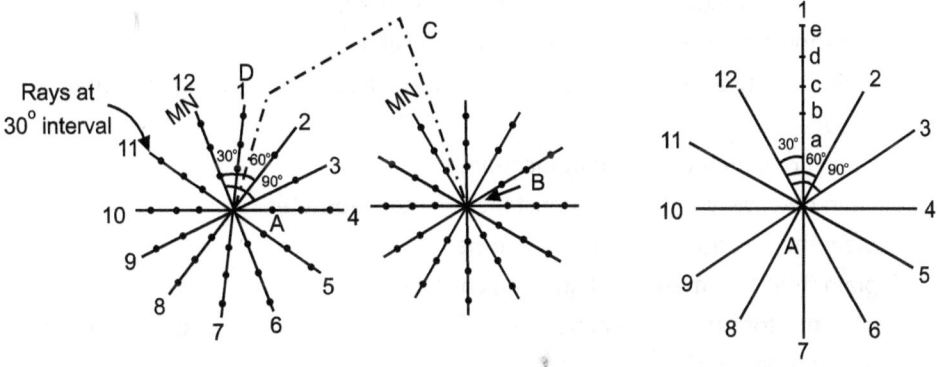

(a) Tacheometric survey　　　　　　(b) Rays shown enlarged at Stn. A

Fig. 3.33

Thus, each station is sighted twice and two values of distance and elevation of each station are obtained, if they agree within the limits of accuracy, the average of the two values may be taken as the value for the distance and elevation of the station.

10. The representative points around the second station and within the range of the instrument are located as stated in (5) above.
11. Similar procedure is used at each of the successive stations C, D etc.
12. Calculation of R.L.s at different points is done simultaneously.

REVIEW QUESTIONS

(1) Define the fundamental axis of theodolite.
(2) State the relationship between the fundamental lines of a transit theodolite.
(3) State the various temporary adjustments of a theodolite.
(4) State the permanent adjustments of a transit theodolite in the order in which they are carried out.
(5) Explain how will you do the elimination of parallax of a theodolite.
(6) Explain cross-hair ring test as a permanent adjustment of a theodolite.
(7) Describe how you would test and adjust the line of collimation of a transit theodolite so as to make it coincide with the axis of the theodolite.
(8) Explain how will you test and adjust the transit theodolite to ensure that the horizontal axis is perpendicular to the vertical axis.
(9) How will you make the line of collimation perpendicular to the horizontal axis.
(10) Define tacheometry and explain the various instruments used in tacheometry.
(11) Explain the various essential characteristics of a tacheometer.
(12) What are the various applications of a tacheometer.
(13) Write short note on 'Advantages of tacheometer'.
(14) Explain the use of anallactic lens in a tacheometer having external focussing telescope.
(15) State various methods used in tacheometry.
(16) Explain how will you find the constants of a tacheometer.
(17) Explain the principle of stadia tacheometry.
(18) Explain fixed hair method of stadia tacheometry.
(19) Derive the formula for distance of staff station and elevation of staff station, when the staff is held inclined but perpendicular to line of sight.
(20) (a) State and define the fundamental axes of a Dumpy level.
(b) How will you test whether the line of collimation is parallel to the axis of bubble tube ?
(21) (a) Describe with a neat sketch Tilting level.
(b) In what respects, a Tilting level differs from the dumpy level ?
(22) (a) Explain the procedure of carrying out the profile levelling and cross sectioning by means of dumpy level and staff.
(b) How will you make the axis of the bubble tube perpendicular to the vertical axis ?
(23) What are the circumstances under which reciprocal levelling is recommended ? How ?

(24) (a) What are the special features of an automatic level ?
(b) Describe briefly the tilt compensator used in self alignment levels.

(25) (a) What are the effects of curvature of earth and atmospheric refraction on the levelling work ? How the staff readings are affected ?

(26) (a) Derive an expression for the correction for (i) curvature of earth and (ii) Refraction.
(b) State the advantages of reciprocal levelling and describe the method.

(27) Write short notes on :
(a) Folding staff.
(b) Fixing the formation line in L - section.
(c) Self-aligning level.

(28) (a) Describe briefly the Construction of a Laser Level.
(b) State the uses of Laser level.

(29) (a) Explain the construction of a Digital Level.
(b) Mention any five uses of Digital Level.

(30) State the advantages of Auto level.

(31) Define the terms 'Contour line', 'Contour interval', 'Horizontal equivalent' and 'Ridgeline'.

(32) Differentiate between :
1. Direct and indirect method of contouring
2. Contour interval and horizontal equivalent.

(33) Compare the following :
1. Contour interval and Horizontal equivalent.
2. Contour lines representing ridgeline and Valley line.

(34) Draw typical contours along with designating (R.L. values) for
(i) Lake (ii) Hill (iii) Ridge (iv) Uniformly slopping ground.

(35) State the different methods of interpolation of counters, Explain any one method in brief.

(36) Show the fallowing features in contour maps :
(i) Steeply sloping and Gently sloping ground,
(ii) Ridge line and Valley line.

(37) With neat sketch explain any four characteristics of contour lines.

(38) Explain in detail the direct method of locating contours and discuss its merits and demerits.

(39) Draw the contour lines showing the following characteristics.
(1) Ridge lines (2) Valley lines (3) Overhanging diff. (4) Hill % Depression or pond.
(40) Write uses of contour maps.
(41) What are the methods of contouring ? Give relative merits and demerits of each.

EXAMPLES

(1) A surveyor recorded the following tacheometric observations in the field work.

Inst. station	Staff station	Vertical angle	Staff reading on vertical held staff
A	B.M.	+ 12° 42'	0.2220, 1.000, 1.780
A	B	+ 9° 36'	0.415, 1.240, 2.065

Reduced level of B.M. is 600 m.
The value of multiplying constant = 100.
Find out the horizontal distance, AB and R.L. of station B.

(2) The following observations are made on vertically held staff with a tacheometer fitted with an anallactic lens. The constants of the instrument are 100 and zero.

Inst. stn.	Height of instrument	Staff station	W.C.B.	Vertical angle	Staff readings
P	1.65	A	250°	+ 3° 30'	1.150, 1.650, 2.150
		B	175°	− 2° 0'	0.750, 1.650, 2.550

The R.L. of the instrument station P = 250 m.
Calculate the length of the line AB, elevations of stations A and B and gradient of line AB.
[**Ans.** : AB = 181.590 m, R.L. of A = 256.093, R.L. of B = 243.722 m

$$\text{Gradient of AB} = \frac{1}{14.678}]$$

(3) The horizontal distance is to be determined from the centre of the road adjoining a river bank and a building on the opposite bank of the river. The following observations were taken by a tacheometer with an anallactic lens having a multiplying constant 100.

Inst. stn.	Height of instrument	Staff station	Vertical angle	Staff readings
Centre of road	1.50 m	Plinth of bldg. at door entrance	9° 15'	1.555, 2.105, 2.655
Centre of road	1.50 m	Top of the terrace of building	12° 12'	1.205, 1.950, 2.625

Determine the height of building above plinth level and R.L. of the plinth if R.L. of centre of road is 525.170 m.

[**Ans.** : Ht. of building = 13.480 m, R.L. of plinth = 542.016]

(4) Following observations were taken with a tacheometer fitted with an anallactic lens. The value of constant multiplier was 100.

Inst. stn.	Height of instrument	Staff station	Reduced bearing	Vertical angle	Staff readings
A	1.50 m	M	N 28° 30' E	+ 6° 24'	0.840, 1.740, 2.640
A	1.50 m	N	N 31 ° 30' W	− 4° 12'	0.610, 1.260, 1.910

Calculate the horizontal distance between stations M and N and the R.L. of M, if R.L. of station A is 280.50 m.

[**Ans.** : MN = 159.165 m, R.L. of M = 300.199 m]

(5) (a) In testing a Dumpy level, reciprocal levels are taken and the following results were obtained.

Instrument at	Staff reading in metres	
	P	Q
P	1.425	1.070
Q	1.060	0.735

Is the line of collimation in adjustment ? What should be the staff reading on P during the second set of the instrument to make the line of collimation truly horizontal ?

[**Ans.** : (i) True difference of level = − 0.340 m.

(ii) Line of collimation is inclined downwards by an amount 0.015 m.]

(6) (a) In a two peg method of Dumpy level, the following readings were observed.

Instrument at	Staff reading on		Remarks
	A	B	
(i) O (midway between A and B)	2.655	2.350	Horizontal distance between A and B is 100 m
(ii) A	2.425	2.115	

Find the staff reading on B so that the line of sight will be horizontal when the instrument is at A.

[**Ans.** : Staff reading on B when the instrument is at A = 2.120].

(7) The following notes refer to reciprocal levels taken with one levelling instrument.

Instrument position	Staff readings in metres on		Remarks (Distance)
	P	Q	
Near P	1.600	2.750	PQ = 1000 m
'Near Q	2.700	1.550	R.L. of P = 125.000 m

Find :

(i) the R.L. of Q,

(ii) the combined correction of curvature and refraction, and

(iii) the collimation error.

[**Ans.** : R.L. of Q = 125.00 m and Collimation error 1.0827 m]

(8) A level is set up at a station O and the reading on the staff held at P 700 m away from O, is 1.470. The reading on the staff at Q 1500 m away is 2 865. Find the true difference in elevation between P and Q.

[**Ans.:** 1.277 m]

(9) Find the distance to the visible horizon from the top of a light house 35 m high. Take the diameter of earth as 12740 km. What is the dip of horizon ?
(Dist. to visible horizon = 22.80 km and dip of horizon = 12.30 minutes).

Unit - IV

CURVES

4.1 INTRODUCTION

The alignment of a communication route like roadway, railways, canals etc. cannot be a straight line in horizontal plane on account of the obligatory points, topographical reasons, geometrical and economical constraints etc. Thus, the direction of alignment of a route needs to be changed in horizontal and vertical plane at so many locations. Curves are inevitable when one has to introduce change in direction of alignment of a route.

4.1.1 Definition of a Curve

The geometrical arc provided at intersection of two straights of communication route such as roads, railways canals etc. is called as curve.

4.1.2 Object behind Provision of Curve

(a) To introduce smooth and gradual change in direction of a route

(b) To introduce smooth and gradual change in slope or gradient of a route.

4.1.3 Principle Types of Curve

(a) Horizontal curve

(b) Vertical curve

4.2 HORIZONTAL CURVE

A geometrical arc provided in plan to round of the direction or to avoid abrupt change in direction is called as horizontal curve. Horizontal curves are required to change the direction of alignment of a route smoothly and gradually in order to make it to pass through some obligatory points or to make it to avoid some obligatory points.

4.2.1 Types of Horizontal Curve

(a) Simple circular curve

(b) Compound circular curve

(c) Reverse circular curve

(d) Transition curve

(a) Simple Circular Curve :

When two straights (say AB and BC as shown in Fig. 4.1) of a route are connected by single circular arc (Say Arc T_1FT_2 as shown in Fig. 4.1) is called as simple circular curve.

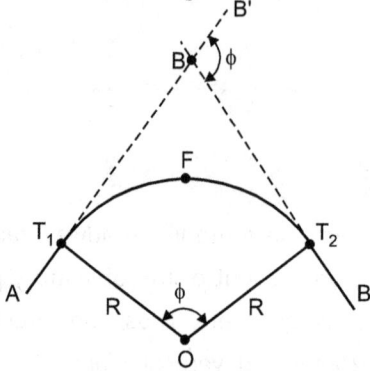

Fig. 4.1 : Simple Circular Curve

(b) Compound Circular Curve :

When two straights (Say AB and BC as shown in Fig. 4.2) of a route are connected by two circular arcs (Say Arc T_1F and FT_2 as shown in Fig. 4.2) of different radii (Say R_1 and R_2) with a common point of tangency (Say F) and centers (O_1 and O_2) being on same side of the common tangent (Say GFH) is called as compound circular curve.

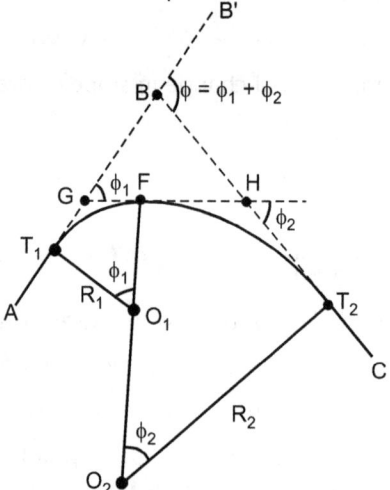

Fig. 4.2 : Compound Circular Curve

(c) Reverse Circular Curve :

When two straights (Say AG and HC as shown in Fig. 4.3 below) of a route are connected by two circular arcs (Say Arc T_1F and Arc FT_2 as shown in Fig. 4.3 below) of same or different radii (Say R_1 and R_2) with a common point of tangency (Say F) and centers (Say O_1 and O_2)

being on opposite side of common tangent (Say GFH) is called as reverse circular curve or serpentine curve.

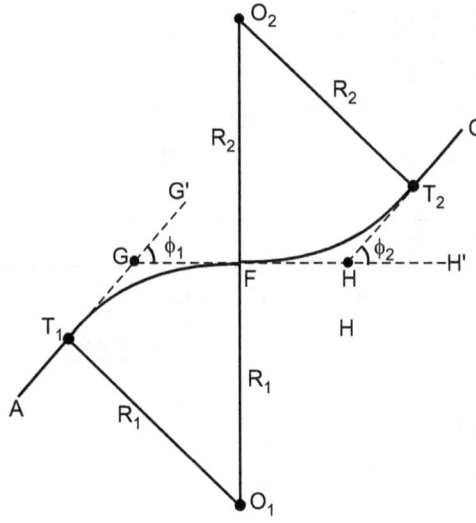

Fig. 4.3 : Reverse Circular Curve

(d) Transition Curve :

It is a curve whose radius gradually changes from infinity to some finite value and vice-versa.

Transition curve needs to be provided in the vicinity of tangent point of circular curve, particularly on the route handling heavy, high speed and steering-less traffic. Transition curves are invariably required on railways or express way.

4.2.2 Principle Points, Lines and Angles on Simple Circular Curve

(a) Principal Points :

1	O	Centre of curve
2	B	Point of intersection (PI)
3	T_1 and T_2	Tangent points
4	T_1	First or rear tangent point or point of curve or tangent - curve
5	T_2	Second or forward tangent point or point of tangency or curve - tangent
6	E	Midpoint of long chord
7	F	Summit or apex point of the curve

(b) Principal Lines :

1.	OT_1, OT_2 and OF	Radius (R) of the curve
2.	AB and BC	Straights to the curve
3.	T_1B and BT_2	Tangents to the curve
4.	T_1B	First or rear or back tangent
5.	T_2B	Second or forward tangent
6.	T_1ET_2	Long chord
7.	T_1FT_2	Curve length
8.	EF	Versed sine or Mid ordinate
9.	FB	Apex distance or External distance

(c) Principal Angles :

1.	$\angle T_1OT_2$	Central angle
2.	$\angle T_1BT_2$	Angle of intersection (I)
3.	$\angle B'BT_2$	Deflection angle (ϕ)

4.2.3 Working out Magnitudes of Angle of Intersection and Central Angle

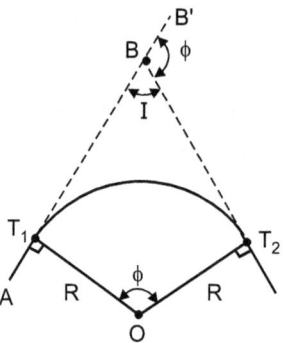

Fig. 4.4 : Working out Magnitudes of Angle of Intersection and Central Angle

(a) Magnitude of Angle of Intersection :

Angle of intersection (I) is the angle subtended by the arc (T_1T_2) of the curve at point of intersection (B) of the straights. In Fig. 4.4 above, $\angle T_1BT_2$ is an angle of intersection (I).

From geometry of Fig. 4.4 it is clear that, $\angle B'BT_2 + \angle T_1BT_2 = 180°$

But $\angle B'BT_2$ is a deflection angle "ϕ" and $\angle T_1BT_2$ is angle of intersection "I"

∴ $\phi + I = 180°$

∴ Angle of intersection ($\angle T_1BT_2$) = I = $(180° - \phi)$

(b) Magnitude of Central Angle :

Central angle is the angle subtended by the arc (T_1T_2) of the curve at centre (O) of the curves. In Fig. 4.4 above, $\angle T_1OT_2$ is a central angle.

We know radius and tangent of a circle are always perpendicular to each other.

Hence, angles between tangents and radii = $\angle BT_1O = \angle BT_2O = 90°$

We know sum of all four internal angles of a quadrilateral is 360°

∴ In quadrilateral BT_1OT_2, $\angle T_1BT_2 + \angle T_1OT_2 + \angle BT_1O + \angle BT_2O = 360°$

∴ $\angle T_1BT_2 + \angle T_1OT_2 = 360° - (\angle BT_1O + \angle BT_2O)$

$= 360° - (90° + 90°)$

$= 180°$

∴ Central angle = $\angle T_1OT_2 = 180° - \angle T_1BT_2$

But $\angle T_1BT_2$ is an angle of intersection (I), and is = $(180° - \phi)$

∴ Central angle = $\angle T_1OT_2 = 180° - (180° - \phi)$

∴ Central angle = $\angle T_1OT_2 = \phi$

That means for a circular curve, central Angle is always equals to Deflection angle.

4.2.4 Elements of Circular Curve

The parameters required to trace the geometry of the circular curve are called as elements of circular curve and it includes

(a) Tangent length

(b) Length of long chord

(c) Length of curve

(d) Versed sine or Mid ordinate

(e) Apex distance

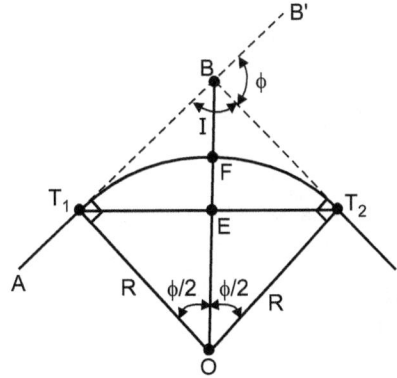

Fig. 4.5 : Elements of a Circular Curve

(a) Tangent Length (l):

We know length of tangent (l) = Length of segment BT_1 or BT_2

We also know for a circular arc tangent and radius are always perpendicular to each other.

∴ $\angle BT_1O = 90°$ and ΔBT_1O is a right angled triangle

In right angled ΔBT_1O, $BT_1 = OT_1 \cdot \tan \angle T_1OB = BT_2$

But $OT_1 = R$ and $\angle T_1OB = \phi/2$

∴ Tangent Length, $l = R \cdot \tan(\phi/2)$

(b) Length of Long Chord:

We know, length of long chord = Length of segment T_1ET_2

But, $T_1ET_2 = T_1E + ET_2$

As E is the midpoint of long chord T_1ET_2, $T_1E = ET_2$

Therefore, Length of long chord $T_1ET_2 = 2(T_1E)$ or $2(ET_2)$

In right angled ΔOET_1, $T_1E = OT_1 \cdot \sin \angle T_1OE$

But T_1E = Semi long chord, $OT_1 = R$ and $\angle T_1OE = \phi/2$

∴ Semi long chord = $R \cdot \sin(\phi/2)$

∴ Length of long chord = $2R \cdot \sin(\phi/2)$

(c) Curve Length (L):

We know, curve length, L = Length of circular arc T_1FT_2

We also know length of circular arc = $R \cdot \phi^c$

Where R is radius of circular arc and ϕ^c is angle in radians, subtended by the circular arc at its centre.

Therefore, Length of curve, L = Length of circular arc $T_1FT_2 = R \cdot \angle(T_1OT_2)c$

But central angle = $\angle(T_1OT_2) = \phi$, and is usually expressed in degrees,

We know $180° = \pi^c$

∴ $\phi° = \left[\dfrac{\pi\phi°}{180}\right]^c$

∴ Length of Curve (L) = $\left[\dfrac{\pi R\phi°}{180}\right]$

(d) Versed Sine (O_0):

We know, versed sine, O_0 = Distance EF

And Distance EF = Distance OF − Distance OE

But, OF = Radius (R) and OE = Adjacent side of $\angle T_1OE$ in right angled ΔOET_1

Hence, $OE = OT_1 \cos \angle T_1OE = R \cdot \cos(\phi/2)$ ------ As $OT_1 = R$ and $\angle T_1OE = (\phi/2)$

∴ Versed sine, O_0 = Dist. EF = Dist. OF − Dist. OE

= $R − R \cdot \cos(\phi/2)$

Or Versed sine, $O_o = R \cdot [1 - \cos(\phi/2)]$
$= R \cdot \text{versine}(\phi/2)$

(e) Apex Distance or External Distance :

We know, apex distance = Distance BF

And Distance BF = Distance OB – Distance OF

But, Distance OB is diagonal of right angle ΔBT_1O and Distance OF = Radius (R).

In right angled ΔBT_1O, $\cos \angle T_1OB = OT_1/OB$

∴ $OB = OT_1/[\cos \angle T_1OB] = OT_1 \cdot \sec \angle T_1OB$
$= R \cdot \sec(\phi/2)$ ------ As $OT_1 = R$ and $\angle T_1OB = (\phi/2)$

∴ Apex distance BF = Dist. OB – Dist. OF = $R \cdot \sec(\phi/2) - R$
$= R \cdot [\sec(\phi/2) - 1]$

4.2.5 Nomenclature for Circular Curve

The circular curve is identified either with its radius or with its degree. On road way the curves are usually referred by their radius. On railways the curves are referred by their degree. Degree of curve is angle subtended by the chord of standard length at centre of curve. On Indian railways usual specified length of this standard chord is 30 metre. Degree of curve is shown by letter 'D'.

4.2.6 Relation between Radius and Degree of a Curve

Let b is the length of the standard chord

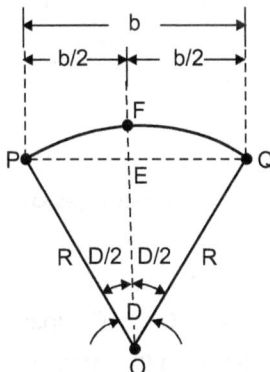

Fig. 4.6 : Working Out Degree of a Curve

In Fig. 4.6 $\angle POQ$ is an angle subtended at centre of the curve by chord PQ of standard length (say b). Hence, $\angle POQ$ may be called as 'Degree of a Curve' and denoted by letter 'D'.

In right angle ΔOEP, EP/OP = $\sin \angle POE$

But, EP = Semi standard chord (b/2) and OP = Radius (R) and $\angle POE = D/2$

∴ $(b/2)/R = \sin(D/2)$ or $b/(2R) = \sin(D/2)$ ... (i)

We know for small angles, their sine ratio ≅ their value in radians

∴ sin (D/2) = (D°/2) converted into radians

Let us convert (D°/2) into radians. We know $180° = \pi^c$,

∴ $(D°/2) = \{[(D°/2)/180] \cdot \pi\}^c = (D°\pi/360)^c$

Hence, sin (D/2) = D°π /360   ... Putting this in equation (i)

b/(2R) = D°π /360

D° = (360 × b) /(2π.R)

D° = 57.296 b/R

This is the relation between Degree and Radians of curve with Standard chord length of b. For flat curve radius is more and degree is less and for sharp curve radius is less and degree is more. That means lower the degree flatter the curve and higher the degree sharper the curve.

The standard chord length is usually 30 m on railways and highways. Hence putting, b = 30 m in above equation.

D° = 57.296 × 30/R = 1718.9/R

D° = 1718.9/R   ... for standard chord length of 30 m

4.2.7 Working out Chainages of Tangent Points T_1 and T_2

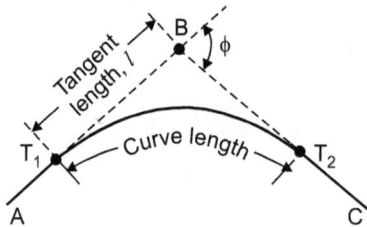

Fig. 4.7 : Working Out Chainages of Tangent Points

If CPI is the chainage of point B of intersection,

Chainage of first tangent point T_1 = CT_1 = Chainage of PI – Tangent length = CPI – l

Chainage of second tangent point T_2 = CT_2 = Chainage of T_1 + Curve length = CT_1 + L

SOLVED EXAMPLES

Example 4.1 : Two straights of a route meet at a deflection angle of 50° at. Radius of the curve is 450 m. Calculate all the elements for this circular curve.

(This type of examples are asked in PU Dec. 2005 and 2006).

Solution : Given: Radius, R = 450 m and Deflection angle, ϕ = 50°

Working out elements for a circular curve means working out tangent length, length of long chord, curve length, versed sine or mid ordinate and apex or external distance.

We know tangent length, $l = R \cdot \tan(\phi/2)$

∴ Tangent length, $l = 450 \cdot \tan(50°/2) = 209.838$ m

We know length of long chord $= 2R \cdot \sin(\phi/2)$

∴ Length of long chord $= 2 \times 450 \times \sin(50°/2) = 380.356$ m

We know length of a curve, $L = \pi R \phi°/180$

∴ Length of a curve, $L = \pi \times 450 \times 50 \div 180 = 392.699$ m

We know versed sine (or mid ordinate), $O_0 = R \cdot [1 - \cos(\phi/2)]$

∴ Verse Sine (or mid ordinate), $O_0 = 450 \times [1 - \cos(50°/2)] = 42.162$ m

We know apex or external distance $= R \cdot [\sec(\phi/2) - 1]$

∴ Apex or external distance $= 450 \times [\sec(50°/2) - 1] = 46.520$ m

Example 4.2 : Work out degree of a curve with radius of 450 m.

Solution : Given: Radius, $R = 450$ m.

We know degree of a curve, $D° = 57.296\ b/R$ ----- where 'b' is standard chord length and R is radius of the curve. When length of standard chord is not given, assume it as 30 m

∴ Degree for a given curve, $D° = 57.296 \times 30/450 = 3.82°$

Example 4.3 : Two straights meets at an angle of 138° are to be connected by a simple curve of 264 m length. Find the radius of the curve and the value of versed sine for a unit chord of 30 m.

Solution : Given: Angle of intersection, $I = 138°$, Length of curve, $L = 264$ m, Unit chord length, $b = 30$ m.

First workout deflection angle, ϕ

We know $I + \phi = 180$, Therefore, Deflection angle, $\phi = 180 - I = 180 - 138 = 42°$.

We also know length of a curve, $L = \pi R \phi°/180$,

∴ $R = 180L/(\pi \phi°) = 180 \times 264/(\pi \times 42°) = 360.145$ m

Now working out versed sine for a unit chord of 30 m.

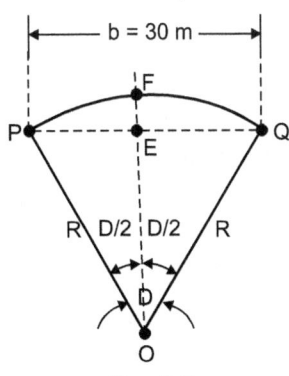

Fig. 4.8

We know angle subtended by standard or unit chord at centre of the curve is the degree D of the curve. Versed sine for unit chord of

30 m $= EF = OF - OE$

$= R - R \cdot \cos(D/2)$

$= R \cdot [1 - \cos(D/2)]$

Where D = Degree of a curve $= 57.296\ b/R$

Here b = unit chord = 30 m and R = Radius = 360.145 m

∴ Degree of a curve, $D = 57.296 \times 30/360.145 = 4.77°$

∴ Versed sine for unit chord of

30 m $= 360.145 \times [1 - \cos(4.77/2)]$

$= 0.312$ m

Example 4.4 : Two tangents intersect at chainage of 3250 m, deflection angle being 32°. Calculate chainages of the tangent points. Assume it as a 4° curve and peg interval is 30 m.

Solution : Given: Chainage of point of intersection, CPI = 3250 m, Deflection angle, ϕ = 32°, Degree of the curve = D = 4° and Peg interval is 30 m.

Knowing degree, first work out radius of the curve.

We know $\quad\quad$ R = 1718.9/ D° $\quad$ ... When standard chord length (Peg interval) is 30m.

Then radius, $\quad$ R = 1718.9 ÷ 4 = 429.725 m

Now work out tangent length l, using the relation, $l = R \cdot \tan(\phi/2)$

Then tangent length, l = 429.725 · tan (32/2) = 123.222 m

∴ Chainage of first tangent point, CT_1 = CPI − l

$\quad\quad$ = 3250 − 123.222

$\quad\quad$ = 3126.778 m

Now work out length L of curve, using the equation, $L = \pi R \phi°/180$

Then length of curve, L = π × 429.725 × 32 ÷ 180 = 240.004 m

∴ Chainage of second tangent point,

$\quad\quad CT_2 = CT_1 + L$

$\quad\quad\quad$ = 3126.778 + 240.004

$\quad\quad\quad$ = 3366.782 m

Example 4.5 : Two straights of a road intersect at a chainage of 2550.5 m. The angle of intersection is 110°. Taking chord length of 30 m, calculate the following:

(i) Radius of curve

(ii) Length of curve

(iii) Tangent length

(iv) Length of long chord

(v) Chainages at starting point and end point.

Solution : Given: Chainage of point of intersection, CPI = 2550.5 m; Angle of intersection, I = 110°; Chord length (i.e. peg interval), P = 30 m.

We know chord length (i.e. peg interval), P = R ÷ 20

∴ $\quad\quad$ Radius of curve = 20 × P = 20 × 30 = 600 m

For reduction of curve length, tangent length and length of long chord, one shall know deflection angle (ϕ). We know, Deflection angle, ϕ = 180° − I = 180° − 110° = 70°.

We know length of a curve, $\quad\quad L = \pi R \phi°/180$

∴ Length of a curve, $\quad\quad\quad\quad\quad$ L = π × 600 × 70 ÷ 180 = 733.038 m

We know tangent length, $\quad\quad\quad\quad\; l = R \cdot \tan(\phi/2)$

∴ Tangent length, $\quad\quad\quad\quad\quad\quad\; l$ = 600 · tan (70°/2) = 420.124 m

We know length of long chord $\quad\quad$ = 2R · sin (ϕ/2)

∴ $\quad\quad$ Length of long chord = 2 × 600 × sin (70°/2) = 688.292 m

Chainage at starting point, $\quad CT_1 = CPI - l$

∴ Chainage at starting point, $\quad CT_1 = 2550.5 - 420.124 = 2130.376$ m

Chainage at end point, $\quad CT_2 = CT_1 + L$

∴ Chainage at second tangent point,

$\quad CT_2 = 2130.376 + 733.038 = 2863.414$ m

4.3 SIMPLE CIRCULAR CURVES

The process of marking the alignment of the proposed curve at the intended location is called as Ranging out or Setting out for the curve. To set out a curve as usual first one will require to establish the control points such as point of intersection, tangent points, points of compound curvature etc. The pegs on the curves then can be located with tape, theodolite, total station etc. With reference to these pre established control points. There are main two methods of curve ranging viz. Linear methods and angular methods.

4.3.1 Linear Methods of Curve Ranging

In these methods, the curve is set out mainly with the help of distance measuring instruments such as chain and tape and use of direction measuring instrument is done minimum. Following are some commonly used linear methods of curve ranging,

1. Method of offsets from the long chord,
2. Method of offset from chords produced,
3. Method of offset from tangent and
4. Method of successive bisection of chords (or arcs).

4.3.1.1 Method of Offsets from the Long Chord

(a) Theory

This method is mainly used to set out short and sharp curves usually that for street kerbs.

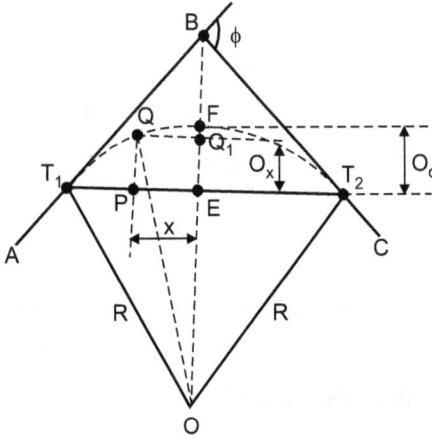

Fig. 4.9 : Method of Offsets from Long Chord

Let O_x is offset from long chord to set out point Q on a circular curve, at a distance x from midpoint E of long chord T_1ET_2 and measured along long chord.

In right angled

ΔOQ_1Q, $(OQ)^2 = (OQ_1)^2 + (QQ_1)^2$ ... (1)

Here $\quad OQ = R$ ... (2)

$\quad OQ_1 = OE + EQ_1 = (OF - EF) + EQ_1$

As $OF = R$, $EF = O_o$ and $EQ_1 = O_x$, therefore $OQ_1 = (R - O_0) + O_x$ ... (3)

Where $\quad O_0 = $ Versed Sine $= R \cdot [1 - \cos(\phi/2)]$

Also $\quad QQ1 = x$ ... (4)

Combining equations (1), (2), (3) and (4),

$$R^2 = [(R - O_0) + O_x]^2 + x^2$$
$$R^2 - x^2 = [(R - O_0) + O_x]^2$$
$$\sqrt{(R^2 - x^2)} = (R - O_0) + O_x$$

Therefore offset from long chord = $\mathbf{O_x = [\sqrt{(R^2 - x^2)}] - (R - O_0)}$

Example 4.6 : Two tangents AB and BC intersect at point B at chainage 210 m. Calculate all data necessary for setting out simple circular curve of radius 100 m and deflection angle of 40° by method of offset from the long chord. Take interval between the ordinates as 5.0 m.

Solution : Given : Chainage of point of intersection, CPI = 210 m, Deflection angle, $\phi = 40°$, Radius of the curve, R = 100 m and Peg interval along long chord, $P_{Long\ Chord} = 5$ m.

Primary Calculations :

Tangent length, $l = R \cdot \tan(\phi/2) = 100 \cdot \tan(40/2) = 36.398$ m.

Chainage of first tangent point, $CT_1 = CPI - l = 210 - 36.398 = 173.602$ m

Length of curve, $L = \pi.R \cdot \phi°/180 = \pi \times 100 \times 40 \div 180 = 69.813$ m

Chainage of second tangent point,

$\quad CT_2 = CT_1 + L$

$\quad\quad = 173.602 + 69.813 = 243.415$ m

Length of long chord $= 2R \cdot \sin(\phi/2) = 2 \times 100 \times \sin(40°/2) = 68.404$ m

Semi long chord $= 68.404 \div 2 = 34.202$ m

Versed sine (or mid ordinate) $= O_0 = R \cdot [1 - \cos(\phi/2)] = 100 \times [1 - \cos(40°/2)] = 6.031$ m

Working out Offsets from Long Chord :

We know length of offset from long chord at chainage x measured along long from midpoint E of long chord = $O_x = [\sqrt{(R^2 - x^2)}] - (R - O_0)$
$= [\sqrt{(100^2 - x^2)}] - (100 - 6.031)$
$= [\sqrt{(10000 - x^2)}] - (93.969)$

Peg on curve	Chainage 'x' of foot of offset, measured from midpoint 'E' of long chord along the long chord	Length of perpendicular offset O_x from long chord $= [\sqrt{(10000 - x^2)}] - (93.969)$	Remark
F	00	$O_0 = 6.031$	Midpoint of long chord
1L or 1R	05	$O_1 = 5.906$	
2L or 2R	10	$O_2 = 5.530$	
3L or 3R	15	$O_3 = 4.900$	
4L or 4R	20	$O_4 = 4.011$	
5L or 5R	25	$O_5 = 2.856$	
6L or 6R	30	$O_6 = 1.425$	
T_1 or T_2	34.202	O_{T1} or $O_{T2} = 00$	Tangent points

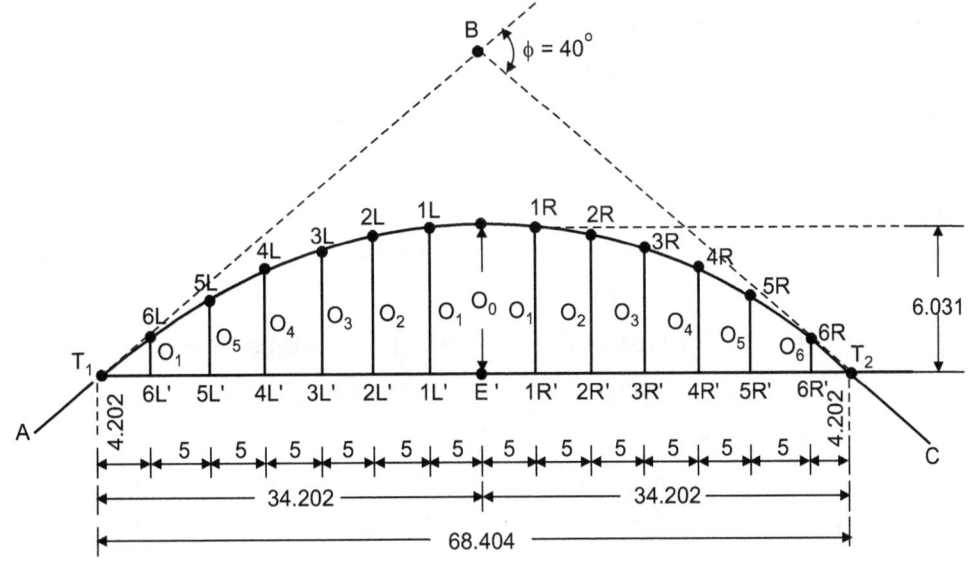

Fig. 4.10 : Sketch to Explain Solution of Example 4.7

4.3.1.1 (b) Field Procedure to set out curve by Method of Offset from Long Chord

1. Knowing point B of intersection and tangent length, get established two more control points T_1 and T_2 on rear straight AB and forward straight BC respectively.
2. Divide long chord T_1T_2 in to an even numbers of equal parts each of length say x. For example, if it is divides in eight parts, we will require tomark down total nine points including the tangent pointsT_1 and T_2. But T_1 and T_2 are already established. That means we will require to mark down only seven points.

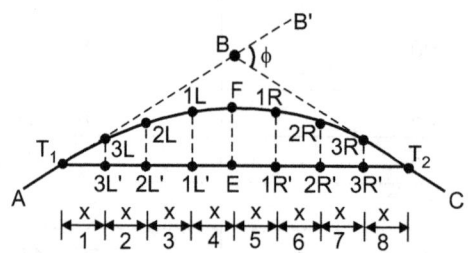

Fig. 4.11 : Method of Offset from Long Chord

3. Amongst these seven points one point will be the vertex or apex point F of the curve. This point F will marked as free end of the offset EF set out at midpoint E of the long chord. Length of offset EF will be equal to versed sine O_0 for the curve = $\{R \cdot [1 - \cos(\phi/2)]\}$. Amongst rest of six points on curve, three points say 1L, 2L and 3L will be on left of vertex F and rest three points say 1R, 2R and 3R will be on right of the same.
4. To set out first point 1L on curve, on left of vertex F, mark a point 1L' on long chord at a distance of x from midpoint E and set out at point 1L' an offset 1L'1L of length.
   = $[\sqrt{(R^2 - x^2)}] - (R - O_0)$. Free end 1L of the offset 1L'1L will be the required point.
5. To set out second point 2L on curve, on left of vertex F, mark a point 2L' on long chord at a distance of 2x from midpoint E and set out at point 2L' an offset 2L'2L of length.
   = $[\sqrt{(R^2 - 4x^2)}] - (R - O_0)$. Free end 2L of the offset 2L'2L will be the required point.
6. To set out third point 3L on curve on left of vertex F, mark a point 3L' on long chord at a distance of x from midpoint E and set out at point 3L' an offset 3L'3L of length.
   = $[\sqrt{(R^2 - 9x^2)}] - (R - O_0)$. Free end 3L of the offset 3L'3L will be the required point.
7. Repeat the procedure on the same ground as like that of steps 4 to 6 to mark three more points 1R, 2R and 3R on curve on right on vertex F.

Example 4.7 : Two straights intersect at a chainage of 2610 m, the deflection angle being 36°. A circular curve of 400 m radius is to be set by "Method of offset from long chord". Calculate the chainages of tangent points and the value of offsets at mid point, 30 m and 60 m. (Take pag interval = 30 m)

Solution : Given : Chainage of point of intersection, CPI = 2610 m, Deflection angle, ϕ = 36°, Radius of the curve, R = 400 m and Peg interval along long chord, $P_{Long\ Chord}$ = 30 m.

Primary Calculations :

Tangent length, l = R · tan (ϕ/2) = 400 · tan (36°/2) = 129.968 m.
Chainage of first tangent point, CT_1 = CPI – l = 2610 – 129.968 = 2480.032 m
Length of curve, L = π · R · ϕ°/180 = π × 400 × 36 ÷ 180 = 251.327 m
Chainage of second tangent point,
$$CT_2 = CT_1 + L$$
$$= 2480.032 + 251.327 = 2731.359 \text{ m}$$
Length of long chord = 2R · sin (ϕ/2) = 2 × 400 × sin (36°/2) = 247.214 m
Semi long chord = 68.404 ÷ 2 = 123.607 m
Versed sine (or mid ordinate) = O_0 = R · [1 – cos (ϕ/2)] = 400 × [1 – cos (36°/2)] = 19.577 m

Working out Offsets from Long Chord :

We know length of offset from long chord at chainage 'x' measured along long chord from midpoint E of long chord = O_x = [$\sqrt{(R^2 - x^2)}$] – (R – O_0)
$$= [\sqrt{(400^2 - x^2)}] - (400 - 19.577)$$
$$= [\sqrt{(160000 - x^2)}] - (380.423)$$

Peg on curve	Chainage 'x' of foot of offset, measured from midpoint 'E' of long chord along the long chord	Length of perpendicular offset O_x from long chord = [$\sqrt{(16000 - x^2)}$] – (380.423)	Remark
F	00	O_0 = 19.577 m	F is apex or vertex point of the curve
1L or 1R	30 m	O_1 = 18.450	
2L or 2R	60 m	O_2 = 15.051	
T_1 or T_2	123.607 m	O_{T1} or O_{T2} = 00	T_1 and T_2 are the Tangent points

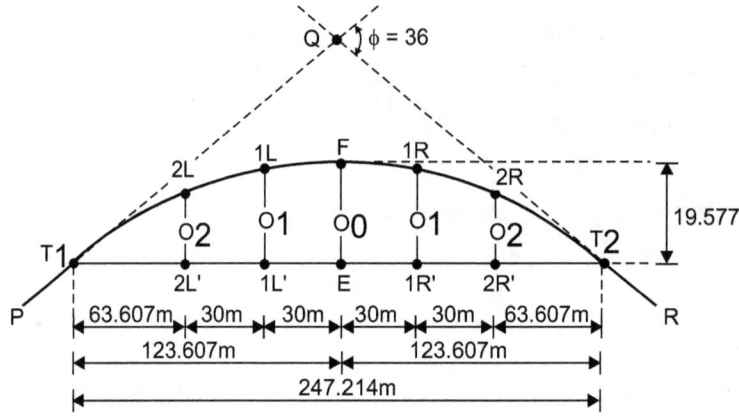

Fig. 4.12: Sketch to Explain Solution of Example 4.7

Example 4.8 : Calculate the ordinate at 25 m interval to set out a circular curve having long chord of 300 m and versed sine of 10 m.

Solution : Given: Peg interval along long chord, $P_{Long\ Chord}$ = 25 m, Length of long chord = 300 m and Versed Sine = 10 m.

The exact formula to work out ordinates form long chord is, $O_x = [\sqrt{(R^2 - x^2)}] - (R - O_0)$. To work out ordinates from long chord by this formula, we will require radius R of the curve. But here radius R of the curve is not given, hence let us work out radius R of the curve first.

We know, Length of long chord, say $X = 2R \cdot \sin(\phi/2)$

$\therefore \quad R \cdot \sin(\phi/2) = X/2$

$\therefore \quad R = \dfrac{X/2}{\sin(\phi/2)}$ ... (1)

We also know, Versed sine, $O_0 = R \cdot [1 - \cos(\phi/2)]$

$\therefore \quad R = \dfrac{O_0}{1 - \cos(\phi/2)}$ ... (2)

As RHS of equations (1) and (2) is same we can equate their RHS.

$\therefore \quad \dfrac{X/2}{\sin(\phi/2)} = \dfrac{O_0}{1 - \cos(\phi/2)}$

$\therefore \quad (X/2) \cdot [1 - \cos(\phi/2)] = O_0 \cdot \sin(\phi/2)$

$\therefore \quad \dfrac{X/2}{O_0} = \dfrac{\sin(\phi/2)}{1 - \cos(\phi/2)}$

We know, $1 - \cos\theta = 2\sin^2\theta$ and $\sin 2\theta = 2\sin\theta \cdot \cos\theta$

$\therefore \quad \dfrac{X/2}{O_0} = \dfrac{2\sin(\phi/4) \cdot \cos(\phi/4)}{2\sin^2(\phi/4)} = \dfrac{\cos(\phi/4)}{\sin(\phi/4)} = \cot(\phi/4)$

$\therefore \quad \tan(\phi/4) = \dfrac{O_0}{X/2}$

∴ $\left(\dfrac{\phi}{4}\right) = \tan^{-1}\left(\dfrac{O_0}{X/2}\right)$

∴ $\phi = 4 \cdot \tan^{-1}\left(\dfrac{O_0}{X/2}\right)$

∴ Here $\phi = 4 \cdot \tan^{-1}\left(\dfrac{10}{150}\right) = 4 \cdot \tan^{-1}\left(\dfrac{1}{15}\right)$

∴ $\phi = 15°15'23''$

Now put $\phi = 15°15'23''$ in equation (1) to obtain radius R of the curve

∴ $R = \dfrac{150}{\sin(\phi/2)} = \dfrac{150}{\sin(15°15'23''/2)} = 1130 \text{ m}$

Working out Offsets from Long Chord :

We know length of offset from long chord at chainage x measured along long from midpoint E of long chord = O_x = $[\sqrt{(R^2 - x^2)}] - (R - O_0)$
= $[\sqrt{(1130^2 - x^2)}] - (1130 - 10)$
= $[\sqrt{(1130^2 - x^2)}] - (1120)$

Peg on curve	Chainage 'x' of foot of offset, measured from midpoint 'E' of long chord along the long chord	Length of perpendicular offset O_x from long chord = $[\sqrt{(1130^2 - x^2)}] - (1120)$	Remark
F	00	$O_0 = 10.000$	Midpoint of long chord
1L or 1R	25	$O_1 = 9.723$	
2L or 2R	50	$O_2 = 8.893$	
3L or 3R	75	$O_3 = 7.508$	
4L or 4R	100	$O_4 = 5.567$	
5L or 5R	125	$O_5 = 3.065$	
T_1 or T_2	150	O_{T1} or O_{T2} = 0.000	Tangent points

4.3.1.2 Method of Offsets from Chord Produced

4.3.1.2 (a) Theory

This method is largely used on flat and long radius road curves. It can be used in confined situations, since all the work is done in close proximity of the curve proper. It is a better method as compared to other linear methods of curve ranging. The only drawback is that error committed in setting out of previous points is carried forward to next points.

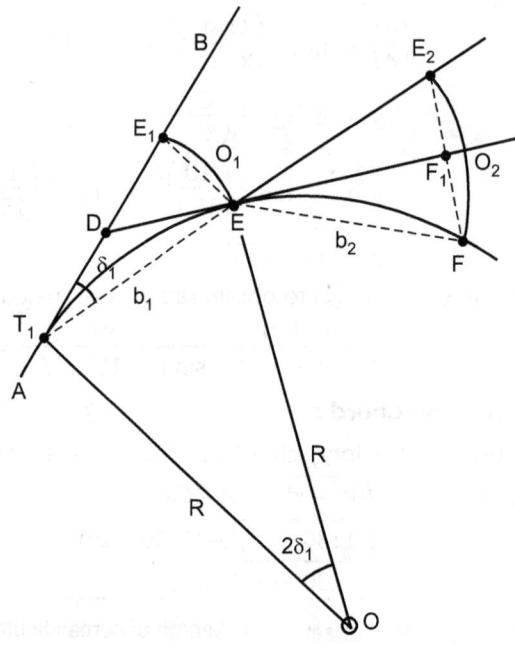

Fig. 4.13 : Method of Offset from Chord Produced

T_1 is first tangent point, E and F are points or pegs on curve, T_1B is a rear tangent.

Let $T_1E_1 = T_1E$ = Length of first chord = b_1

Let Length of arc T_1E = Length of chord $T_1E = b_1$ and $\angle BT_1E = \delta_1$,

Then $\angle T_1OE = 2 \cdot \delta_1$ and b_1 = Arc $T_1E = R \cdot 2\delta_1$

∴ $\qquad \delta_1 = b_1 / 2R$

Similarly Offset O_1 = Chord E_1E = Arc $E_1E = b_1 \cdot \delta_1$, but $\delta_1 = b_1/2R$

∴ $\qquad O_1 = b_1^2 / 2R$ ... (1)

EE_2 is prolongation of T_1E beyond E, such that EE_2 = Length of second chord = b_2

Rotate EE_2 about E to cut prolongation of tangent DE at F_1 and the curve at F,

Then isosceles ΔE_2EF_1 and ΔE_1T_1E may be assumed similar.

Hence, $(E_2F_1/EE_2) = (E_1E/T_1E_1)$ but $EE_2 = b_2$, $E_1E = O_1$ and $T_1E_1 = b_1$,

∴ $\qquad (E_2F_1/b_2) = (O_1/b_1)$ or $E_2F_1 = (b_2/b_1) \cdot O_1$

But from equation (1), $O_1 = b_1^2/2R$

∴ $\qquad E_2F_1 = \dfrac{b_2}{b_1} \times \dfrac{b_1^2}{2R} = b_2 \cdot b_1/2R$

From Fig. 4.12, Offset $\quad O_2 = E_2F_1 + F_1E$,

We can prove that, $F_1E = b_2^2/2R$ and $E_2F_1 = b_2 \cdot b_1/2R$

Hence offset to set out 2nd peg on curve = $O_2 = b_2 \cdot b_1/2R + b_2^2/2R$

$$O_2 = b_2 \cdot (b_1 + b_2)/2R$$

Same way, Offset to set out 3rd peg on curve = $O_3 = b_3 \cdot (b_2 + b_3)/2R$

Offset to set out 4th peg on curve = $O_4 = b_4 \cdot (b_3 + b_4)/2R$

Hence offset to set out nth peg on curve = $\mathbf{O_n = b_n \cdot (b_{n-1} + b_n)/2R}$

Example 4.9 : The chainage of the intersection point of two straights is 2105.59 m and the deflection angle is 45°20'. A circular curve of 250.00 m radius is to be set out to connect the two straights. Calculate the necessary data for setting out a curve by method of offset from chord produced.

Solution : Given : Chainage of point of intersection, CPI = 2105.59 m, Deflection angle, ϕ = 45°20', Radius of the curve, R = 250 m.

Primary Calculations :

Tangent length, $l = R \cdot \tan(\phi/2)$

$= 250 \times \tan(45°20'/2)$

$= 104.406$ m

Chainage of first tangent point,

$CT_1 = CPI - l$

$= 2105.59 - 104.406$

$= 2001.184$ m

Length of curve, $L = \pi \cdot R \cdot \phi°/180$

$= \pi \times 250 \times 45°20' \div 180$

$= 197.804$ m

Chainage of second tangent point,

$CT_2 = CT_1 + L$

$= 2001.184 + 197.804$

$= 2198.988$ m

Peg interval on curve, $P = R/20$

$= 250/20$

$= 12.5$ m

Chainage of peg on rear straight prior to T_1 = CS = [Integer part of $(CT_1 \div P_{Straight})] \times P_{Straight}$.

Where $P_{Straight}$ is the peg interval on straight. It is also not given, hence assuming it as peg interval P (12.5 m) on curve.

$\therefore$ CS = [Integer part of $(2001.184 \div 12.5)] \times 12.5$

= [Integer part of (160.095)] × 12.5

= [160] × 12.5 = 2000 m

Chainage of first peg on curve, CP_1 = CS + P = 2000 + 12.5 = 2012.5 m ... this is > CT_1 i.e. 2001.184 m, therefore alright.

Length of sub-chord at beginning of the curve,

b_1 = $CP_1 - CT_1$

= 2012.5 − 2001.184 m

= 11.316 m

Number of unit chords = n = Integer part of $[(L - b_1) \div P]$

= Integer part of [(197.804 − 11.316) ÷ 12.5]

= Integer part of [(186.488) ÷ 12.5]

= Integer part of [14.919]

= 14

Length of sub-chord at end of the curve,

b_{T2} = $L - n \cdot P - b_1$

= 197.804 − 14 × 12.5 − 11.316

= 11.488 m

Working out Offsets from Long Chord :

We know offset from chord produced to set out n^{th} peg = $O_n = b_n \cdot (b_{n-1} + b_n)/2R$

$= b_n \cdot \dfrac{(b_{n-1} + b_n)}{(2 \times 250)}$

$= b_n \cdot \dfrac{(b_{n-1} + b_n)}{500}$

SURVEYING - S.E. CIVIL (NMU)　　　　　　　　　　　　　　　　　　　　CURVES

Peg on Curve	Chord length to set out n^{th} peg, b_n m	Chainage in m	Offset from Chord Produced to set out n^{th} peg $O_n = b_n \cdot (b_{n-1} + b_n)/500$	Remark
T_1	---	2001.184	---	First Tangent Point
1	$b_1 = 11.316$	2012.5	$O_1 = b_1 \cdot (b_0 + b_1)/500$ $= 11.316 \times (00 + 11.316)/500$ $= 0.256$ m	There are 14 unit chords and 2 sub chords, means total number of chords is $(14 + 2) = 16$. Hence to set out this curve we will require total $(16 + 1)$ i.e. 17 pegs including pegs at first tangent point T_1 and second tangent point T_2. That means we will require to set out total 15 pegs in between T_1 and T_2 and excluding pegs at T_1 and T_2.
2		2025.0	$O_2 = b_2 \cdot (b_1 + b_2)/500$ $= 12.5 \times (11.316 + 12.5)/500$ $= 0.595$ m	
3		2037.5		
4		2050.0		
5		2062.5		
6		2075.0		
7	b_2 to $b_{15} = 12.5$	2087.5		
8		2100.0	O_3 to $O_{15} = b_3 \cdot (b_2 + b_3)/500$ $= 12.5 \times (12.5 + 12.5)/500$ $= 0.625$ m	
9		2112.5		
10		2125.0		
11		2137.5		
12		2150.0		
13		2162.5		
14		2175.0		
15		2187.5		
T_2	$b_{T2} = 11.488$	2198.988	$O_{T2} = b_{T2} \cdot (b_{15} + b_{T2})/500$ $= 11.488 \times (12.5 + 11.488)/500$ $= 0.551$ m	Second Tangent Point

4.3.1.2 (b) Field Procedure to Set out Curve by Method of Offsets from chord Produced

1. Knowing point B of intersection and tangent length, get established two more control points T_1 and T_2.
2. Mark point E_1 on rear tangent T_1B, at a distance equal to length b_1 of chord to set out first peg E on the curve.
3. Set out offset E_1E of length O_1 at E_1, free end E of this offset is the first point E on the curve.
4. To set out second point F on curve, prolong chord T_1E upto E_2, so that EE_2 is equal to length b_2 of second chord.
5. Set out offset E_2F of length O_2 at E_2, free end F of this offset is the second point F on the curve.

6. Repeat the process until the end point T_2 of the curve is reached. The last point thus fixed should coincide with initially located T_2. If not find closing error and express it as % of length of curve.

Example 4.10 : Two tangents intersect at a chainage 2052 m deflection angle 60°30'. Calculate the necessary data for setting out a curve of 300 m radius to connect two tangents. It is intended to set out curve the curve by offsets from chord produced.

Take peg interval = 20 m. Length of chain being used = 20 m.

Solution : Given: Chainage of point of intersection, CPI = 2052 m; Deflection angle, ϕ = 60°30'; Radius of the curve, R = 300 m; Peg interval, P = 20 m; Length of chain being used 20 m.

Primary Calculations :

Tangent length, $l = R \cdot \tan(\phi/2) = 300 \times \tan(60°30'/2) = 174.955$ m.
Chainage of first tangent point, CT_1 = CPI − l = 2052 − 174.955 = 1877.045 m
Length of curve, $L = \pi \cdot R \cdot \phi°/180 = \pi \times 300 \times 60°30' \div 180 = 316.777$ m
Chainage of second tangent point,
$$CT_2 = CT_1 + L$$
$$= 1877.045 + 316.777 = 2193.822 \text{ m}$$

Peg interval on curve, P = 20 m ... Given in the problem itself.

As length of chain being used is 20 m, adopting peg interval greater than 20 m will create inconvenience in setting out.

Chainage of peg on rear straight prior to T_1 = CS = [Integer part of ($CT_1 \div P_{Straight}$)] × $P_{Straight}$.

Where $P_{Straight}$ is the peg interval on straight. It is not given, hence let us assume it as peg interval P (i.e. 20 m) on curve.

$\therefore$
$$CS = [\text{Integer part of } (1877.045 \div 20)] \times 20$$
$$= [\text{Integer part of } (93.852)] \times 20$$
$$= 93 \times 20 = 1860 \text{ m}$$

Chainage of first peg on curve, CP_1 = CS + P = 1860 + 20 = 1880 m, and this is > CT_1 i.e. 1877.045 m, therefore alright.

Length of sub-chord at beginning of the curve,
$$b_1 = CP_1 - CT_1$$
$$= 1880 - 1877.045$$
$$= 2.955 \text{ m}$$

Number of unit chords = n = Integer part of [(L − b_1) ÷ P]
$$= \text{Integer part of } [(316.777 - 2.955) \div 20]$$
$$= \text{Integer part of } [(313.822) \div 20]$$
$$= \text{Integer part of } [15.691]$$
$$= 15$$

Length of sub-chord at end of the curve,
$$b_{T2} = L - n \cdot P - b_1$$
$$= 316.777 - 15 \times 20 - 2.955$$
$$= 13.822 m$$

Working out Offsets from Long Chord :

We know offset from chord produced to set out n^{th} peg = $O_n = b_n \cdot (b_{n-1} + b_n)/2R$
$$= b_n \cdot (b_{n-1} + b_n)/(2 \times 300)$$
$$= b_n \cdot (b_{n-1} + b_n)/600$$

Peg on Curve	Chord length to set out n^{th} peg, b_n m	Chainage in m	Offset from Chord Produced to set out n^{th} peg $O_n = b_n \cdot (b_{n-1} + b_n)/600$	Remark
T_1	--	1877.045	--	T_1 is First Tangent Point
1	$b_1 = 2.955$	1880	$O_1 = b_1 \cdot (b_0 + b_1)/600$ $= 2.955 \times (00 + 2.955)/600$ $= 0.015 m$	
2		1900	$O_2 = b_2 \cdot (b_1 + b_2)/600$ $= 20 \times (2.955 + 20)/600$ $= 0.765 m$	There are 15 unit chords and 2 sub-chords, means total number of chords is $(15 + 2) = 17$. Hence to set out this curve we will require total $(17 + 1)$ i.e. 18 pegs including pegs at first tangent point T_1 and second tangent point T_2. That means we will require to set out total 16 pegs in between T_1 and T_2 and excluding pegs at T_1 and T_2.
3	b_2 to $b_{16} = 20$	1920	O_3 to $O_{16} = b_3 \cdot (b_2 + b_3)/600$ $= 20 \times (20 + 20)/600$ $= 1.333 m$	
4		1940		
5		1960		
6		1980		
7		2000		
8		2020		
9		2040		
10		2060		
11		2080		
12		2100		
13		2120		
14		2140		
15		2160		
16		2180		
T_2	$b_{T2} = 13.822$	2193.822	$O_{T2} = b_{T2} \cdot (b_{16} + b_{T2})/600$ $= 13.822 \times (20 + 13.822)/600$ $= 0.779 m$	T_2 is Second Tangent Point

Example 4.11 : Tabulate the data necessary for setting out the curve by offset from chord produced for the following data :
  (i) Radius of curve = 650 m
  (ii) Deflection angle of curve = 22°
  (iii) Chainage of intersection point = 2100 m
  (iv) Peg interval = 20 m

Solution : Given : Radius of the curve, R = 650 m; Deflection angle, ϕ = 22°; Chainage of point of intersection, CPI = 2100 m; Peg interval, P = 20 m.

Primary Calculations :

Tangent length, l = R · tan (ϕ/2) = 650 × tan (22°/2) = 126.347 m.
Chainage of first tangent point, CT_1 = CPI − l = 2100 − 126.347 = 1973.653 m
Length of curve, L = π · R · ϕ°/180 = π × 650 × 22° ÷180 = 249.582 m
Chainage of second tangent point,

$$CT_2 = CT_1 + L$$
$$= 1973.653 + 249.582 = 2223.235 \text{ m}$$

Peg interval on curve,   P = 20 m   ... Given in the problem itself.

Chainage of peg on rear straight prior to T_1 = CS = [Integer part of (CT_1 ÷ $P_{Straight}$)] × $P_{Straight}$.

Where $P_{Straight}$ is the peg interval on straight. It is not given, hence let us assume it as peg interval P (i.e. 20 m) on curve.

$\therefore$ CS = [Integer part of (1973.653 ÷ 20)] × 20
       = [Integer part of (98.683)] × 20
       = 98 × 20 = 1960 m

Chainage of first peg on curve, CP_1 = CS + P = 1960 + 20 = 1980 m, and this is > CT_1 i.e. 1973.653 m, therefore alright.

Length of sub-chord at beginning of the curve,

$$b_1 = CP_1 − CT_1$$
$$= 1980 − 1973.653$$
$$= 6.347 \text{ m}$$

Number of unit chords = n = Integer part of [(L − b_1) ÷ P]
               = Integer part of [(249.582 − 6.347) ÷ 20]
               = Integer part of [(243.235) ÷ 20]
               = Integer part of [12.161]
               = 12

Length of sub-chord at end of the curve,
$$b_{T2} = L - n \cdot P - b_1$$
$$= 249.582 - 12 \times 20 - 6.347$$
$$= 3.235 \text{ m}$$

Working out Offsets from Long Chord :

We know offset from chord produced to set out n^{th} peg = $O_n = b_n \cdot (b_{n-1} + b_n)/2R$
$$= b_n \cdot (b_{n-1} + b_n)/(2 \times 650)$$
$$= b_n \cdot (b_{n-1} + b_n)/1300$$

Peg on Curve	Chord length to set out n^{th} peg, b_n m	Chainage in m	Offset from Chord Produced to set out n^{th} peg $O_n = b_n \cdot (b_{n-1} + b_n)/1300$	Remark
T_1	--	1973.653	--	T_1 is First Tangent Point
1	$b_1 = 6.347$	1980	$O_1 = b_1 \cdot (b_0 + b_1)/600$ $= 6.347 \times (00 + 6.347)/1300$ $= 0.031$ m	
2		2000	$O_2 = b_2 \cdot (b_1 + b_2)/600$ $= 20 \times (6.347 + 20)/1300$ $= 0.405$ m	There are 12 unit chords and 2 sub chords, means total number of chords is (12 + 2) = 14. Hence to set out this curve we will require total (14 + 1) i.e. 15 pegs including first tangent point T_1 and second tangent point T_2. That means we will require to set out total 13 pegs in between T_1 and T_2 and excluding pegs at T_1 and T_2.
3	b_2 to $b_{13} = 20$	2020	O_3 to $O_{16} = b_3 \cdot (b_2 + b_3)/650$ $= 20 \times (20 + 20)/1300$ $= 0.615$ m	
4		2040		
5		2060		
6		2080		
7		2100		
8		2120		
9		2140		
10		2160		
11		2180		
12		2200		
13		2220		
T_2	$b_{T2} = 3.235$	2223.235	$O_{T2} = b_{T2} \cdot (b_{13} + b_{T2})/1300$ $= 3.235 \times (20 + 3.235)/1300$ $= 0.779$ m	T_2 is Second Tangent Point

4.3.1.3 Method of Offset from Tangent

This method can be used when deflection angle and radius of curvature both are relatively small i.e. when the curve is of small length. Once up on time, the method was common in use to set out railway curves. The offset from tangent may be either radial or perpendicular.

4.3.1.3.1 Method of Radial Offsets from Tangent

4.3.1.3.1 (a) Theory

This method of offsets form tangent is preferred when centre of the curve is accessible. Let we have to set out point P on a circular curve from rear tangent T_1B.

Extend radius OP beyond the circular arc till it cuts rear tangent T_1B at P_1.

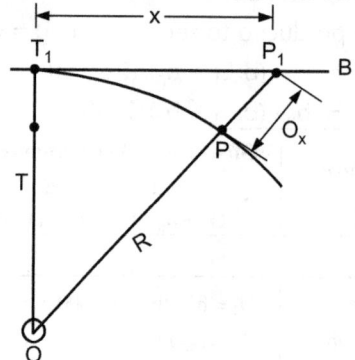

Fig. 4.14 : Method of Radial Offsets from Tangent

Then $P_1P = O_x$ is the radial offset to set out point P on the curve, point P_1 is the foot of said offset and distance $T_1P_1 = x$ is the chainage of foot of said offset with respect to rear or first tangent point T_1.

In right angled $\triangle OT_1P_1$, $OP_1^2 = OT_1^2 + T_1P_1^2$ ... (1)

But $\quad OP_1 = OP + PP_1$

$\quad\quad\quad = R + O_x$ ... As $OP = R$ and $PP_1 = O_x$ ... (2)

Combining equations (1) and (2)

$$(R + O_x)^2 = OT_1^2 + T_1P_1^2$$

But OT_1 = Radius 'R' of the circular curve and T_1P_1 is chainage 'x' of the foot P_1 of the radial offset P_1P.

$\therefore \quad\quad (R + O_x)^2 = R^2 + x^2$

$\therefore \quad\quad (R + O_x) = \sqrt{(R^2 + x^2)}$

$\therefore \quad O_x = [\sqrt{(R^2 + x^2)}] - R$ ... Relation to work out length of radial offset from tangent.

Check that length of last offset i.e. an offset set out at point of intersection is equal to external distance or apex distance.

Example 4.12 : Two straights of a route intersect at an angle of 110°. Calculate all the data to set out a curve of radius 150 m by method of radial offsets from the tangents. Assume chainage of point of intersection as 3550 m and peg interval along tangent as 20 m.

Solution : Given : Angle of intersection, I = 110°; Radius of the curve, R = 150 m; Chainage of point of intersection, CPI = 3550 m; Peg interval along tangent, P = 20 m.

Primary Calculations :

Deflection Angle, $\phi = 180° - I = 180° - 110° = 70°$

Tangent length, $l = R \cdot \tan(\phi/2) = 150 \cdot \tan(70°/2) = 105.031$ m

Chainage of first tangent point, $CT_1 = CPI - l = 3550 - 105.031 = 3655.031$ m

Length of curve, $L = \pi \cdot R \cdot \phi°/180 = \pi \times 150 \times 70 \div 180 = 183.260$ m

Chainage of second tangent point,

$$CT_2 = CT_1 + L$$
$$= 3655.031 + 183.260 = 3838.291 \text{ m}$$

Apex or external distance = $R \cdot [\sec(\phi/2) -] = 150 \cdot [\sec(70°/2) - 1] = 33.116$ m

Working out Radial Offsets from Tangent :

We know length of radial offset from tangent at chainage 'x' measured along tangent from tangent point T_1 or $T_2 = O_x = [\sqrt{(R^2 + x^2)}] - R$

$$= [\sqrt{(150^2 + x^2)}] - 150$$
$$= [\sqrt{(22500 + x^2)}] - 150$$

Peg on curve	Chainage 'x' in m of foot of offset, measured from tangent point 'T_1 or T_2' along the tangent towards point of intersection.	Length of radial offset O_x in m from tangent $= [\sqrt{(22500 + x^2)}] - 150$	Remark
T_1 or T_2	00	O_{T1} or $O_{T2} = 00$	Tangent points
1	20	$O_1 = 1.327$	
2	40	$O_2 = 5.242$	
3	60	$O_3 = 11.555$	
4	80	$O_4 = 20.000$	
5	100	$O_5 = 30.278$	
F	105.031	$O_F = 33.116$	Apex point

Check : Length of last offset must be = External distance or Apex distance.

4.3.1.3.1 (b) Field Procedure to set out curve by Method of Radial Offsets from Tangents

1. Knowing point B of intersection and tangent length l, get established two more control points T_1 and T_2 on rear straight AB and forward straight BC respectively.
2. Mark the points 1', 2', 3' ....., B indicating feet of offsets $O_1, O_2, O_3, ..., O_F$ at a distance x, 2x, 3x, ..., l from tangent point T_1 towards the point of intersection B.
3. Set out radially, towards centre of curvature, the offsets 1'1, 2'2, 3'3 ....., BF of length $O_1, O_2, O_3, ..., O_F$ at previously marked points 1', 2', 3' ....., B on rear tangent T_1B.

4. Free ends 1, 2, 3, ..., F of these offsets 1'1, 2'2, 3'3 ....., BF are the points 1, 2, 3, ..., F on the curve.
5. Check: Length of last offset must be = External distance or apex distance.
6. Set out remaining half of the curve from the second tangent point.
7. When the offset becomes too long, the central portion of the curve may be set out from the third tangent passing through apex point F of the curve.
8. It should be noted that the points on curve are not located at regular interval and as we go away from tangent point, the offsets become too long and error due to laying down of the long offsets is likely to come in to play.

4.3.1.3.2 Method of Perpendicular Offsets from Tangent

4.3.1.3.2 (a) Theory

This method of offsets form tangent is preferred when centre of the curve is inaccessible.

Let we have to set out point P on a circular curve from rear tangent T_1B.

Draw a line PP_1 through P cutting first or rear tangent T_1B at P_1.

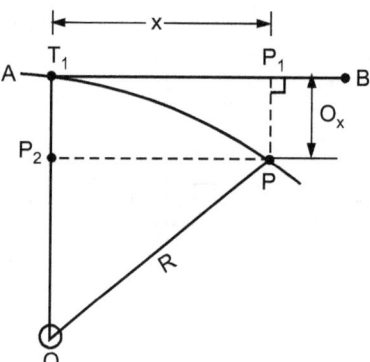

Fig. 4.15 : Method of Perpendicular Offsets from Tangent

Then $P_1P = O_x$ is the perpendicular offset to set out point P on the curve, point P_1 is the foot of said offset and distance $T_1P_1 = x$ is the chainage of foot of said offset with respect to rear or first tangent point T_1.

Through point P on the curve draw line PP_2 parallel to AB and cutting radius OT_1 at P_2.

We know radius and tangent of circular arc are always perpendicular to each other, hence being parallel to rear tangent T_1B, line PP_2 will also be cutting radius OT_1 at right angles and hence $\triangle OP_2P$ is a right angled triangle.

In right angled ΔOP_2P, $OP^2 = OP_2^2 + P_2P^2$ ... (1)

But
OP = Radius 'R',
$OP_2 = OT_1 - P_2T_1$
$= R - O_x$ As OT_1 = Radius 'R' of circular curve and
P_2T_1 = Length of Perpendicular Offset $PP_1 = O_x$
P_2P = Chainage T_1P_1 of foot P_1 of perpendicular offset $PP_1 = x$

Putting values of OP, OP_2 and P_2P in equation (1)

$\therefore \quad R^2 = (R - O_x)^2 + x^2$
$\therefore \quad R^2 - x^2 = (R - O_x)^2$
$\therefore \quad \sqrt{(R^2 - x^2)} = R - O_x$
$\therefore \quad O_x = R - [\sqrt{(R^2 - x^2)}]$

Relation to work out length of perpendicular offset from tangent.

Example 4.13 : Two straights of a route intersect at an angle of 110°. Calculate all the data to set out a curve of radius 150 m by method of radial offsets from the tangents. Assume chainage of point of intersection as 3550 m and peg interval along tangent as 20 m.

Solution : Given : Angle of intersection, I = 110°; Radius of the curve, R = 150 m; Chainage of point of intersection, CPI = 3550 m; Peg interval along tangent, P = 20 m.

Primary Calculations :

Deflection Angle, $\phi = 180° - I = 180° - 110° = 70°$
Tangent length, $l = R \cdot \tan(\phi/2) = 150 \cdot \tan(70°/2) = 105.031$ m.
Chainage of first tangent point,
$CT_1 = CPI - l = 3550 - 105.031 = 3655.031$ m
Length of curve, $L = \pi \cdot R \cdot \phi°/180 = \pi \times 150 \times 70 \div 180 = 183.260$ m
Chainage of second tangent point,
$CT_2 = CT_1 + L$
$= 3655.031 + 183.260 = 3838.291$ m
Apex or external distance = $R \cdot [\sec(\phi/2) -] = 150 \cdot [\sec(70°/2) - 1] = 33.116$ m

Working out Radial Offsets from Tangent :

We know length of radial offset from tangent at chainage 'x' measured along tangent from tangent point T_1 or $T_2 = O_x = R - [\sqrt{(R^2 - x^2)}]$
$= 150 - [\sqrt{(150^2 - x^2)}]$
$= 150 - [\sqrt{(22500 - x^2)}]$

Peg on curve	Chainage 'x' in m of foot of offset, measured from tangent point 'T$_1$ or T$_2$' along the tangent towards point of intersection.	Length of perpendicular offset O$_x$ in m from tangent $= 150 - [\sqrt{(22500 + x^2)}]$	Remark
T$_1$ or T$_2$	00	O$_{T1}$ or O$_{T2}$ = 00	Tangent points
1	20	O$_1$ = 1.339	
2	40	O$_2$ = 5.432	
3	60	O$_3$ = 12.523	
4	80	O$_4$ = 23.114	
5	100	O$_5$ = 38.197	
6	105.031	O$_6$ = 42.909	

4.3.1.3.2 (b) Field Procedure to set out curve by Method of Perpendicular Offsets from Tangents

1. Knowing point B of intersection and tangent length *l*, get established two more control points T$_1$ and T$_2$ on rear straight AB and forward straight BC respectively.
2. Mark the points 1', 2', 3' ..... indicating feet of offsets O$_1$, O$_2$, O$_3$, ... at a distance x, 2x, 3x, ... from tangent point T$_1$ towards the point of intersection B.
3. Set out perpendicularly, towards centre of curvature, the offsets 1'1, 2'2, 3'3 ..... of length O$_1$, O$_2$, O$_3$, ..., at previously marked points 1', 2', 3' ..... on rear tangent T$_1$B.
4. Free ends 1, 2, 3, ... of these offsets 1'1, 2'2, 3'3 ..... are the points 1, 2, 3, ... on the curve.
5. Set out remaining half of the curve from the second tangent point.
6. Check: Free end of the last offsets set out from both tangents must be one and the same point.
7. When the offset becomes too long, the central portion of the curve may be set out from the third tangent passing through apex point F of the curve.
8. It should be noted that the points on curve are not located at regular interval and as we go away from tangent point, the offsets become too long and error due to laying down of the long offsets is likely to come in to play.

4.3.1.4 Method of Successive Bisection of Chords (or Arcs)

It is also known as 'Versine Method'. This method is suitable when the land outside the curve is unsuitable for chaining.

1. Knowing point B of intersection and tangent length *l*, get established two more control points T$_1$ and T$_2$ on rear straight AB and forward straight BC respectively.

2. Join first or rear tangent point T_1 and second or forward tangent point T_2 by a chord. Bisect chord T_1T_2 at point E.

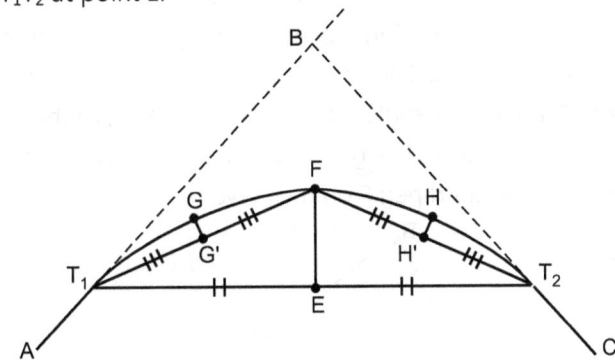

Fig. 4.16 : Method of Successive Bisection of Chords (or Arcs)

3. Set out offset EF at E, so that EF = Versed sine for arc T_1T_2 = R.[1 − cos (φ/2)]. Then E is a point on curve.
4. Join T_1 and F and T_2 and F by the chords. Bisect chords T_1F and T_2F at G' and H' respectively.
5. Set out offsets G'G and H'H at G' and H' respectively, so that length each of these offsets = Versed sine for arc T_1F or T_2F = R · [1 − cos (φ/4)]. Then G and H are two more points on the curve.
6. Continue the process till sufficient numbers of points on the curve are marked.
7. It should be noted that accuracy of setting out the curve by this method is governed by number of bisections of chords.

4.3.2 Angular Methods of Curve Ranging

In these methods, the curve is set out mainly with the help of angle measuring instruments such as theodolite and use of distance measuring instrument is done optimum. Angular methods are preferred to set out very long and flat curves as in case of railways and expressways. There are two angular methods to set out the circular curves. One is Rankine's method of tangential/deflection angles and another is two theodolite method.

4.3.2.1 Rankine's Method of Tangential/Deflection Angles

(a) Theory

Before going to discussions on the Rankine's method of tangential/deflection angles, we will get clarified some commonly used terms in this method.

Chord (Unit Chord or Sub Chord) : It is a line joining peg under consideration on the curve to its immediate previous peg. In a Fig. 4.17 below straights T_1D, DE, EF are chords.

Whole Chord : It is a line joining peg under consideration on the curve to rear/first or forward/second tangent point. In a Fig. 4.17 below T_1D, T_1E, T_1F are whole chords.

Tangential Angles or Individual Tangential Angle : It is a angle made by chord under consideration with a tangent drawn at its start point. It is usually denoted by δ. In Fig. 4.17 below $\delta_1, \delta_2, \delta_3$ are individual deflection angles for first peg D, second peg E and third peg F on the curve respectively. Tangential angles are also called as deflection angles.

Total Tangential Angles: It is angle made by whole chord to that peg on the curve with the rear tangent. It is denoted by Δ. In Fig. 4.17 below $\Delta_1, \Delta_2, \Delta_3$ are total deflection angles for first peg D, second peg E and third peg F on the curve respectively.

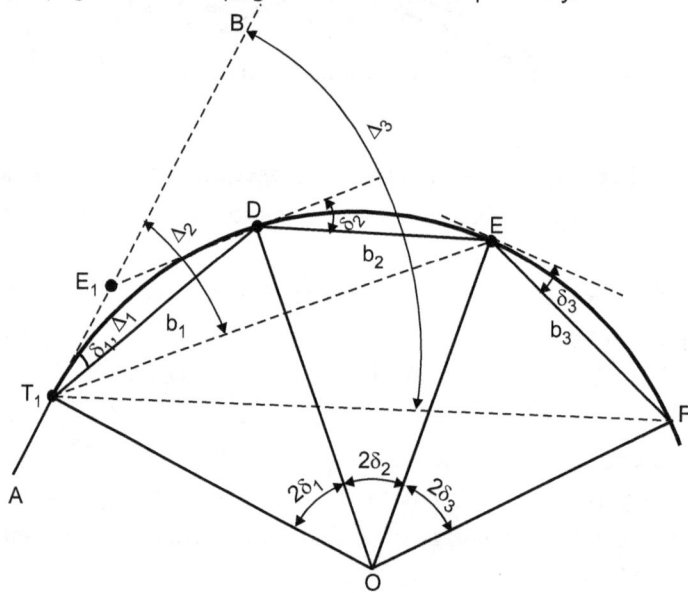

Fig. 4.17 : Rankine's Method of Deflection Angles

Relation for Individual Tangential/Deflection Angle (δ_n) for n^{th} peg :

Let $\angle BT_1D = \delta_1$ = Individual tangential/deflection angle to set out first peg D on the curve.

As AB is perpendicular to OT_1, $\angle DT_1O = 90 - \delta_1 = \angle T_1DO$

∴ $\angle T_1OD = 180 - 2 \cdot (90 - \delta_1) = 2 \cdot \delta_1$

Let us assume that length b_1 of chord T_1D = Arc T_1D

∴ $b_1 = R \cdot [(\angle T_1OD)^c] = R \cdot [\pi \cdot (\angle T_1OD)°/180]$ but $\angle T_1OD = 2\delta_1$

∴ $b_1 = R \cdot [\pi \cdot (2\delta_1)°/180] = \pi \cdot R \cdot \delta_1°/90$

∴ $\delta_1° = 90 \cdot b_1/(\pi \cdot R)$

$\delta_1° = 28.648 \cdot b_1/R$

Same way $\delta_2° = 28.648 \cdot b_2/R$, $\delta_3° = 28.648 \cdot b_3/R$, $\delta_4° = 28.648 \cdot b_4/R$,

Hence individual tangential/deflection angle for n^{th} peg = **$\delta n° = 28.648 \cdot b_n/R$**

Since $b_2 = b_3 = ... = b_{n-1}$ = Unit chords, Individual tangential angles $\delta_2 = \delta_3 = ... = \delta_{n-1}$

Relation for Total Tangential/Deflection Angle (Δ_n) for n^{th} peg :

Total tangential/deflection angle for 1st peg D on curve = $\angle BT_1D = \Delta_1 = \delta_1$
Total tangential/deflection angle for 2nd peg E on curve = Δ_2
And $\Delta_2 = \angle BT_1E = \angle BT_1D + \angle DT_1E$
But $\angle BT_1D = \Delta_1$ and $\angle DT_1E$ is the angle subtended by the chord DE in opposite segment, and therefore = Tangential $\angle \delta_2$.
$\therefore$ Total deflection angle for 2nd peg = $\Delta_2 = \Delta_1 + \delta_2$
Same way total tangential/deflection angle for 3rd peg F on curve = Δ_3
And $\Delta_3 = \angle BT_1F = \angle BT_1E + \angle ET_1F = \Delta_2 + \delta_3$
Same way $\Delta_4 = \Delta_3 + \delta_4$, $\Delta_5 = \Delta_4 + \delta_5$, $\Delta_6 = \Delta_5 + \delta_6$, and so on
Total deflection angle to set out n^{th} peg $\Delta_n = \Delta_{n-1} + \delta_n$

Example 4.14 : Two tangents intersect at chainage of 1250 m. The angle of intersection is 150°. Calculate all data necessary for setting out a curve of radius 250 m by deflection angle method. The peg interval may be taken as 20 m.

Solution : Given : Chainage of point of intersection, CPI = 1250 m, Angle of intersection, I = 150°, Radius of the curve, R = 250 m. Peg interval (on curve), P = 20 m

Primary Calculations :

Deflection angle, ϕ = 180 – I = 180 – 150 = 30°.
Tangent length, $l = R \cdot \tan(\phi/2) = 250 \times \tan(30°/2) = 66.987$ m
Chainage of first tangent point,
CT_1 = CPI – l = 1250 – 66.987 = 1183.013 m
Length of curve, $L = \pi \cdot R \cdot \phi°/180 = \pi \times 250 \times 30° \div 180 = 130.900$ m
Chainage of second tangent point,
$CT_2 = CT_1 + L$
= 1183.013 + 130.900 = 1313.913 m
Peg interval on curve, P = 20 m ... Given
Chainage of peg on rear straight prior to T_1,
= CS = [Integer part of ($CT_1 \div P_{Straight}$)] × $P_{Straight}$.

Where $P_{Straight}$ is the peg interval on straight. It is also not given, hence assuming it as peg interval P (20 m) on curve.

$\therefore$ CS = [Integer part of (1183.013 ÷ 20)] × 20
= [Integer part of (59.151)] × 20
= [59] × 20 = 1180 m

Chainage of first peg on curve, CP_1 = CS + P = 1180 + 20 = 1200 m
This is > CT_1 i.e. 1183.013 m, therefore alright.
Length of sub chord at beginning of the curve,

$$b_1 = CP_1 - CT_1$$
$$= 1200 - 1183.013 \text{ m}$$
$$= 16.987 \text{ m}$$

Number of unit chords = n = Integer part of $[(L - b_1) \div P]$
$$= \text{Integer part of } [(130.900 - 16.987) \div 20]$$
$$= \text{Integer part of } [(113.913) \div 20]$$
$$= \text{Integer part of } [5.696]$$
$$= 5$$

Length of sub-chord at end of the curve,
$$b_{T2} = L - n \cdot P - b_1$$
$$= 130.900 - 5 \times 20 - 16.987$$
$$= 13.913 \text{ m}$$

Working out Deflection Angles :

We know, individual tangential/deflection angle for n^{th} peg = $\delta n = (28.648 \cdot b_n/R)°$

∴ Chord length to set out first peg is 16.987 m, therefore individual deflection angle to set out first peg = $\delta_1 = (28.648 \times 16.987 \div 250)° = 1.947° = 1°56'48''$.

Chord length to set out 2nd to 6th peg is 20 m, therefore individual deflection angle to set out 2nd to 6th peg = δ_2 to $\delta_6 = (28.648 \times 20 \div 250)° = 2.292° = 2°17'31''$.

Chord length to set out last peg, T_2 is 13.913 m, therefore individual deflection angle to set out last peg, $T_2 = \delta_{T2} = (28.648 \times 13.913 \div 250)° = 1.594° = 1°35'40''$.

Peg on Curve	Chord length to set out n^{th} Peg, b_n m	Chainage in m	Deflection Angle $\delta n° = 28.648 \cdot b_n/R$	Total Deflection Angle, Δ_n		Remark
				Calculated Value $\Delta_n = \Delta_{n-1} + \delta_n$	Value for setting out with 20" Theodolite	
T_1	---	1183.013	---	---	---	First tangent Point
1	$b_1 = 16.987$	1200	$\delta_1 = 1°56'48''$	$\Delta_1 = \delta_1 = 1°56'48''$	1°56'40"	
2	$b_2 = 20$	1220	δ_2 to $\delta_6 =$ 2°17'31"	$\Delta_2 = \Delta_1 + \delta_2 = 4°14'19''$	4°14'20"	
3	$b_3 = 20$	1240		$\Delta_3 = \Delta_2 + \delta_3 = 6°31'50''$	6°31'40"	
4	$b_4 = 20$	1260		$\Delta_4 = \Delta_3 + \delta_4 = 8°49'21''$	8°49'20"	
5	$b_5 = 20$	1280		$\Delta_5 = \Delta_4 + \delta_5 = 11°6'52''$	11°7'00"	
6	$b_6 = 20$	1300		$\Delta_6 = \Delta_5 + \delta_6 = 13°24'23''$	13°24'20"	
T_2	$b_{T2} = 13.913$	1313.913	$\delta_{T2} = 1°35'40''$	$\Delta_{T2} = \Delta_6 + \delta_{T2} = 15°0'3''$	15°0'0"	Second Tangent Point

Check : Last total deflection angle, Δ_{T2} must be equal to $\phi/2$. Here ϕ is 30° and Δ_{T2} is 15°, therefore alright.

4.3.2.1 (b) Field Procedure to Set out Curve by Rankine's Method of Deflection Angles

1. Knowing point B of intersection and tangent length, get established two more control points T_1 and T_2 on rear straight AB and forward straight BC respectively, so that $T_1B = BT_2 = $ Tangent length (l).
2. Set up a theodolite at rear tangent point T_1, set horizontal circle window A to 0°0'0" and by rotating instrument about outer spindle bisect point B of intersection.
3. Set horizontal circle window A to Δ_1 by rotating instrument about inner spindle and bring line of sight along T_1D.
4. Open the tape through b_1, by holding its zero end at T_1. Swing other end of the tape in stretched condition till it comes in line of sigth of theodolite at T_1 to mark 1st peg D on curve.
5. Again by rotating the instrument about inner spindle Set horizontal circle window A to Δ_2 and bring line of sight along T_1E.
6. Open the tape through b_2, by holding its zero end at D. Swing other end of the tape in stretched condition till it comes in line of sigth of theodolite at T_1 to mark 2nd peg E on curve.
7. Repeat the process till you mark last point T_2 on curve. Measure the distance between T_2 initially marked as control point and T_2 marked finally in the process of setting out and record this distance as closing error. Express the closing error as % of total length of curve.

Example 4.15 : Tabulate the data required for setting out a circular curve by the deflection angle method, considering the following information:
  (i) Angle of intersection = 135°
  (ii) Chainage of point of intersection = 1620 m
  (iii) Degree of curve = 5°
  (iv) Peg interval = 30 m

Solution : Given : Chainage of point of intersection, CPI = 1620 m, Angle of intersection, I = 135°, Degree of the curve, D = 5°. Peg interval (on curve), P = 30 m

As primary calculations can not be carried ahead without radius 'R' of the curve and deflection angle 'ϕ', hence let us first workout radius 'R' and deflection angle 'ϕ' for the curve from its given degree 'D' angle of intersection 'I'.

We know, Radius of curve, R = 1718.9/ D°
When standard chord length (i.e. peg interval) is 30 m.

Then radius, R = 1718.9 ÷ 5 = 343.78 say 344 m
We know, Deflection angle, ϕ = 180 − I = 180 − 135 = 45°.

Primary Calculations

Tangent length, l = R · tan (ϕ/2) = 344 × tan (45°/2) = 142.490 m
Chainage of first tangent point, CT_1 = CPI − l = 1620 − 142.490 = 1477.51 m
Length of curve, L = π · R · ϕ°/180 = π × 344 × 45° ÷ 180 = 270.177 m
Chainage of second tangent point,
$$CT_2 = CT_1 + L$$
$$= 1477.51 + 270.177 = 1747.687 \text{ m}$$

Peg interval on curve, P = 30 m ... Given
Chainage of peg on rear straight prior to T_1 = CS = [Integer part of (CT_1 ÷ $P_{Straight}$)] × $P_{Straight}$.

Where $P_{Straight}$ is the peg interval on straight. It is not given, let us assume it same as like that of peg interval P (i.e. 30 m) on curve.

∴ CS = [Integer part of (1477.51 ÷ 30)] × 30
= [Integer part of (49.250)] × 30
= [49] × 30 = 1470 m

Chainage of first peg on curve, CP_1 = CS + P = 1470 + 30 = 1500 m
This is > CT_1 i.e. 1477.51 m, therefore alright.
Length of sub-chord at beginning of the curve,
$$b_1 = CP_1 - CT_1$$
$$= 1500 - 1477.51 \text{ m}$$
$$= 22.49 \text{ m}$$

Number of unit chords = n = Integer part of [(L − b_1) ÷ P]
= Integer part of [(270.177 − 22.49) ÷ 30]
= Integer part of [(247.687) ÷ 30]
= Integer part of [8.256]
= 8

Length of sub-chord at end of the curve,
$$b_{T2} = L - n \cdot P - b_1$$
$$= 270.177 - 8 \times 30 - 22.49$$
$$= 7.687 \text{ m}$$

There are 8 unit chords and 2 sub chords, means total number of chords is (8 + 2) = 10. Hence, to set out this curve we will require total (10 + 1) i.e. 11 points including first tangent point T_1 and second tangent point T_2. That means we will require to set out total 9 pegs in between T_1 and T_2 and excluding pegs at T_1 and T_2.

Working out Deflection Angles :

We know, individual tangential/deflection angle for n^{th} peg = δn = $(28.648 \cdot b_n/R)°$

Chord length to set out first peg is 22.49 m, therefore individual deflection angle to set out first peg = δ_1 = $(28.648 \times 22.49 \div 344)°$ = $1.873°$ = $1°52'23"$.

Chord length to set out 2nd to 9th peg is 30 m, therefore individual deflection angle to set out 2nd to 9th peg = δ_2 to δ_9 = $(28.648 \times 30 \div 344)°$ = $2.498°$ = $2°29'54"$.

Chord length to set out last peg, T_2 is 7.687 m, therefore individual deflection angle to set out last peg, T_2 = δ_{T2} = $(28.648 \times 7.687 \div 344)°$ = $0.640°$ = $0°38'25"$.

Sr. No.	Peg on Curve	Chord length to set out n^{th} Peg, b_n in m	Chainage in m	Individual Deflection Angle $\delta n°$ = 28.648 $\cdot$ $b_n \div R$	Total Deflection Angle, Δ_n Calculated Value $\Delta_n = \Delta_{n-1} + \delta_n$	Value for setting out with 20" Theodolite	Remark
1	T_1	--	1477.51	--	--	--	T_1 is First Tgt. Point
2	1	b_1 = 22.49	1500	δ_1 = 1°52'23"	Δ_1 = δ_1 = 1°52'23"	1°52'20"	
3	2	b_2 = 30	1530		Δ_2 = Δ_1 + δ_2 = 4°22'17"	4°22'20"	
4	3	b_3 = 30	1560		Δ_3 = Δ_2 + δ_3 = 6°52'11"	6°52'20"	
5	4	b_4 = 20	1590		Δ_4 = Δ_3 + δ_4 = 9°22'05"	9°22'00"	
6	5	b_5 = 30	1620	δ_2 to δ_9 = 2°29'54"	Δ_5 = Δ_4 + δ_5 = 11°51'59"	11°52'00"	
7	6	b_6 = 30	1650		Δ_6 = Δ_5 + δ_6 = 14°21'53"	14°22'00"	
8	7	B_7 = 30	1680		Δ_7 = Δ_6 + δ_5 = 16°51'47"	16°51'40"	
9	8	B_8 = 30	1710		Δ_8 = Δ_7 + δ_8 = 19°21'41"	19°21'40"	
10	9	B_9 = 30	1740		Δ_9 = Δ_8 + δ_9 = 21°51'35"	21°51'40"	
11	T_2	b_{T2} = 7.687	1747.687	δ_{T2} = 0°38'25"	Δ_{T2} = Δ_9 + δ_{T2} = 22°30'00"	15°0'0"	T_2 is Second Tgt. Point

Check : Last total deflection angle, Δ_{T2} must be equal to $(\phi/2)$. Here ϕ is 45° and Δ_{T2} is 22°30', therefore alright.

4.4 COMPOUND CURVES

When two straights (Say AB and BC) of a route are connected by two circular arcs (Say Arc T_1F and FT_2) of different radii (Say R_1 and R_2) with a common point of tangency (Say F) and centres (O_1 and O_2) being on same side of the common tangent (Say GFH) is called as compound circular curve.

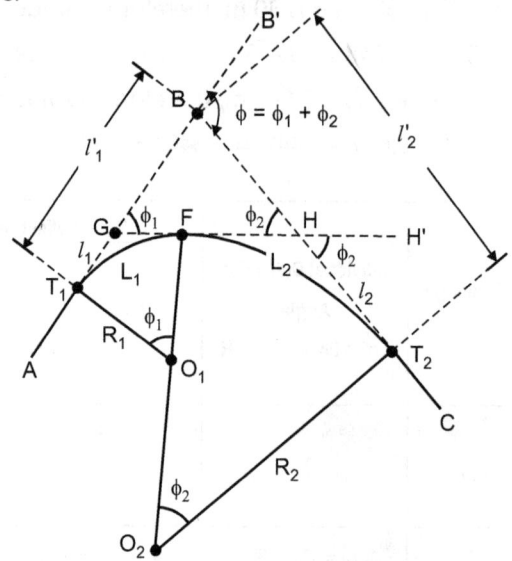

Fig. 4.18 : Compound Circular Curve

- B = Point of intersection of the straights.
- O_1 and O_2 = Centres of the first (T_1F) and second (FT_2) circular arcs.
- T_1 = Point of tangency for first circular arc T_1F with rear tangent T_1B
- T_2 = Point of tangency for second circular arc FT_2 with forward tangent BT_2
- F = Point of Compound Curvature or Common Point of Tangency
- G = Point of intersection of the common tangent GH with rear straight AB
- H = Point of intersection of the same common tangent GH with forward straight BC
- AB and BC = Straights of a route.
- R_1 and R_2 = Radii of the first and second circular arcs.
- T_1G and GF = Tangent lengths for first circular arc = l_1.
- FH and HT_2 = Tangent lengths for 2nd circular arc = l_2.
- GH = Length of common tangent
- T_1B = Length of rear tangent to the compound circular arc $T_1FT_2 = l_1'$.
- BT_2 = Length of forward tangent to the compound circular arc $T_1FT_2 = l_2'$.

4.4.1 Elements of Compound Curve

1. **Deflection Angles :**
   Deflection angle for first circular arc = $\angle BGH = \phi_1$
   Deflection angle for second circular arc = $\angle H'\, H\, T_2 = \phi_2$
   Total Deflection Angle = $\angle B'\, BC = \phi = \phi_1 + \phi_2$

2. **Tangent Lengths :**
   Tangent lengths for first circular arc = T_1G and $GF = l_1 = R_1 \cdot \tan(\phi_1/2)$
   Tangent lengths for second circular arc = FH and $HT_2 = l_2 = R_2 \cdot \tan(\phi_2/2)$
   Length of common tangent $GH = GF + FH = l_1 + l_2$

3. **Curve Lengths :**
   Length of first circular arc = Length of circular arc $T_1F = L_1 = \pi \cdot R_1 \cdot \phi_1°/180$
   Length of first circular arc = Length of circular arc $FT_2 = L_2 = \pi \cdot R_2 \cdot \phi_2°/180$

4. **Length of Tangents to Compound Arc :**
   Length of Rear Tangent to the compound circular arc T_1FT_2 = Length $T_1B = l_1'$
   And $\quad l_1' = T_1B = T_1G + GB = l_1 + GB$
   But $\quad GB = \dfrac{GH \cdot \sin(GHB)}{\sin(GBH)} = \dfrac{(l_1 + l_2) \times \sin\phi_2}{\sin[180 - (\phi_1 + \phi_2)]} = \dfrac{(l_1 + l_2) \times \sin\phi_2}{\sin\phi}$
   $\therefore \quad l_1' = l_1 + \dfrac{(l_1 + l_2) \times \sin\phi_2}{\sin\phi}$

   Length of Forward Tangent to the compound circular arc T_1FT = Length $BT_2 = l_2'$
   And $\quad l_2' = BT_2 = HT_2 + BH = l_2 + BH$
   But $\quad BH = \dfrac{GH \cdot \sin(HGB)}{\sin GBH} = \dfrac{(l_1 + l_2) \times \sin\phi_1}{\sin[180 - (\phi_1 + \phi_2)]} = \dfrac{(l_1 + l_2) \times \sin\phi_1}{\sin\phi}$
   $\therefore \quad l_2' = l_2 + \dfrac{(l_1 + l_2) \times \sin\phi_1}{\sin\phi}$

   To work out the data necessary for setting out, out of the parameters R_1, R_2, ϕ, ϕ_1, ϕ_2, l_1', l_2' four must be known in addition to the chainage CPI of point of intersection, rest three may be worked out with equations stated above.

   To set out a compound curve the surveyor shall know the chainages of the control or key points such as T_1, G, F H and T_2.

4.4.2 Working out Chainages of Key or Control Points for a Compound Curve

Chainage of point B of intersection = CPI ... (Usually given or known)
Chainage of first or rear tangent point T_1 of compound curve = CT_1
$\quad CT_1 = CPI - l_1'$

where l_1' = Length of first or rear tangent to compound curve.

Chainage of point F of compound curvature = CF

$$CF = CT_1 + L_1$$

where L_1 is length of first circular arc T_1F.

Chainage of second or forward tangent point T_2 of compound curve = CT_2

$$CT_2 = CF + L_2$$

where L_2 is length of second circular arc FT_2.

4.4.3 Field Procedure to set out a Compound Curve

1. Mark rear tangent point T_1 on straight AB at a distance l_1' from point B of intersection. l_1' is the length of rear tangent T_1B to a compound curve.
2. Mark forward tangent point T_2 on straight BC at a distance l_2' from point B of intersection. l_2' is length of forward tangent BT_2 to a compound curve. T_1, B and T_2 are primary control points for the process of setting out.
3. Mark point G on straight AB in between T_1 and B at a distance l_1 so that distance $T_1G = l_1 \cdot l_1$ is the tangent lengths for first circular arc.
4. Mark point H on straight BC in between B and T_2 at a distance l_2 so that distance $T_2H = l_2 \cdot l_2$ is the tangent lengths for second circular arc.
5. Ascertain that field length common tangent GH tallies with its calculated value. Mark point F on GH at a distance l_1 from G or l_2 from H. Points G, H and F are secondary control points.
6. Ascertain that field length of long chord T_1F for first circular arc = $2R_1 \cdot \sin(\phi_1/2)$ and field length of long chord FT_2 for second circular arc = $2R_2 \cdot \sin(\phi_2/2)$ or ascertain that
$$\angle T_1FT_2 \text{ is} = \left\{180 - \left(\frac{\phi_1}{2} + \frac{\phi_2}{2}\right)\right\} = \left\{180 - \frac{(\phi_1 + \phi_2)}{2}\right\}$$
7. Now set out first circular arc from rear tangent point T_1 and second circular arc from point F of compound curvature either by method of offset from chord produced or by method of deflection angles or any other suitable method.

Example 4.16 : Two straight lines AB and BC are intersected by a line MN. The angle AMN and MNC are 145° and 140° respectively. The radius of first curve is 400 m and that of second curve is 600 m. Find the chainages of tangent points and the point of compound curvature, given that the chainage of the point of intersection is 5555 m.

Solution : Given : Chainage of point B of intersection = CPI = 5555 m.

Angle of intersection for first circular arc = ∠AMN = I_1 = 145°
Angle of intersection for second circular arc = ∠MNC = I_2 = 140°
Radius of first circular arc = R_1 = 400 m.
Radius of second circular arc = R_2 = 600 m.

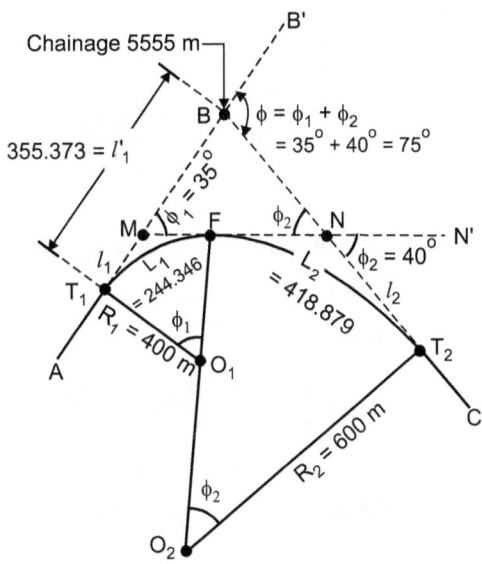

Fig. 4.19 : Figure to support Example 4.16 on Compound Curve

1. **Deflection Angles :**
   Deflection angle for first circular arc = ∠BMN = ϕ_1 = 180 − ∠AMN = 180 − 145° = 35°
   Deflection angle for second circular arc = ∠N'N T_2 = ϕ_2 = ∠MNB = 180 − ∠MNC
   = 180 − 140° = 40°
   Total Deflection angle = ∠B'BC = ϕ = ϕ_1 + ϕ_2 = 35° + 40° = 75°

2. **Tangent Lengths :**
   Tangent lengths for first circular arc = T_1M and
   MF = l_1 = R1 · tan (ϕ_1/2) = 400 · tan (35/2) = 126.120 m
   Tangent lengths for second circular arc = FN and
   NT_2 = l_2 = R_2 · tan (ϕ_2/2) = 600 · tan (40/2) = 218.382 m
   Length of common tangent MN = MF + FN = l_1 + l_2 = 126.120 + 218.382 = 344.502

3. **Curve Lengths :**
   Length of first circular arc = Length of circular arc T_1F = L_1 = π · R_1 · ϕ_1°/180
   = π × 400 × 35 ÷ 180
   = 244.346 m

Length of second circular arc = Length of circular arc $FT_2 = L_2 = \pi \cdot R_2 \cdot \phi_2°/180$

$= \pi \times 600 \times 40 \div 180$

$= 418.879$ m

4. **Length of Tangents to Compound Arc :**

   Length of Rear Tangent to the compound circular arc T_1FT_2 = Length $T_1B = l_1'$

   And $l_1' = T_1B = T_1M + MB = l_1 + MB$

   $= l_1 + \dfrac{(l_1 + l_2) \times \sin \phi_2}{\sin \phi}$

   $= 126.120 + \dfrac{(344.502) \times \sin 40}{\sin 75}$

   ∴ $l_1' = 126.120 + 229.253 = 355.373$

   Length of Forward Tangent to the compound circular arc T_1FT_2 = Length $BT_2 = l_2'$

   And $l_2' = BT_2 = NT_2 + BN = l_2 + BN$

   $= l_2 + \dfrac{(l_1 + l_2) \times \sin \phi_1}{\sin \phi}$

   $= 218.382 + \dfrac{(344.502) \times \sin 35}{\sin 75}$

   ∴ $l_2' = 218.382 + 204.569 = 422.95$

5. **Chainages of Key or Control Points for a Compound Curve :**

   Chainage of first or rear tangent point T_1 of compound curve = CT_1

   $CT1 = CPI - l_1'$

   $= 5555 - 355.373$

   $= 5199.627$ m

   Chainage of point F of compound curvature = CF

   $CF = CT_1 + L_1$

   $= 5199.627 + 244.346$

   $= 5443.973$ m

   Chainage of second or forward tangent point T_2 of compound curve = CT_2

   $CT_2 = CF + L_2$

   $= 5443.973 + 418.879$

   $= 5862.852$ m

Example 4.17 : A road is to be curved to avoid an obstacle. The forward straight deflects right of the rear straight through an angle of 145°. It is a compound curve. The radii of the left and right component curves of this compound curve are 480 m and 300 m respectively. The distance between point of intersection rear and forward straight and the tangent point at which left curve of radius 480 m leaves the straight is 1240.8 m Calculate length of forward tangent and curve length for whole curve.

Solution : Given : Radius of left component curve (R_1) = 480 m, Radius of right component curve (R_2) = 300 m. Length of rear tangent for whole curve (l_1') = 1240.8 m. Deflection angle through which forward straight deflects with respect to rear straight (ϕ) = 145°.

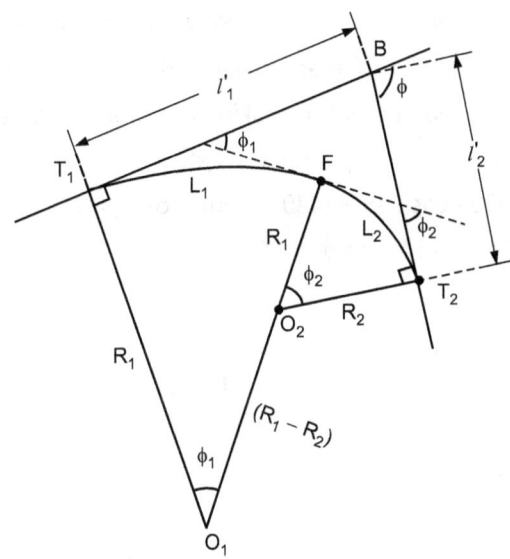

Fig. 4.20 : Figure to support Example 4.17 on Compound Curve

The equations for a compound curve can also be derived by considering traverse $O_1T_1BT_2O_2$ as a closed traverse and applying usual condition of a closed traverse.

Assuming the direction O_1T_1 as north, the particulars required to apply the usual check are tabulated below.

Line	WCB (θ_n)	Length (l_n)	Latitude, $L_n = l_n \cdot \cos \theta_n$	Departure, $D_n = = l_n \cdot \sin \theta_n$
O_1T_1	00°	R_1	R_1	00
T_1B	90°	l_1'	00	l_1'
BT_2	90° + ϕ	l_2'	$l_2' \cdot \cos(90° + \phi) = - l_2' \cdot \sin \phi$	$l_2' \cdot \sin(90° + \phi) = l_2' \cdot \cos \phi$
T_2O_2	180° + ϕ	R_2	$R_2 \cdot \cos(180° + \phi) = - R_2 \cdot \cos \phi$	$R_2 \cdot \sin(180° + \phi) = - R_2 \cdot \sin \phi$
O_2O_1	180° + ϕ_1	$R_1 - R_2$	$(R_1 - R_2) \cdot \cos(180° + \phi_1) = - (R_1 - R_2) \cdot \cos \phi_1$	$(R_1 - R_2) \cdot \sin(180° + \phi_1) = - (R_1 - R_2) \cdot \sin \phi_1$

We know for a closed traverse, $\Sigma L_n = 00$ and $\Sigma D_n = 00$

$\therefore \quad \Sigma L_n = R_1 - l_2' \cdot \sin \phi - R_2 \cdot \cos \phi - (R_1 - R_2) \cdot \cos \phi_1 = 00 \quad \ldots (1)$

$\therefore \quad \Sigma D_n = l_1' + l_2' \cdot \cos \phi - R_2 \cdot \sin \phi - (R_1 - R_2) \cdot \sin \phi_1 = 00 \quad \ldots (2)$

And we know, for a compound curve,

$$\phi_1 + \phi_2 = \phi \quad \ldots (3)$$

Actually there are seven unknowns l_1', l_2', R_1, R_2, ϕ_1, ϕ_2 and ϕ, but only three equilibrium equations are available, hence out of these seven unknowns four must be known so that values of rest of three can be worked out by making use of above three equations.

Putting values R_1, R_2, l_1' and ϕ, in equation (1) first

$480 - l_2' \cdot \sin 145° - 300 \cdot \cos 145 - (480 - 300) \cdot \cos \phi_1 = 00$

$480 - 0.574 \, l_2' + 245.746 - 180 \cdot \cos \phi_1 = 00$

$\quad -0.574 \, l_2' - 180 \cos \phi_1 = -725.746 \quad \ldots (3)$

Now putting values R_1, R_2, l_1' and ϕ, in equation (2)

$1240.8 + l_2' \cos 145 - 300 \cdot \sin 145 - (480 - 300) \cdot \sin \phi_1 = 00$

$1240.8 - 0.810 \, l_2' - 172.073 - 180 \cdot \sin \phi_1 = 00$

$\quad -0.810 \, l_2' - 180 \cdot \sin \phi_1 = -1068.727 \quad \ldots (4)$

Solving equations (3) and (4) simultaneously,

$\phi_1 = 75°,$

$l_2' = 1183.6 \text{ m} \quad \ldots \text{Ans (1)}$

Putting $\phi_1 = 75°$, $\phi_2 = 145° - 75° = 70°$

Curve length for whole curve = $L_1 + L_2 = (\pi \cdot R_1 \cdot \phi_1°/180) + (\pi \cdot R_2 \cdot \phi_2°/180)$

$\qquad = (\pi \times 480 \times 75°/180) + (\pi \times 300 \times 70°/180)$

$\qquad = 627.9 + 366.3$

$\qquad = 994.2 \text{ m}$

4.5 TRANSITION CURVE

4.5.1 Introduction and Definition

In case of simple circular curve at the point of tangency the radius of curvature suddenly changes from infinity that is the radius of straight line to some finite value that is the radius of circular curve or vice versa.

The special curve introduced between the straight and the circular arc and whose radius gradually varies from infinity that is the radius of straight to some finite value that is the radius of circular curve or vice versa is called as transition curve.

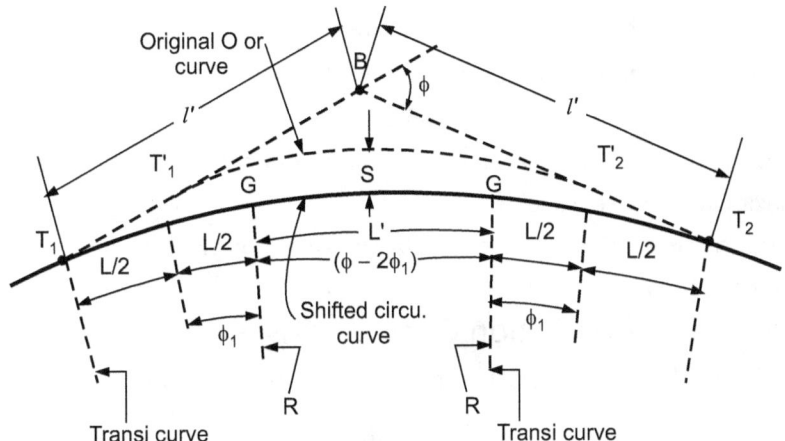

Fig. 4.21: Transition Curve

4.5.2 Reasons for or Objects behind the Provision of the Transition Curve (OR Where and Why – the Transition Curve?)

In case of vehicles without steering arrangement like that of rolling stock (i.e. wagons, oaches and locomotives) on railways or in case of vehicles moving at high speed on expressways, if the direction of vehicle is not changed or assisted to change gradually from straight to circular arc or vice versa by the route itself, the vehicle will follow the same path on which it is moving while approaching the curved section and will get derailed/derouted. Hence a transition curve will required to be introduced in between the straight and circular arc which will change in case of steeringless vehicles or assist to change in case of steeringed vehicles the direction gradually from straight to circular arc and vice a versa.

We know that on circular path the vehicle of mass M experiences the centrifugal force, $F = (M \cdot v^2/g \cdot R)$, where v is speed of vehicle and R is radius of curve. If speed v of the vehicle is constant then the magnitude of centrifugal force solely and inversely depends on radius R of the curved path. On straight path radius is infinity, hence the centrifugal force F is zero and thus no super elevation is required. On circular curved path, radius is finite and centrifugal force is maximum and thus maximum super elevation is required. That means at point of tangency of circular curve, the super elevation shall change suddenly from zero to maximum, which is practically not possible from safety and comfort point of view. Thus super elevation shall change gradually from zero to maximum or vice a versa. To obtain zero super elevation, radius of curvature shall be infinity and to obtain maximum super elevation radius shall be equal to R that is the radius of adopted circular curve. Thus one will require introducing a transition curve between the straight and the circular or vice versa.

4.5.3 Functions of the Transition Curves
1. To introduce gradually, the curvature from that of the straight tangent to that of the circular arc.
2. To provide medium for gradual change for introduction of super elevation from zero to maximum and vice versa.
3. To allow smooth, safe and comfortable movement of traffic at entry and exit sections of the circular curve.

4.5.4 Advantages of Transition Curve
1. It eliminates dangers of derailment or deroutement, overturning and side slipping of the vehicles.
2. It permits provision of super elevation in proportion to increase in curvature from that of the straight to that of the circular arc.
3. It eliminates discomfort to the passengers on account of sudden change in degree of curvature.

4.5.5 Requirements of an Ideal Transition Curve
1. It should meet the straight and circular curve tangentially.
2. Its curvature should be zero at its origin on the straight.
3. Its radius at the junction with circular curve should match that of the circular curve.
4. Its curvature shall increase at the same rate as like that of the super elevation.
5. Its length should be sufficient to allow attainment of full super elevation at its end.

4.5.6 Various Forms/Shapes/Types of the Transition Curve
Following are the commonly used types or forms of the transition curves:
(a) Clothoid or true Spiral, (b) Cubic Parabola and (c) Lemniscate.

1. Clothoid or True Spiral :

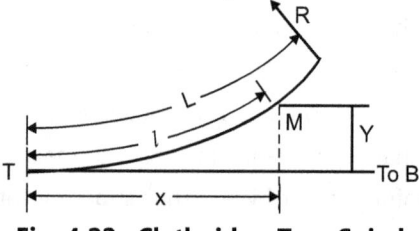

Fig. 4.22 : Clothoid or True Spiral

The equation of this curve is
$$y = \frac{l^3}{6RL}\left(1 - \frac{l^4}{56R^2 L^2}\right)$$
where y is perpendicular offset to any point M from initial tangent TB, l is the distance of point M from origin T of the transition curve being measured along the curve, L is the total length of transition curve and R is radius of circular curve.

Such type of curves is more preferred on railways.

2. Cubic Parabola :

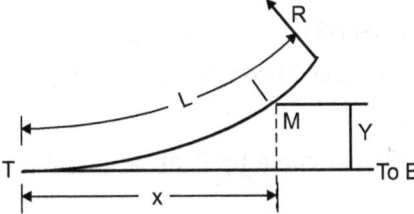

Fig. 4.23 : Cubic Parabola

The equation of this curve is

$$y = \frac{x^3}{6RL}$$

where y is perpendicular offset to any point M from initial tangent TB,

x is the distance of point M from origin T of the transition curve being measured along the X axis, L is the total length of transition curve and R is radius of circular curve.

Such type of curves is most convenient on railways. Indian Railways is using it from long back.

3. Lemniscate Curve :

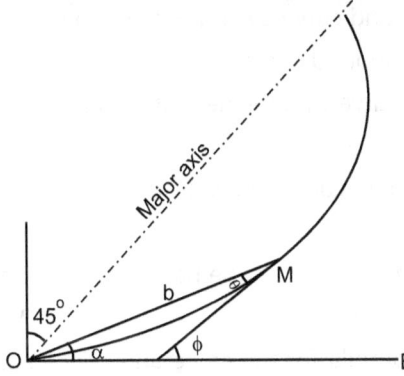

Fig. 4.24 : Lemniscate

It is easier to work with polar coordinates in case of Bernoulli's Lemniscate. The polar equation of Bernoulli' lemniscates is

$$b = K\sqrt{(\sin 2\alpha)}$$

where b is length OM of polar ray, α is polar deflection angle and K is constant.

For the lemniscates, the deviation angle (ϕ) is exactly equal to three times the polar deflection angle (α). For clothoid or cubic parabola this relation is approximately true.

Lemniscates are used in preference to the spirals on highways.

REVIEW QUESTIONS

(1) Define a simple circular curve and derive a relation between its degree and radius, assuming a unit chord of 30 m length.
(2) Classify the curves into different types. Draw a sketch of simple circular curve showing its various elements.
(3) Define degree of curve. Derive relation between radius and degree of curve.
(4) Write a note on use of curves in highways and railways.
(5) What are the different types of curves? Draw neat sketch of each.
(6) Draw an illustrative sketch of a simple circular curve.
(7) State various types of horizontal curves.
(8) State and derive elements of simple curve.

(9) Draw a neat sketch of a circular curve and show its various elements there upon.
(10) Describe the method of setting out circular curve by offset from chord produced.
(11) Describe how to set a circular curve by perpendicular offsets from the long chord with the help of neat sketch.
(12) Explain the procedure of setting out a simple circular curve by Rankine's method of deflection angles.
(13) List the various methods of setting out simple circular curve. Explain briefly the Rankine's method of deflection angles.
(14) Describe the method of setting out a simple circular curve by Rankine's method of deflection angles using two theodolites.
(15) Draw a neat sketch of a compound curve and show the various elements on it.
(16) Explain the field procedure of setting out compound curve by angular method.
(17) Derive the equations for various elements of compound curve.
(18) Explain the procedure of setting out compound curve with the help of a sketch.
(19) Draw an illustrative sketch of a compound curve.
(20) What are the requirements of a good transition curve? How is the length of a transition curve computed?
(21) Derive an expression for the length of the transition curve on the basis of an arbitrary gradient.
(22) What is shift of curve? State clearly. Give the formula for the same and hence state the reason, why it is necessary to be introduced.
(23) What is meant by transition curve? What are the objectives of providing transition curve? What are the requirements of ideal transition curve?
(24) What is a transition curve? When and why is it used?
(25) State the various formulae to calculate the length of transition curve and also state the meaning of terms involved.
(26) What are the methods of determining the length of a transition curve? Explain any one.
(27) Explain the functions of transition curve.
(28) What is transition curve ? What are the objectives of providing transition curve?
(29) State clearly any four conditions to be fulfilled when a transition curve is introduced between the tangent and the circular curve.

(30) What is reverse curve? Where is a reverse curve used? What are its disadvantages? Illustrate your answer with a neat sketch.
(31) Draw a neat sketch of reverse curve and explain the various notations used on it.
(32) Write short note on location and uses of reverse curves.
(33) Write a short note on use of reverse curves in highways.
(34) Draw an illustrate sketch of a reverse curve to show its various elements.
(35) Explain the use of reverse curves in highways. Also draw a neat labelled sketch of reverse curve.
(36) What is reverse curve? What are its advantages? Draw an illustrative sketch to show all the elements of this curve.
(37) What are the various types of vertical curves? Discuss each with neat sketch.
(38) Draw a neat sketch of circular curve and show thereupon all principal points, lines and angles.
(39) Enumerate the elements of a circular curve and derive the relations for the same.
(40) Enlist the common difficulties in setting out curves. Explain briefly how to overcome them.
(41) Compare the linear method of curve ranging with the angular methods in the context of ease in computations, difficultness in setting out, instruments required, speed of work, suitability against nature of terrain etc.
(42) Suggest a method to set out a curve for street kerb and explain stepwise how to set out the curve by the method suggested.
(43) A client wants to get set out a long and flat curve on railway. Suggest a proper method to do so and explain step by step the procedure for the method suggested.
(44) A curve is to be set out on a reasonably broken barren ground. It is very difficult to follow linear measurements. State which method of curve ranging can be suggested in this case and also describe the procedure to follow in the method suggested.
(45) Explain stepwise procedure to set out a circular curve by the method of radial offsets from tangents.
(46) Explain stepwise procedure to set out a circular curve by the method of perpendicular offsets from tangents.
(47) Explain the procedure of setting out compound curve by linear method.
(48) Define transition curve. State why and where it is essential to introduce a transition curve. Enlist the requirements of an ideal transition curve.

(49) List down various forms of the transition curve and compare them with each other. State which form is more preferred on Indian Railways.

(50) Define vertical curve and with help of suitable sketches bring out difference between two principle types of the vertical curves.

EXAMPLES

1. Two tangents intersect at the chainage 1190 m, the deflection angle being 36°. Calculate tangent length, length of the curve, length of the first and last sub–chord and mid–ordinate. Take radius of curve (R) = 300 m and Peg interval = 30 m.

2. The chainage of the intersection of the two straights having the deflection angle of 50° is 1680.50 m. If the radius of the curve is 450 m, calculate Length of curve, Degree of curve, apex distance and Mid-ordinate.

3. Two tangents AB and BC intersect at a point B at chainage 210 m. Calculate all necessary data for setting out simple circular curve of radius 100 m and deflection angle of 40° by method of offsets from the long chord. Take interval between ordinates as 5.0 m.

4. Calculate the ordinates at 10 m interval for setting out a circular curve of 200 m radius for a deflection angle of 60°. Use method of offsets from the long chord.

5. The chainage of the intersection point of two straights is 2105.59 m and the deflection angle is 45° 20′. A circular curve of 250.00 m radius is to be set out to connect the two straights. Calculate the necessary data for setting out a curve by method of offset from the chord produced.

6. Two tangents AB and BC intersect at chainage 1100 m. The angle of intersection is 140°. Calculate all data necessary for setting out a circular curve of radius 250 m by deflection angle method. The peg interval taken is 20 m. Calculate data for field checking.

7. Calculate the necessary data for setting out a simple circular curve of 350 m radius to connect the two tangents intersecting at the chainage 1238 m, the deflection angle being 36°. Take the peg interval equal to 30 m. Use Rankine's method of deflection angles.

8. Two tangents PQ and QR intersect at chainage 2100 m. The angle of deflection is 40°. Calculate all data necessary for setting out a circular curve of radius 250 m by deflection angle method. The peg interval taken is 20 m. Calculate data for field checking.

9. Two straights AB and BC are intersected by a line MN. The angles AMN and MNC are 145° and 140° respectively. The radius of the first curve is 400 m and that of second curve is 600 m. Find the chainage of tangent points and the point of the compound curvature, given that the chainage of the point of intersection is 5555 m.

10. A compound curve consisting of two simple circular curves of radii 350 m and 500 m, is to be laid out between two straights. The angle of intersection between the tangents and the two straights 25° and 55°. Calculate: Length of common tangent, Length of main tangent.

11. Two straight lines AB and BC intersect at a point B of chainage 1000 m. To avoid an obstacle, another line EF is taken to connect AB and BC so that angle AEF = 135° and angle EFC = 145°. The radius of the first arc is 400 m and that of the second is 200 m. Calculate the chainages of: The tangent points and the points of the compound curvature.

12. Two straight lines intersect at a chainage of 1800 m with a deflection angle of 34°. It is proposed to intersect a circular curve of 575 m radius with a cubic parabolic transition curve 110 m long at each end. Find the chainage of: The beginning and end point of the combined curve; and the junction points. Draw a neat sketch to illustrate your answer.

13. Calculate the length of transition curve, when rate of radial acceleration is 0.3 m/s³, allowable speed on curve is 40 km/hr and the radius of circular curve is 250 m.

14. The chainage of point of intersection is 2750 m, radius of curve is 140 m, angle of intersection is 162°. Calculate chainage of beginning and end of the circular curve. Also find lengths of subchords and length and number of unit chords.

15. A curve for a street kerb is to be set out by method of offsets from long chord. Angle of intersection is 95°. Radius of curve is 60 m. Assume peg interval along long chord as 10m. Work out all necessary data for setting out.

16. Two straights of a road way meet at a deflection angle of 26°. Chainage of point of intersection is 6500 m. Assuming radius of circular curve as 175 m, calculate all the data required to set out the circular curve by method of offset from long chord. Take peg interval as 15 m.

17. Calculate the radial offsets from tangent at 25 m interval (along tangent) to set out a circular curve. Assume radius of curve as 400 m and deflection angle as 60°.

18. Calculate the perpendicular offsets from tangent at 25 m interval (along tangent) to set out a circular curve. Assume radius of curve as 400 m and deflection angle as 60°.

19. Two straights of a railway are proposed to be connected by a circular arc of 2.865°. Deflection angle is 10°. Chainage of point of intersection is 1800 m. Calculate all the data required to set out a curve by angular method of deflection angles with a 20" theodolite. Take peg interval as R/20.

20. Two straight lines PQ and QR intersect at a point Q having chainage 3200 m. To avoid an obstacle, another line AB is taken to connect PQ and QR so that angle PAB = 140° and angle ABR = 150°. The radius of the first arc is 300 m and that of the second is 450m. Calculate length of all tangents and the chainages of all the tangent points.

21. Length of rear tangent (l_1') to the compound arc is 100 m, radius (R_1) of left or first circular arc is 140 m, deflection angle (ϕ_1) for first circular arc is 18°15′, total deflection angle (ϕ) is 42°10′ and chainage of point (B) of intersection 1519.7 m. Calculate – Length of forward tangent (l_2'), radius (R_2) of right or second circular arc, deflection angle (ϕ_2) for second circular arc, chainage of point (F) of compound curvature and chainages of points (T_1 and T_2) of tangency.

22. Two straights AB and BC intersect at chainage of 9000 m, the deflection angle being 46°. It is proposed to insert a right handed circular curve of 600 m radius with a cubic parabolic curve 120 m length at each end. Find the chainages at beginning and end point of combined curve, and also chainages of junction points of circular curve and transition curve.

Unit - V

PLANE TABLE SURVEYING

5.1 INTRODUCTION

Plane Table Survey :

This is simple convenient and quick method of surveying. The main characteristics of this method is that the field observations and the plotting on the land features on a drawing sheet fixed on the horizontal surface of a plane and task proceeds simultaneously.

The table is shifted from one station to the other station for plotting the land details. The map of the filed is already prepared just when the survey is complete.

5.2 OBJECTIVES OF PLANE TABLE SURVEY

After Studying this plane table surveying, you should be able to :
- Know the basic principle of plane table surveying, their advantages and disadvantages.
- Recognize the equipment and accessories used in plane tabling.
- Define the adjustments of plane table.
- Define the procedure of setting up the plane table.
- Know the procedures of recording observations.
- Know various methods of resection.
- Define the possible errors in plane tabling.

5.3 EQUIPMENT REQUIRED FOR PLANE TABLE SURVEY

The main equipments used in plane table surveying are :
(1) Plane Table
(2) U frame with Plumb bob
(3) Alidade
(4) Trough compass
(5) Spirit level

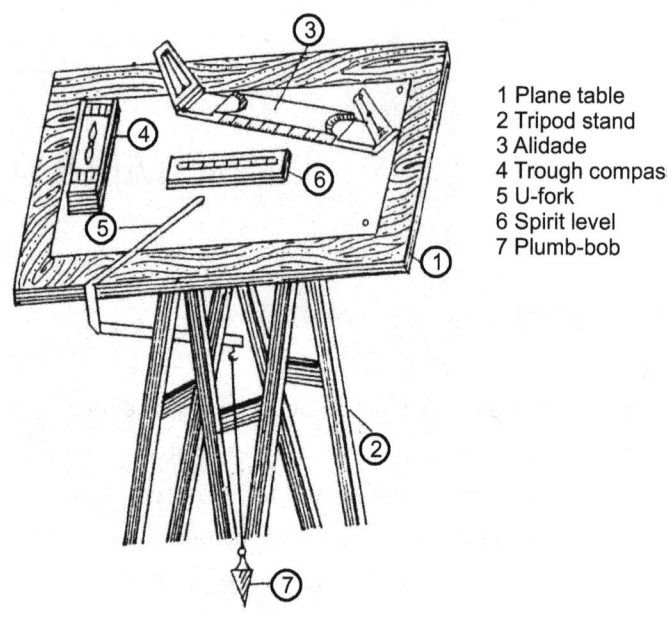

Fig. 5.1 : Equipments in Plane Table Surveying

1 Plane table
2 Tripod stand
3 Alidade
4 Trough compass
5 U-fork
6 Spirit level
7 Plumb-bob

(1) Plane Table :

It is required for providing horizontal surface for the drawing sheet. The top may be adjusted to the horizontal positions at different set up points in the field. The top should be capable of being tilted about two manually perpendicular axes on its surface. For orientation the table should be capable of being rotated about its vertical axis. For the portability the top should be detachable as well as clamped in position while plotting the work. Plane table consists of 'Drawing Board' made up of Pine or Teak having smooth finish. It is having ball and socket arrangement. It is mounted on a tripod (open type foldable frame provided with pointed iron shoes).

(2) U Fork with Plumb Bob :

Used in transferring the station point on the ground vertically above on the drawing sheet on the horizontal plane of the table. U shaped frame with one of its leg horizontal, carrying a pointed end which lies on the vertical line indicated by a plumb line suspended from its other end.

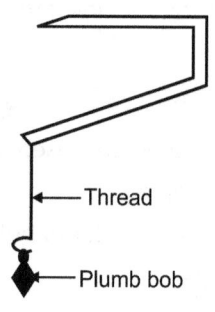

Fig. 5.2 : Indicator Point

(3) Alidade :

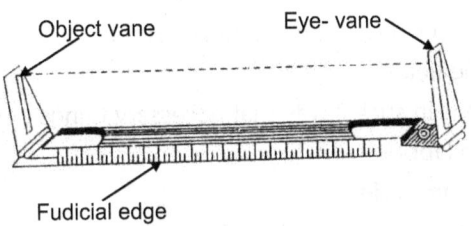

Fig. 5.3 : Alidade

This is employed for drawing rays on the drawing sheet in required directions for locating the field details on the map. It is a combination of a slighting device and a straight edge ruler. One of its edge is levelled and graduated for scaling off line on the map. This working edge is called fiducial edge. It is made up of wood or brass. The sighting device is constituted on two sighting vanes one near the eye of the observer called sight vane with vertical slit, other at the far end of the ruler called object and provided with vertical wire. Both the vanes are hinged to the ruler for the convenience of folding against it.

Requirements for the Workability of an Alidade :

The slit and wire must be vertical when the alidade is placed on the horizontal surface of the table. The alidade cannot be employed for its purpose. For the convenient working of the alidade the length of the alidade should be as nearly as possible equal to the longer dimension of the plane table.

(4) Trough Compass :

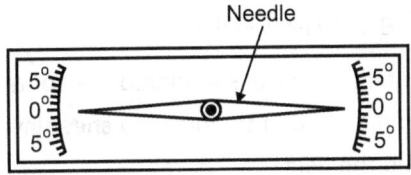

Fig. 5.4 : Trough Compass

It is required for orientation of the drawing sheet with respect to the field by comparing the drawn magnetic North-South line of the field and magnetic North-South line shown on the map with the orientation of the magnetic needle in the trough compass.

(5) Spirit Level :

It is used to ascertain the horizontality of the plane surface.

(6) Drawing sheet, pencil, eraser, engineering drawing, instrument.

(7) Water proof cover.

5.3.1 Procedural Steps in Plane Tabling

(1) Reconnaissance and selection of station points :
- Move around the field.
- Select the stations in such a way that necessary things may be incorporated.
- Use of minimum labour.

(2) Setting up the plane table :
- Drawing paper is to be mounted on the board.

(3) Applying the methods of plane table.

(4) Step 2 and 3 are to be repeated at all the station points.

Mounting of Drawing Sheet on the Plane Table :

(1) Preparation of Drawing Sheet :
- The sheets absorb moisture from the atmosphere and is dried subsequently under the sun.
- It leads to the unequal expansion and contraction of the sheet.
- It introduces error between the plotting and reading of the map.
- The expansion and contraction should be minimum.
- The sheet should be exposed to moisture and drying.
- Zinc and celluloid sheet may be used.

(2) Mounting of the Sheet on the Plane Table :
- The sheet should be so mounted that there may not be any slip between the sheet and the table.
- Sheet should be fixed for the pins and clips.

5.3.2 Setting Up of the Plane Table

(1) Levelling : The plane table surface is rendered horizontal.

(2) Orientation : The plane table and the drawing sheet laying on it, is placed parallel to its position at other stations on the field.

(3) Centring : The transferring of the station point on the ground vertically above it on to the drawing sheet on the table is called *centring*.

(1) Levelling of the Table :

The tripod stand carrying the board is to be placed suitable over the station point such that the point on the map representing the station point lies on the vertical passing through the station point over which the board is to be placed.

The Board is to be tilted about its two mutually perpendicular axis by operating its mechanism till the bubble in the spirit level occupies central position when it is placed parallel to both the axes.

(2) Orientation of the Table :

The table may be placed parallel to its previous positions at other stations by two methods.

(a) Method of orientation by the Magnetic needle.

(b) Method of orientation by Back sighting.

5.3.3 Method of Orientation by the Magnetic Needle

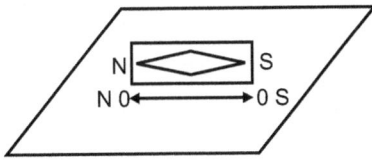

Fig. 5.5

Fig. 5.5 shows North-South direction.

The trough compass is to be placed on the magnetic North-South line already drawn on the drawing sheet in such a way that 0-0 line of the trough compass is along the magnetic meridian line on the drawing sheet. If the orientation is not perfect the axis of the magnetic needle will remain deflected from the line 0-0. For this, the table has to be rotated in clockwise or anticlockwise direction till the angle between the 0-0 and the magnetic axis of the needle vanishes.

Orientation by Back Sighting :

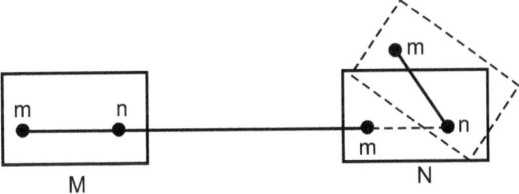

Fig. 5.6

M Station : MN is a leg of transverse. MN is drawn to scale on drawing sheet. The table is on station M and mn is bisected.

N Station : The table is to be placed over the station N as exactly as possible and the table surface is rendered horizontally. For the orientation of back sighting, the fiducial edge of the alidade is centred on n and placed along nm. The board is now rotated till a vertically held long rod M is bisected through the vertical slit at the other end of it. nm on the drawing sheet is now over and along the line NM. The table is not parallel to its previous station.

Centring of the Table :

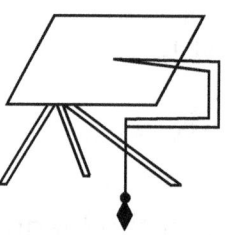

Fig. 5.7

For centring the table over the station point, U frame is to be held with respect to the drawing board. Such that wooden peg marking the station point lies just below the pointed end of the plumb bob hanging from one arm of the U frame. If the point located on the drawing sheet by the indicator point of the U frame does not coincide with the point already marked on the sheet as the station point over which the table is being set up, the table has to be moved suitably to that end.

5.4 METHODS OF PLANE TABLING

The methods of plane tabling are as follows :
- (A) Radiation
- (B) Intersection
- (C) Traversing
- (D) Resection

[A] Radiation :

In this method, the point is located on plan by drawing a ray from the plane table station to the point and plotting to scale along the ray and the distance measured from the station to the point. This method is suitable for the survey of the small areas which can be commanded from a single station.

Procedure :

(1) Select a point P so that all points to be located are visible from it.

(2) Set up the table at point P and after levelling it, clamp the board.

(3) Select a point P on the sheet so that it is exactly over the station P on the ground by the use of U frame. The point represents on the sheet the instrument station P on the ground.

(4) Mark the direction of the magnetic needle with the help of the compass in the top corner of the sheet.

(5) Centring the alidade at P. Sight the various points ABCDE and draw rays along the fiducial edge of the alidade lightly with a chisel pointed pencil.

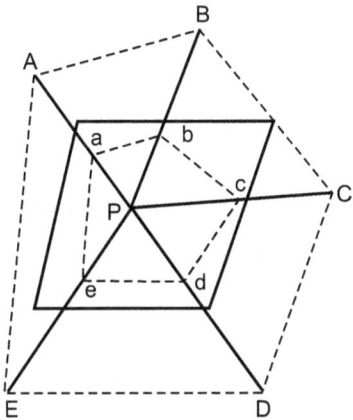

Fig. 5.8 : Radiation

(6) Measure the distances PA, PB, PC, PD, PE from P to the various points with the chain or tape and plot them to scale along the corresponding rays. Join the points to give the outline of the survey. Care must be taken that the alidade is touching the point P while the sights are being taken.

(7) The field work can be checked by measuring the distances AB, BC, CD etc. and comparing them with their plotted lengths ab, bc, cd.

[B] Intersection :

In this method, the point is fixed on plan by the intersection of the rays drawn from the intersection of the rays drawn from the two instrument stations. The line joining these stations is called the base line. The method requires only the linear measurement of this line. This method is commonly employed for locating the,

(1) Detail.
(2) The distance and in accessible points.
(3) The broken boundaries.
(4) The rivers.
(5) The points which may be used subsequently as the instrument stations.

Procedure :

(1) Select two points P and Q in a commanding position so that all points to be plotted are visible from both P and Q.
(2) The line joining the station P and Q is known as the base line.
(3) With a table set up and levelled at P, select a suitable point P on the paper so that it is over the instrument station P on the ground. Mark the direction of the magnetic meridian by means of the compass.

(4) With the alidade pivoted on the point P, sight the station Q and other objects A, B, C, D, E, F and draw rays along the fiducial edge of the alidade towards Q, A, B, C etc.

(5) Measure the distance PQ accurately with the steel tape and set it on to scale along the ray drawn to Q and thus fix the position of q on the sheet.

(6) Shift the table and set it up at centre of the table so that the point q is directly above the point Q on the ground and level it.

(7) Place the alidade along qp and after orienting the table by back sighting on P. Clamp it.

(8) With the alidade touching q sight the same objects and draw rays. The intersection of these rays with the corresponding rays drawn from P, determine the position of the object A, B, C etc. on the sheet. Care should be taken to avoid very acute or obtuse intersections. The extreme limits for the angles of intersection being 30° and 120°.

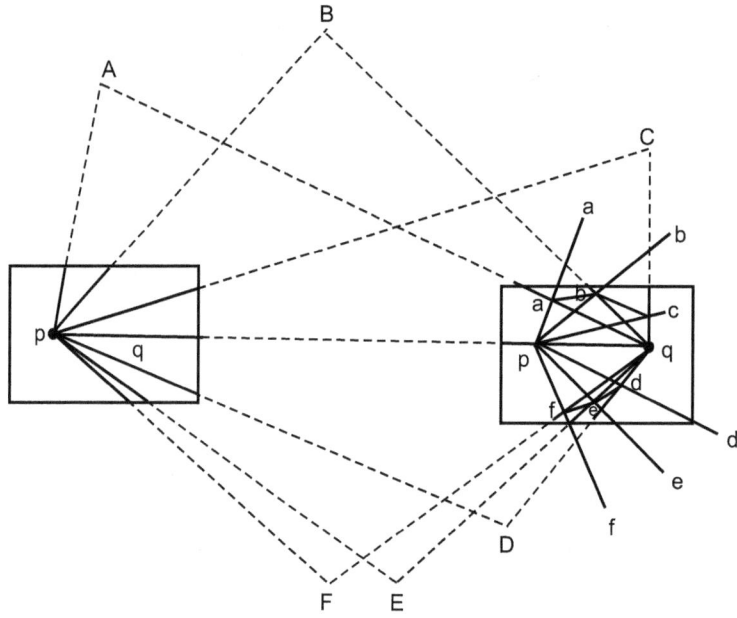

Fig. 5.9 : Intersection

[C] Traversing :

This method is similar to that of compass or transit traversing. It is used for running survey lines between stations which have been previously fixed by other methods of surveying to locate the topographical features. It is used for the survey of roads, rivers etc.

Procedure :

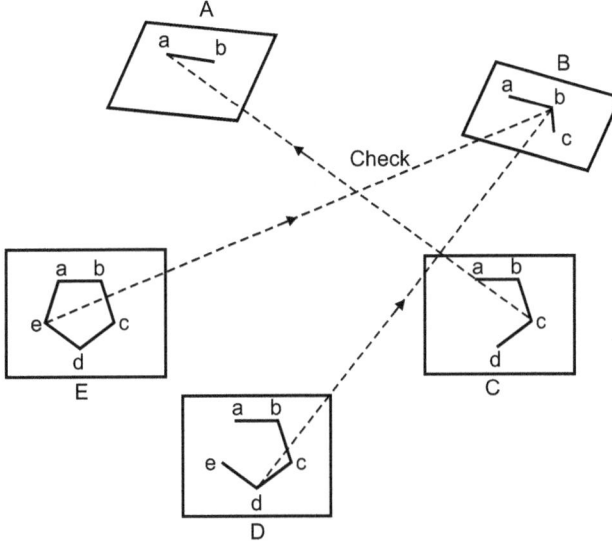

Fig. 5.10 : Traversing

(1) Select the traverse stations A, B, C, D etc.
(2) Set up the table at A select the point a suitably on the sheet. Centre and level the table when the board is clamped.
(3) Mark the direction of the magnetic meridian on the sheet.
(4) Centring the alidade on a, sight the ranging rod at B and draw a ray along the levelled edge of the alidade.
(5) Measure the distance AB with the chain or tape and lay it off to scale on the ray drawn towards B, thus fixing the position of b on the sheet, which represents the station B on the ground.
(6) Locate the surrounding details by radiation or by offsets taken in the usual way and the distant objects by intersection.
(7) Shift the instrument and set it at B having centred and levelled the table. Orient it by back sighting on A with the alidade along ba and then clamp the board.
(8) With the alidade pivoted on b, sight the station C and draw a ray along the fiducial edge of the alidade.
(9) Measure the distance BC with the chain or tape and set it off to scale on the ray drawn to c to fix the point c on the sheet. The nearby detail is located as before.
(10) Continue the process until all the remaining stations are plotted.

[D] Method of Resection :

This method is used for establishing the instrument stations only. After fixing the station the details are located either by radiation or intersection. The characteristics feature of resection is that the point plotted on plan is the station occupied by the plane table.

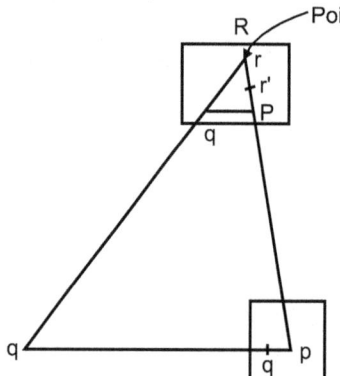

Fig. 5.11 : Resection

Procedure :

(1) Select a base line PQ on the ground. Measure it accurately with steel tape and plot it to scale on the sheet as pq in a suitable position.
(2) Set up the table at P. Centre it so that p is vertically over P and level it.
(3) Place the alidade along pq. Orient the table by turning the board until the signal at Q is bisected and then clamp it.
(4) With the alidade touching P, sight the station R, which is to be located by resection and draw array along the ruling edge of the alidade. Mark the point r' along the ray by estimation (rough estimate Pr' and plot).
(5) Shift the table and set it up at R with r over R. Orient the table by taking a back sight on P and clamp it.
(6) With the alidade centred on q, sight the station Q and draw array. The point of intersection of this ray and that previously drawn from P gives the required point r.
(7) Continue the process to establish other station points.
(8) This method is also called as back ray method. It is necessary to draw a ray from the preceding station to be occupied by the instrument.

5.5 ADVANTAGES OF PLANE TABLING

(1) Surveying and plotting proceed simultaneously. When the survey is over the map of plot surveyed is already prepared.
(2) Surveying and plotting being done by the same person, there is little change of any omission of any detail.

(3) Angular measurements are totally eliminated and the linear measurements are reduced to minimum excepting where such measurements are to be supplemented as a matter of convenience.

(4) It does not require any device for angular measurement, it does not involve any costly instrument. With no angular measurement and least number of linear measurement and it can be accomplished with least number of labour. It is cheap method of surveying.

(5) No need of field book. The errors occurring out of mistakes in field book recording are totally eliminated. The method provides scopes for checking the accuracy of any plotting from any point of work.

(6) It is an excellent method of filling the interior details of any old map where the advantage of the method is unique.

(7) Plane tabling is a convenient and rapid method of locating points on different contours and the plotting is very accurate in case of small scale map.

(8) The skill required for plane tabling is not great and can be acquired within a very short time.

5.6 DISADVANTAGES OF PLANE TABLING

(1) Scale is a very important factor for the accurate execution of plane table survey. In case of a very large scale map much error may be introduced by the plane tabling methods and as such the methods are not suitable.

(2) Much error is introduced due to expansion and contraction of the drawing sheet when plane tabling is carried out under the fluctuating humidity condition of weather.

(3) The method works on the visibility of the vertically held ranging rod at the location of the plot details. This method is not suitable in the survey of a wooded piece of plot.

(4) Absence of field notes and field book recording does not permit the map to be drawn in scale other than one chosen during the survey work with plane table. This also possess inconvenience in the computation of areas and earthworks concerned with the plot surveyed.

5.7 ERRORS OF PLANE TABLE SURVEYING

The sources of errors in plane tabling may be classified as :
1. Instrumental errors.
2. Errors of manipulation and sighting.
3. Errors of plotting.

(1) Instrumental Errors :
(i)   The surface of the plane table not being perfectly levelled and even.
(ii) The working edge of the alidade not being straight.
(iii) The fitting of the table and tripod may be loose.
(iv) Defective trough compass which affects the orientation.
(v)   Sight vanes of alidade not being perpendicular to the base of ruler.
(vi) Line of sight not being exactly over the ruling edge.

(2) Errors of Manipulation and Sighting : Errors of manipulation and sighting may be due to :
(i)   The board not being horizontal - This error affects chiefly the measurement of vertical angles.
(ii) The table not being accurately centred. The plotted position of the occupied station not being exactly over the station on the ground.
(iii) The table not being correctly oriented. To prevent this error, the orientation of the table should be checked at as many stations as possible by backsighting or by magnetic meridian.
(iv) The table being displaced from its initial position. There is likely to be slight rotation or other displacement of the table. Frequent check-sights should be taken to detect and correct any displacement.
(v)   The defective sighting - The objects not being correctly sighted. The resulting errors, however, will tend to compensate and are relatively unimportant.

(3) Errors of Plotting : These include
(i)   Drawing too thick lines and drawing a line which does not coincide with the edge of the alidade or not parallel to it.
(ii) Careless pricking of points of intersection.
(iii) Mistakes in laying off distances to scale. Such errors can only be minimised by constant care in drawing and in use of scales.
(iv) Errors due to contraction and expansion of drawing paper. It can be eliminated by using good quality paper.

5.8 MINOR INSTRUMENTS

5.8.1 Abney Clinometer (Abney Level)

Abeny level is one of the various forms of clinometers used for the measurement of slopes, taking cross-sections, tracing contours, setting grades and all other rough levelling operations. It is a light, compact and hand instrument with low precision as compared to engineer's level. The Abney level consists of the following :

(1) A square sighting tube having peep hole or eye-piece at one end and a cross-wire at the other end. Near the objective end, a mirror is placed at an angle of 45° inside the tube and occupying half the width, as in the hand level. Immediately above the mirror, an opening is provided to receive rays from the bubble tube placed above it. The line of sight is defined by the line joining the peep hole and the cross-wire.

(2) A small bubble tube, placed immediately above the openings attached to a vernier arm, which can be rotated either by means of milled headed screw or by rack and pinion arrangement. The image of the bubble is visible in the mirror.

When the line of sight is at any inclination, the milled-screw is operated till the bubble is bisected by the cross-wire. To vernier is thus moved from its zero position, the amount of movement being equal to the inclination of the line of sight.

(3) A semi-circular graduated arc is fixed in position. The zero mark of the graduations coincides with the zero of the vernier. The reading increases from 0° to 60° (or 90°) in both the directions, one giving the angles of elevation and the other angles of depression. In some instruments, the values of the slopes, corresponding to the angles, are also marked. The vernier is of extended type having least count of 5' or 10'.

If the instrument is to be used as a hand level, the vernier is set to read zero on the graduated arc and the level is then used as an ordinary hand level.

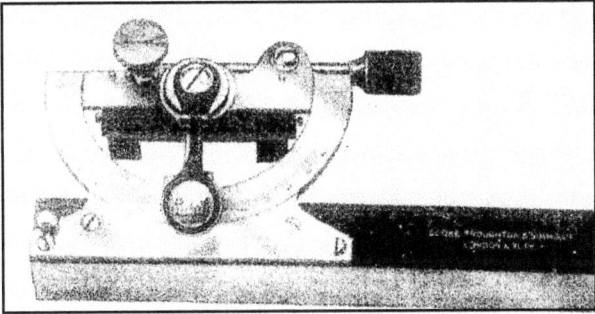

Fig. 5.12 : Abney Level

The Abney level can be used for (i) measuring vertical angles, (ii) measuring slope of the ground, and (iii) tracing grade contour.

(i) Measurement of vertical angle :

(1) Keep the instrument at eye level and direct it to the object till the line of sight passes through it.

(2) Since the line of sight is inclined, the bubble will go out of centre. Bring the bubble to the centre of its run by the milled-screw. When the bubble is central, the line of sight must pass through the object.

(3) Read the angle on the arc by means of the vernier.

(ii) Measurement of slope of the ground :

(1) To take a target, having cross-marks, at observer's eye height and keep it at the other end of the line.
(2) Hold the instrument at one end and direct the instrument towards the target till the horizontal wire coincides with the horizontal line of the target.
(3) Bring the bubble in the centre of its run.
(4) Read the angle on the arc by means of the vernier.

Testing and Adjustment of Abney Level :

(1) Fix two rods, having marks at equal heights h (preferably at the height of observer's eye), at two points P and Q, about 20 to 50 metres apart.
(2) Keep the Abney level at the point A against the rod at P and measure the angle of elevation α_1 towards the point B of the rod Q.
(3) Shift the instrument to Q, hold it against B and sight A. Measure the angle of depression α_2.

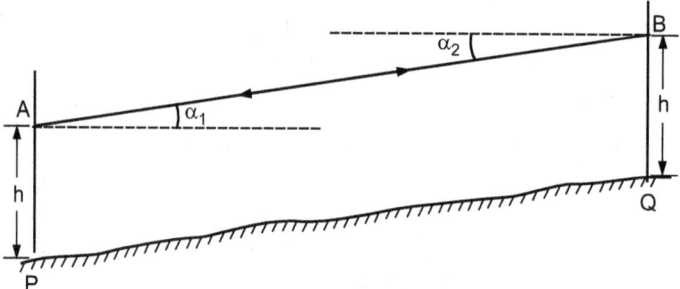

Fig. 5.13

(4) If α_1 and α_2 are equal, the instrument is in adjustment i.e. the line of sight is parallel to the axis of the bubble tube when it is central and when vernier reads zero.
(5) If not, turn the screw so that the vernier reads the mean reading $\dfrac{\alpha_1 + \alpha_2}{2}$. The bubble will no longer be central.

Bring the bubble to the centre of its run by mans of its adjusting screws. Repeat the test till correct.

Note : If the adjustment is not done, the index error equal $\dfrac{\alpha_1 - \alpha_2}{2}$, may be noted and the correction may be applied to all the observed readings.

5.8.2 Box Sextant

The box sextant is small pocket instrument used for measuring horizontal and vertical angles, measuring chain angles and locating inaccessible points. By setting the vernier to 90°, it may be used as an optical square. Fig. 5.14 shows a box sextant.

A box sextant consists of the following parts :

(1) A circular box about 8 cm in diameter and 4 cm high.
(2) A fixed horizon glass, silvered at lower half and plain at upper half.
(3) A movable index glass fully silvered.
(4) An index arm pivoted at the index glass and carrying a vernier at the other end.
(5) An adjustable magnifying glass, to read the angle.

(a)

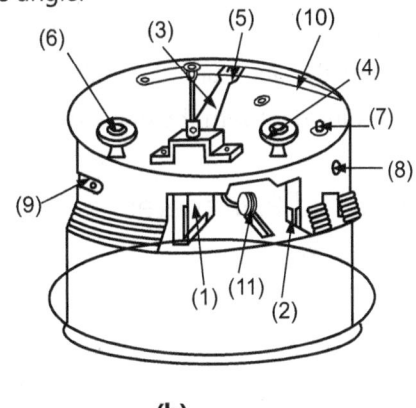
(b)

Fig. 5.14 : Box Sextant

1. Index mirror
2. Horizon glass
3. Index arm
4. Screw for setting the index arm
5. Vernier
6. Adjusting key
7., 8. Keys for adjusting the horizon glass
9. Eye hole
10. Graduated arc
11. Coloured glasses for controlling the solar rays

A milled-headed screw to rotate the index glass and the index arm. An eye hole or peep hole or a telescope for long distance sighting. A pair of coloured glass for use in bright sun. A slot in the side of the box for the object to be sighted.

Measurement of Horizontal Angle with Box Sextant :

1. Hold the instrument in the right hand and bring the plane of the graduated arc into the plane of the eye and the two points to be observed.

2. Look through the eye hold at the left hand object through the lower unsilvered portion of the horizon glass.

3. Turn the milled-headed screw slowly so that the image of the right-hand object, after double reflection, is coincident with the left-hand object; view directly through the upper half of the horizon glass. Clamp the vernier. If a slow motion screw is provided, bring the images of object into exact coincidence.

The reading on the vernier gives directly the angle.

Note : The vertex (V) of an angle measured is not exactly at the eye but at the intersection of the two lines of sight which, for small angels, is considerably behind the eye. For this reason, there may be an appreciable error in the measurement of the angles less than say, 15°.

Measurement of Vertical Angle with Sextant :

Vertical angels may be measured by holding the sextant so that its arc lies in a vertical plane. If it is required to measure the vertical angle between two points, view the lower object directly, and turn the milled headed screw until the image of the higher object appears coincident with the lower one.

5.8.3 Digital Planimeter

A digital planimeter can be used to find area of an irregular surface quickly. The planimeter works on inbuilt nickel cadmium storage battery. The Fig. 5.15 shows different parts of a digital planimeter, PLACOM KP 90 M manufactured by Koizomi 50 Sokki CO – of Japan. There is a rotary encoder, which has replaced the integrating wheel of the mechanical planimeter. An electronic circuit measures the pulses of the rotary encoder and the area is displayed in digital form.

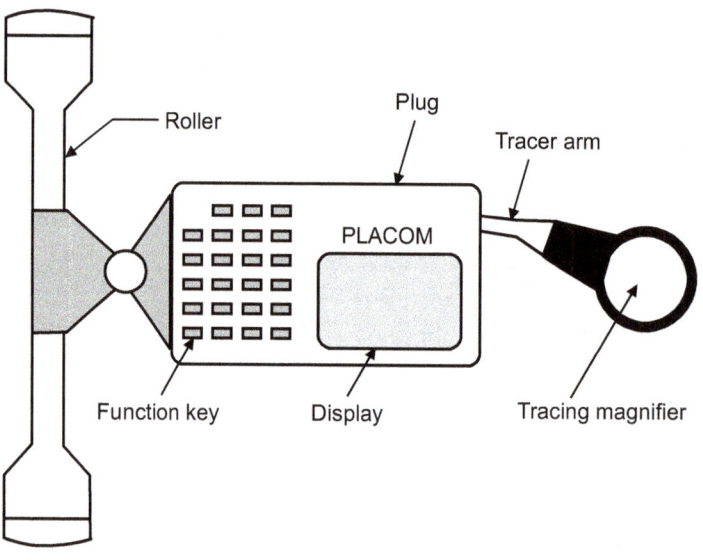

Fig. 5.15 : Digital Planimeter

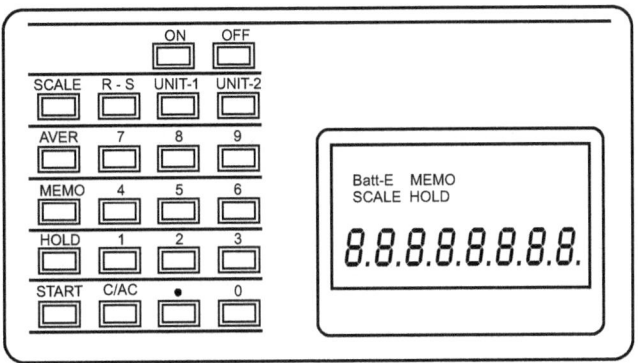

Fig. 5.16 : Function Keys

| ON | — Power Supply ON key
| OFF | — Power Supply OFF key
| C/AC | — Clear and all clear key
| START | — It is a start key for starting measurement. When the key pressed, buzzer sounds lightly.
| HOLD | — By pressing this key, measured value is (stored) held in memory.
| MeMo | — It is a key for holding an intermediate measurement in memory.
| AVER | — It is a key for calculating average value.
| UNIT -1 | — It is a key for selecting unit system i.e. Metric system or for British system.
| UNIT-2 | — It is a shift key of the unit within each unit system. Such as $km^2 \rightarrow m^2 \rightarrow cm^3$ or acre – Ft^2 – in^2
| SCALE | — Pressing this key causes the setting of the reduced scale
| R–S | — Pressing this key confirms the setting of reduced scale
| . | — Decimal point key
| 0 ~ 9 | — Numerical key

Measurement:

Suppose an area 'P' as shown in Fig. 5.17 is to be measured.

(a) **Preparation:** Paste or fix the drawing paper containing the area on a drawing board. Place the roller at the position which will make a right angle with the main body. By tracing the outline of the figure, if any inconvenient movement of the roller is found, then the position of the roller is adjusted.

Procedure:

(b) Press ON key to switch on the power supply.

(c) Select the unit by using 2 keys of UNIT-1 and UNIT-2.

(d) Put a mark like 'A' on the outer periphery of the figure to use it as a starting point.

(e) Press START key, the buzzer sounds lightly. Confirm that display shows 0. Then trace the figure by lens (tracing point) clockwise round the circumference of the figure and close on starting point. The area of figure will be displayed on display panel.

(f) Bigger areas are subdivided into two or three parts of convenience.

(g) By the use of MEMO and AVER keys, the same area can be measured a number of times and its mean value can be obtained for increased measuring accuracy.

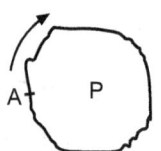

Fig. 5.17 : Measurement

Special Features:

1. Measurement of area of regular and irregular figures.
2. It measures both in Metric and British system of units i.e. mm, cm, m, km, in, ft. etc.
3. The higher unit is shifted automatically if the measured number exceeds 8 figures during operation.
4. The resolution in the line measurement is as high as 0.05 mm.

5. It provides a wide range of scale ratio or magnifying ratio covering from $\frac{1}{10^{-7}}$ to $\frac{1}{10^{+7}}$.

6. It has a rechargeable Ni-Cd battery as the power source with a life of approximately 40 h.

Applications:
(i) To find the area of an irregular figure directly in digital form to the desired scale.
(ii) Averaging of the area is done to get the mean area accurately.
(iii) It is possible to find the perimeter (length) of an irregular shaped area.

REVIEW QUESTIONS

(1) Draw a sectional elevation of a prismatic compass and name all the parts.
(2) Differentiate between the following :
    (a) Quadrantal bearing and Whole circle bearing.
    (b) Fore bearing and Back bearing.
    (c) Magnetic meridian and True meridian.
(3) Explain the temporary adjustments of a prismatic compass.
(4) Which compass is used to obtain the Reduced bearings of lines ? Sketch the graduations of dial.
(5) (a) Explain how the bearing of a line is measured using prismatic compass.
    (b) Why zero is marked at the south end ?
(6) (a) Differentiate between a closed traverse and an open traverse.
    (b) List the equipments required for carrying out a chain and compass survey.
(7) Convert the following whole circle bearings to reduced bearings :
    (i) 142° 30', (ii) 237° 45', (iii) 74° 15', (iv) 304° 20', (v) 114° 30'
(8) Convert the following reduced bearings to whole circle bearings.
    (i) S 24° 15' E, (ii) N 64° 30' E, (iii) N 55° W, (iv) S 70° 40' W, (v) S 71 45' E
(9) Write a note on local attraction.
(10) List the various methods of plane table surveying and explain any one in detail.
(11) Give any three advantages and three disadvantages of plane table surveying.
(12) What are the various sources of error in plane table surveying ? Explain briefly the influence of inaccurate centring in plane table surveying.

(13) (a) What do you understand by the term 'Magnetic declination' ?
(b) Describe in brief the variations of Magnetic declination.

(14) What are the various sources of errors in plane table surveying ? Explain briefly the influence of inaccurate centring in plane table surveying.

(15) What are the different methods of plane table surveying ? Explain the limitations of each one of them.

(16) Describe the errors affecting the degree of precision in plane table surveying. Assuming your own data, bring out clearly how the scale of the map influences the tolerable centring accuracy.

(17) Describe the method of traversing in the plane table surveys ? When is the method of traversing suitable ?

(18) Explain the method of intersection in plane tabling.

(19) Under what conditions, radiation method is used ?

(20) What is the advantage of telescope alidade over plain alidade ?

SURVEYING - S.E. CIVIL (NMU)   MARCH 2015

University Question Paper
MARCH 2015

Time : Three Hours   **Max. Marks : 80**

Instruction to Candidates :
1. Do not write anything on question paper except Seat No.
2. Graph or diagram should be drawn with the black ink pen being used for writing paper or black HB pencil.
3. Students should note, no supplement will be provided.
4. Attempt **any two** questions from each unit.
5. Non-programmable calculator is allowed.
6. Assume suitable data wherever necessary.

UNIT - I

1. (a) Explain :
   (i) Height of instrument method. [8]
   (ii) Rise and fall method.
   (b) Explain curvature and refraction correction in short and derive an expression for curvature and refraction correction with neat sketch. [8]
   (c) Following reciprocal readings were taken with level. [8]

Instrument at	Staff reading on		Remark
	A	B	
A	1.156	2.597	Distance between A and B = 1200 m
B	0.987	2.418	RL of A = 625.555

   Find :
   (i) The true reduced level of B.
   (ii) The combined correction for curvature and refraction.
   (iii) The error in the collimation adjustment of the instrument.

UNIT - II

2. (a) Enlist various fundamental lines of transit theodolite and explain the relation between them. [8]
   (b) Explain measurement of horizontal angle by repetition method and errors that are eliminated by this process. [8]

(c) The following are the lengths and bearings of the sides of a traverse ABCD. The bearings are referred to the magnetic meridian, the value of the magnetic declination being 5°30' W. Convert the observed bearings to the true bearings and find the error of closure. [8]

Line	Length in m	Bearing
AB	470.00	343°52'
BC	635.00	87°50'
CD	430.00	172°40'
DA	563.00	265°12'

UNIT - III

3. (a) Derive an expression for horizontal distance and RL of a point, when the line of collimation is inclined to the horizontal and staff is held vertically. [8]
   (b) Describe fully with sketches, the characteristics of contours and explain the uses of contour maps. [8]
   (c) What do you understand by tachometry ? Explain the circumstances under which this type of survey is preferred ? [8]

UNIT - IV

4. (a) Explain with neat sketch, the procedure of setting out a simple circular curve by 'Rankine's method' of deflection angles. [8]
   (b) What is meant by transition curve ? What are the types and uses of transition curve ? [8]
   (c) Explain horizontal and vertical curves and their purposes. [8]

UNIT - V

5. (a) Write short notes on Abney level and Box Sextant. [8]
   (b) What is orientation ? Explain methods of orientation. [8]
   (c) Enumerate advantages, disadvantages and errors in plane table surveying. [8]